Badiou

Published:

Jeremy Ahearne, *Michel de Certeau*
Peter Burke, The French Historical Revolution: *The Annales School 1929–1989*
Michael Caesar, *Umberto Eco*
M. J. Cain, *Fodor*
Filipe Carreira da Silva, *G. H. Mead*
Rosemary Cowan, *Cornel West*
George Crowder, *Isaiah Berlin*
Maximilian de Gaynesford, *John McDowell*
Reidar Andreas Due, *Deleuze*
Eric Dunning, *Norbert Elias*
Matthew Elton, *Daniel Dennett*
Chris Fleming, *Rene Girard*
Edward Fullbrook and Kate Fullbrook, *Simone de Beauvoir*
Andrew Gamble, *Hayek*
Neil Gascoigne, *Richard Rorty*
Nigel Gibson, *Fanon*
Graeme Gilloch, *Walter Benjamin*
Karen Green, *Dummett*
Espen Hammer, *Stanley Cavell*
Christina Howells, *Derrida*
Fred Inglis, *Clifford Geertz*
Simon Jarvis, *Adorno*
Sarah Kay, *Žižek*
Valerie Kennedy, *Edward Said*
Chandran Kukathas and Philip Pettit, *Rawls*
Moya Lloyd, *Judith Butler*
James McGilvray, *Chomsky*
Lois McNay, *Foucault*
Dermot Moran, *Edmund Husserl*
Michael Moriarty, *Roland Barthes*
Stephen Morton, *Gayatri Spivak*
Harold W. Noonan, *Frege*
James O'Shea, *Wilfrid Sellars*
William Outhwaite, *Habermas, 2nd Edition*
Kari Palonen, *Quentin Skinner*
John Preston, *Feyerabend*
Chris Rojek, *Stuart Hall*
William Scheuerman, *Morgenthau*
Severin Schroeder, *Wittgenstein*
Susan Sellers, *Helene Cixous*
Wes Sharrock and Rupert Read, *Kuhn*
David Silverman, *Harvey Sacks*
Dennis Smith, *Zygmunt Bauman*
James Smith, *Terry Eagleton*
Nicholas H. Smith, *Charles Taylor*
Felix Stalder *Manuel Castells*
Geoffrey Stokes, *Popper*
Georgia Warnke, *Gadamer*
James Williams, *Lyotard*
Jonathan Wolff, *Robert Nozick*

Badiou

A Philosophy of the New

Ed Pluth

polity

Copyright © Ed Pluth 2010

The right of Ed Pluth to be identified as Author of this Work has been asserted in accordance with the UK Copyright, Designs and Patents Act 1988.

First published in 2010 by Polity Press
Reprinted 2011

Polity Press
65 Bridge Street
Cambridge CB2 1UR, UK

Polity Press
350 Main Street
Malden, MA 02148, USA

All rights reserved. Except for the quotation of short passages for the purpose of criticism and review, no part of this publication may be reproduced, stored in a retrieval system, or transmitted, in any form or by any means, electronic, mechanical, photocopying, recording or otherwise, without the prior permission of the publisher.

ISBN-13: 978-0-7456-4277-2 (hardback)
ISBN-13: 978-0-7456-4278-9 (paperback)

A catalogue record for this book is available from the British Library.

Typeset in 10.5 on 12 pt Palatino
by Toppan Best-set Premedia Limited
Printed and bound in Great Britain by the MPG Books Group

The publisher has used its best endeavours to ensure that the URLs for external websites referred to in this book are correct and active at the time of going to press. However, the publisher has no responsibility for the websites and can make no guarantee that a site will remain live or that the content is or will remain appropriate.

Every effort has been made to trace all copyright holders, but if any have been inadvertently overlooked the publisher will be pleased to include any necessary credits in any subsequent reprint or edition.

For further information on Polity, visit our website: www.politybooks.com

Contents

Guide to Abbreviations of Badiou's Publications	vi
Introduction	1
1 Badiou's Philosophical Background	17
2 *Being and Event*	29
3 Situations and Events	48
4 *Logics of Worlds*	67
5 Infinity and Truth	85
6 Badiou's Theories of the Subject	104
7 Ethics and Affects	128
8 Politics	154
Conclusion	175
Select Bibliography	186
Index	188

Guide to Abbreviations of Badiou's Publications

AF	"The Adventure of French Philosophy"
B	*Briefings on Existence*
BE	*Being and Event*
C	*The Century*
Con	*Conditions*
E	*Ethics*
I	*De l'idéologie*
IT	*Infinite Thought*
LM	*Logiques des mondes*
M	*Manifesto for Philosophy*
Meta	*Metapolitics*
NN	*Number and Numbers*
NR	*Le Noyau rationnel de la dialectique hégélienne*
P	*Polemics*
PB	"Philosophy as Biography"
Po	"Politics: A Non-Expressive Dialectics"
PP	*Peut-on penser la politique?*
S	*De quoi Sarkozy est-il le nom?*
SA	"The Subject of Art"
SP	*Saint Paul*
TC	*Théorie de la contradiction*
TS	*Théorie du sujet*
TW	*Theoretical Writings*
WL	"What is to Live?"

Introduction

Ni Dieu ni homme [Neither god nor man]

(C 216n53)

"One is right to revolt against the reactionaries..."

In a candid moment at a recent conference, Alain Badiou expressed his frustration and surprise at the fact that so many of his peers – he had in mind the generation of student and worker activists known as *soixante-huitards*, or "68ers" – developed a strong hostility toward their former militant engagement. Although his comment was delivered almost as a passing remark, it was more than that: his dismay about people turning against something they once believed is directly connected to one of his philosophy's overarching concerns. Badiou is interested in the conditions of conversion, conviction, resolution, persistence, and then, on the other side, wavering, doubt, and retreat. His philosophy is interested in describing the conditions under which a militant engagement changes into a reaction against that engagement itself, and how someone can suddenly become opposed to the very possibility of a similar engagement ever happening again. And what are the conditions under which a militant engagement can continue, instead of burning out or reversing? Badiou came up with a little ethical formula once that captures his orientation quite nicely: "love what you will never believe twice." It is a bit obscure, but it should mean something like "do not be ashamed about being convinced of something that you feel you actually should not be convinced of, and have great difficulty justifying..."

Badiou asks these kinds of questions not only with respect to political movements (although these do seem to have pride of place) but also for all sorts of things that enthuse human beings every so often, such as romances, scientific discoveries, and artistic innovations. In fact, along with politics, love, science, and art are the four fields of human practice in which what he calls "truths" are possible. And although his experience with lapses in faith may have been the trigger for much of his philosophical activity, it is safe to say that he is actually more concerned with describing (and defending) the possibility of fidelity within all of these domains; fidelity to those events that can lead human beings to put their happiness, and sometimes even their livelihood at stake, often against their better judgment, for what appears to be (and may well be) nothing more than a stupid idea: something as silly, say, as a new way of doing mathematics, or a hunch that a new way of making sound has musical value.

The most common reference in Badiou's work is, as I mentioned, politics, and most of his key examples, and many of his key concepts, come from political theory and political history, with a strongly Marxist inflection. But not always. Using an unfamiliar but colorful term, Badiou describes as Thermidorian the type of reaction he witnessed, and was vexed by, among members of his generation after 1968. Students of the French Revolution would recognize the term, since it is usually used to describe the period just after Robespierre's infamous reign of terror. The Thermidorian period (named after one of the months of the French Revolutionary calendar – covering mid-July to mid-August) was characterized by social and political moderation. Now, Badiou is not saying that anything about May 1968 and its long aftershocks compares to the intensity of the French Revolution, as far as its achievements and actual historical significance goes. Nor does it compare to other revolutionary events of the twentieth century – the Russian Revolution of 1917, and the Cultural Revolution in China, to use two more of Badiou's standard references. Badiou does want to say, however, that despite the difficulty in determining the significance of May 1968, the period that followed can be characterized as another Thermidorian reaction. And to such a period corresponds a distinctive form of subjectivity, one based on the cessation of a previous and also always possible revolutionary fervor. Thus, the Thermidorian is not just any political conservative, but someone who is saying no to something he or she once encountered, to something he or she once was, or to something he or she once believed. A Thermidorian is someone who "renounces his revolutionary enthusiasm and sells his rallying to the order of proprietors" (P 85). A more typical conservative might be opposed to certain social movements for any number of reasons; but the Thermidorian is a distinct type who brings a particular sort of passion to her reaction, one that is motivated by a subjective experience with the other side.

We see in this discussion of Thermidorian reaction how two interests are present in Alain Badiou's work, and I will be making a similar point about Badiou's philosophy throughout this introduction. On the one hand, it shows how he is interested in studying different types of subject-positions, each expressing a different attitude about its world: some will be characterized by a fidelity to a new development (in a situation such as art, think of Cubism, or twelve-tone music) and some will be reacting against one, like the Thermidorians of the French Revolution in politics. And, on the other hand, Badiou is interested in mapping out the resemblances among different historical periods and discerning something like the overall structure of such situations. Thus, there are two distinct interests in Badiou's philosophy: an interest in a theory of the subject, and a theory that details the structures within which subjects appear. It is his study of both that is crucial to his ability to build a case for fidelity, or faithful subjectivity.

A large part of Badiou's work, then, is interested in pursuing the formal resemblances among different historical periods. This results in the production of a conceptual framework, a philosophical system, that can be used to outline the structure of such disparate situations as the living things in a park, the works that make up a twentieth-century artistic movement, the geology of a mountain range millions of years ago, and the love between Abélard and Héloïse in the eleventh century. Yet another significant part of Badiou's work studies something altogether different from structure – what are called events, truths, and subjects.

This makes Badiou's philosophy rather distinctive on the contemporary scene. Badiou himself has proposed thinking of twentieth-century French philosophy in terms of an ongoing debate between vitalism and formalism. Vitalism could be described as a philosophy that promotes the centrality of things like life, change, nature, and becoming (Badiou thinks of the early twentieth-century philosopher Henri Bergson as well as the more recent Gilles Deleuze in these terms), while formalism is a philosophical orientation interested in issues like the organization of objects, their identities and differences, or the overall structures in which they fit (Lévi-Strauss, the early Foucault, Lacan – structuralism, in a word). Thinking of the debate in French philosophy this way is almost like thinking of it in terms of a debate that goes back to the pre-Socratics, when Heraclitus argued that you can never step into the same river twice – nothing stays the same, all is flux – and Parmenides argued that all is one, and change and movement are illusions. Badiou sees himself bringing these two sides of an old debate together. Putting the debates that went on during his formative years yet another way, he writes:

> From the start of the [twentieth] century, then, French philosophy presents a divided and dialectical character. On one side, a philosophy of life; on the other, a philosophy of the concept. This debate between life and concept will be absolutely central to the period that follows. At stake in any such discussion is the question of the human subject, for it is here that the two orientations coincide. (AF 69)

The claim that the two orientations "coincide" in a theory of the subject is critical to Badiou, and to his own contribution to his history – for this coincidence was also being hammered out in the mid-1960s by people such as Sartre, Althusser, and Lacan, all of whom made important and differing claims about the nature of the subject. If the key conflict on the theory of the subject during Badiou's philosophical training was "Sartre versus Althusser" – as he has claimed – this is like saying the conflict was between the assertion of the rights and privileges of the free, conscious human subject (Sartre) versus the assertion of the predominance of a-subjective, non-conscious processes and systems, with a devaluing of the (humanist) subject as a thing of pure ideology (Althusser). A theory of the subject (as such) would be about how to think of the mixture of the two, of vitalism and formalism. This is where Badiou's main philosophical contribution will reside: in thinking of the subject as something like a site where vitalism and formalism, life and structure, change and being, come together.

Yet despite all the ink Badiou has spilled in the presentation of his philosophical system – worked out so far in the two massive tomes of a series called *Being and Event* – he claims that "the motif of the subject unifies in the long run my endeavor in thought" (LM 548). And accompanying this interest in developing an ambitious philosophical system has been a series of studies of (which are always equally defenses of) what he calls a "faithful subjectivity"; a type of subject that is characterized not by reaction but by the

Introduction 5

embrace of, or, perhaps better, possession by, a transforming encounter with an event and its consequences.

On the faithful subject

What is faithful subjectivity supposed to be about? Going back to another historical moment, this time the slave revolt led by Spartacus in 73 BC, Badiou describes how this revolt was, from a certain perspective, perhaps nothing all that new or special: slave revolts were not uncommon in the Roman world. But, subjectively, Badiou wants to say that this particular revolt was something different. To see this, one has to look at the way the members of the revolt saw what they were doing, and how this related to the situation they were in. When this is taken into account, Badiou thinks we can see that what these slaves were doing amounted to "the realization in the present of a previously unknown possible" (LM 60). The slaves were actively demonstrating the existence of, and were already living in, a present that was different from the social and political "present" that had constituted their lives as slaves; they were creating a present that rivaled and effectively split in two the social and political situation they were living in.

In a few words, this is what a faithful subjectivity always does – it is engaged in the construction of a new present: a construction whose process and end result Badiou also calls a truth. Such is what Badiou has in mind when he writes of the human capacity to be seized by an eternal truth. A truth is in large part defined by the way in which its construction contests the reigning present not simply with a critique, but with the actual presence of an alternative within that present itself. This alternative scrambles the situation in question: it redraws the relations among members or inhabitants of that situation. It organizes the world in question differently. For example, in the case of the Spartacan rebellion there was the actualization of an idea that was itself highly dubious, or perhaps deemed to be beyond the pale, unacceptable in their present moment: the idea of equality among members of the human community, slaves and citizens. It is as if the members of the revolt were saying "we are already no longer simply the slaves you say we are, and that we indeed are, officially; but we are also, right now, already something else."

Badiou's fusion of a study of structures with a study of events, along with an interest in discerning the position of the subject in each, is really an attempt then to develop a theory of change, or a theory of the emergence of genuine novelty in human situations. And this theory – quite detailed and complex, as we shall see – is able to develop an ethic, one that Badiou thinks could be useful to individuals when they are involved in truth procedures.

But why would they need such help? Why aren't they fine on their own? In other words, why is Badiou doing what he is doing? Does it stem from mere intellectual curiosity? A consideration of Badiou's encounter with his philosophical nemeses, the *nouveaux philosophes*, or "new philosophers," provides an answer to these questions – these are the contemporary Thermidorians to which Badiou frequently alludes. Some in this group of thinkers that emerged in the late 1970s had indeed been involved in radical political movements in the 1960s and 1970s, and they gained media attention for writing repentant books that claimed to see in these student and workers' movements a direct route to the Gulag. One of them even claimed that the Soviet Gulag was "the logical application of Marxism," the inevitable end result of the Marxism many of the students and workers were embracing. One of the key ideas promoted by them – and a basic reactionary technique, according to Badiou – is that periods of terror and social-political repression are not mere accidents that follow from periods of revolutionary fervor, but rather are their logical outcomes, and are even what the movements are really about, no matter how much the members of the movements claim to be rallying for emancipation and equality. In this way, the *nouveaux philosophes* were able to portray themselves as defenders of the humanist values of the liberal, parliamentarian nation-state. From their perspective, Badiou writes,

> every effort to unite people around a positive idea of the Good, let alone to identify Man with projects of this kind, becomes in fact the real source of evil itself. [...] Every revolutionary project stigmatized as "utopian" turns, we are told, into totalitarian nightmare. Every will to inscribe an idea of justice or equality turns bad. Every collective will to the Good creates Evil. (E 13)

Terrorists, totalitarians, religious fundamentalists, and leftist radicals are all cut out of the same cloth according to the Thermidorian point of view: their utopian ambitions are really just a pretext for the realization of a violent desire to destroy the present, and to destroy human life.

There is, of course, something to such fears, given the experiences of the twentieth century. As Badiou himself notes:

the century was haunted by the idea of changing man, of creating a new man. It's true that this idea circulates between the various fascisms and communisms, that their statues are more or less the same: on the one hand, the proletarian standing at the threshold of an emancipated world, on the other, the exemplary Aryan, Siegfried bringing down the dragons of decadence. Creating a new humanity always comes down to demanding that the old one be destroyed. (C 8)

The dreams of destruction and renewal that pervaded the twentieth century are now the stuff of our political nightmares. Badiou adds:

What is intriguing is that today these categories are dead and buried, that no one gets involved any more with the political creation of a new man. On the contrary, what we hear from all sides is the demand for the conservation of the old humanity, and of all endangered species to boot. (C 20–21)

Such a claim is of a piece with Badiou's view that reaction has become a dominant mode of subjectivity today. In his defense of fidelity over reaction, Badiou claims to have learned a different lesson from the twentieth century: it is that human beings can do remarkable things as they already are. The twentieth-century desire to destroy one version of being human in order to replace it with another can be abandoned, he thinks, while something of the revolutionary creativity and fidelity that blossomed in the past century can still be preserved. In this respect, Badiou does not wish to succumb to the well-grounded fears of the reactionary, who can be said to be giving up on the creation of a new present, wishing instead to preserve the present roughly as it is, since all the alternatives are terror-prone, and thus far worse.

While destruction is no longer something Badiou can be said to be an advocate of – at one time, he was, as we shall see – he does hold that a romance with destruction remains a key temptation for any faithful subject. But it is a temptation that Badiou believes is still worth risking. In a much-cited phrase, he wrote that a disaster is better than a dis-being [*désêtre*] – by which he means a dismantling and abandoning of what is genuinely and uniquely human. The reactionary wishes to avoid the temptation of destruction altogether, but at too high a cost: at the cost of our very capacity to create a new present and expose ourselves to our intrinsically human capacity to produce truth. Thus, Badiou wishes to turn the tables, and announces that there is an unexpected threat in the protective and pro-life ethic of the reactionary; it is a hedge against terror, yes, but at the same time, it blocks our capacity to experience and develop what he calls truths.

Badiou's philosophy as an anti-humanism in defense of the human

Thus, from his perspective, our contemporary respect for life and human rights (and even animal rights) comes along with a rejection of what is in fact crucial about being human, which is precisely the ability to be seized by an eternal truth, as potentially destructive as that is. Without this exposure to the risk of destruction what we are left with is a life Badiou describes in a variety of sharply negative ways: as a basically animal life, a life of "passive nihilism" endorsing an "artificial individualism" (C 98), tinged with an obsession over security (C 124) while amusing ourselves with what he describes as a "Tibetan pornography":

> Lenin remarked that during times when critical and revolutionary political activity is very weak, what the sorry arrogance of imperialism produces is a mixture of mysticism and pornography. That's exactly what we are getting today in the form of formal romantic vitalism. We have universal sex, and we have oriental wisdom. A Tibetan pornography: that would fulfill the wish of this century, which is putting off inventing its birth. (P 139)

This is not a very flattering and upbeat assessment of the current moment; indeed, Badiou's assessment sounds rather dour and even moralistic. What's wrong with creature comforts and Tibetan pornography, whatever the latter would be? But what Badiou is saying here is that our interest in security, our interest in avoiding division, our defense of pleasures that harm no one as the private good and divine right of each individual ... all of this is actually de-humanizing us. We know well the risks that an exposure to what Badiou calls truths entails: an overzealous enthusiasm, an intolerance of difference, a disregard for simple happiness and simple pleasures, and an inability to compromise with others and find common ground. (I should note that Badiou does not exactly buy this: he thinks a truth is in principle a unifying thing, because it is universal and addressed to all – all can become subject to it, there is no elitism here. Nevertheless, he is keenly aware of the divisiveness of what he calls a truth procedure; this, in fact, is one of its hallmarks.) To worry about this too much is to succumb to a false dilemma. He wants to say that we can risk terror, without having terror. We can be militants for a truth in a particular situation, without becoming zealots or succumbing to the urge to let destruction and intolerance run rampant. In fact, Badiou believes that his philosophy can even provide guidelines for avoiding what, in his own terms, would really be evil: the disappearance or non-existence of any truth whatsoever, or the disappearance of the value of truth. And, in this respect, his philosophy is as much about developing an ethic of truths as it is about settling obscure issues concerning being, structures, and the nature of the subject.

On philosophy's status and task

If Alain Badiou has any notoriety today (and this is still mostly in France), it is perhaps for the positions he has staked out on current events and politics, and not for the subtle and complex positions he stakes out on being, multiplicity, truth, and the subject. His enemies consider him to be either a kind of quaint and antiquated leftist, dreaming of destruction, who imagines himself to be an old-school public intellectual; or else a dangerous terrorist sympathizer, who is politically and morally wildly irresponsible by still advocating for communism, and for being unapologetic about his Maoist past.

His positions on current events are easy to grasp, and easy to surprise. This is not the case for his philosophy. Yet his philosophical orientation does guide his position on politics and current events. Badiou's positions on any number of contemporary issues – take his claim that cinema is not really an art form, or that not voting is a significant political gesture – rest firmly on the foundations that his philosophy provides. Badiou has intriguing positions on the nature of being (it is radically multiple, but also identical to "the void"), on infinity (it exists, and there are even an infinite number of infinities), on existence itself (there are degrees of it, which means that for any given situation or world some things can be said to exist more than others), mathematics (it is the study of being qua being), logic (it tells us about the consistency of worlds), and immortality (although humans are mortal creatures, their relation to truths allows them to become immortals). One might think it possible to arrive at all of Badiou's conclusions on contemporary issues without having to ground them or argue for them in the way he does. Perhaps it is. But Badiou certainly feels that his philosophical labors in areas such as mathematics have allowed him to gain clarity on the positions he takes now, and he undoubtedly feels – he has argued as much – that it is partly due to a philosophical shortcoming, a theoretical oversight, that faithful subjectivity is so objectionable and difficult today. If philosophers had taken note of developments in mathematics earlier, Badiou's hunch is that perhaps reaction would be a little less tempting.

This amounts to saying that philosophy has not been doing its job, and has, for quite a long time, misunderstood its job. Badiou argues that philosophy has been genuflecting before the superiority of either the sciences (in anglophone philosophy, generally) or the arts, and poetry in particular (in the Romantic tradition, strongest in continental philosophy). Yet the resources of philosophy, and philosophy alone, are required to preserve and detect the emergence of truths: Badiou can call himself a follower of Plato on this point, who famously opposed mere opinion to truth. Philosophy cannot push the emergence and development of a truth, but without a certain type of philosophy the pursuit of truths in politics, art, science, or love may wither away, for a lack of advocacy and a lack of justification.

It may sound, then, as if Badiou is ready to give a vigorous defense of philosophy, and that he is eager to restore it to its position as Queen of the sciences. But there are some rather unexpected things he has to say about it that would rule such a reinstatement out. For example, he holds that there is no such thing as a philosophical truth. Philosophy "does not establish any truth but it sets a locus of truths" (M 37). In other words, philosophy itself does not lead us to any truths of its own. It relies on, is parasitic upon, the truths that are developed in particular situations.

The practice of philosophy for Badiou is not about developing a credo, then, that would lead one to a truth about the way the world is. Philosophy will not tell one what particular position to take in politics or the sciences, for example. Truths are produced in these other, non-philosophical walks of life: in particular, in the four situations of love, art, politics, and science. Badiou says little about the status of his own philosophy: while his own philosophy cannot be true in the sense he uses, because that term pertains only to a particular type of process in a particular type of situation, it would seem as if Badiou is committed to at least the correctness of his philosophy's description of being, event, situations, and so on. In this respect, he is neither a skeptic, nor a relativist. (It is likely the case that he would describe his own philosophy as "veridical" rather than true: the distinction between veridical and true is discussed in chapter 5.)

To get an idea of how Badiou sees the relation between his philosophical endeavors and human practice, broadly construed, consider Badiou's discussion of a figure from the Paris Commune of 1871 (another one of Badiou's preferred historical reference points) who, at a crucial and pressure-filled moment at the end of the Commune's turbulent existence, was not able to give the Communards at the barricades, starting to panic and about to face down an onslaught from government troops invading from Versailles, a simple order – any order at all. At a moment that required speed and ingenuity, this figure, faced with people demanding to know what the orders were, could only manage to say that he needed to be left alone: he needed some peace in order to think things over, he claimed. Badiou's point is that this poor man did not have a theory, a general framework, that allowed him to see quickly what should be done. His hesitation exemplifies the tragedy that can occur when theory and philosophy fail to do their job. At the end of his preface to *Theory of the Subject*, in which this example is first given, Badiou claims that he wrote the work in the hopes that neither he, nor his readers, would ever become those who "at the great due dates of history, can once and for all only distribute herring vouchers" (TS 15). For that is what this figure was reduced to – passing out food coupons in desperation; nice, perhaps, but nothing that would save them from the coming slaughter! Badiou makes the same point about his work in a more recent text, *Polemics*, which also contains a study of the Paris Commune of 1871: "all of my philosophical efforts aimed to contribute, however slightly, to preventing us (as the inheritors of the Cultural Revolution and May 1968) from becoming 'dealers in herring vouchers'" (P 281).

And given that philosophy is, by Badiou's own account, parasitic upon other things, what is it that a philosophy can do, then, when it is not doing something as useless as distributing herring vouchers? Philosophy is able to isolate the truths that are emerging in human practice, and is able to give some kind of support to their novelty. To strike another Platonic note, philosophy's job is to defend truth against established opinions and conventional wisdom. And, without a proper philosophical defense, it may well be the case that no one bothers to advocate for a truth – preferring, rather, to avoid the conflict, division, uncertainty, and frequent isolation that truth creates.

Badiou is arguing, then, that we live in an ideological climate in which any militants for a truth will naturally worry that they are flirting with some kind of terror or madness by continuing with their projects. They will be tempted by the subjectivities of reaction and obscurity, tempted to avoid the apparent inhumanity of what their projects are doing not only to them but to others. Lovers will balk at the changes to their lives that their love entails, and will succumb to the pressure to pursue easy pleasure and routine in their everyday lives; artists will be tempted to produce the familiar and marketable, when they secretly believe they are on to something else no one understands, but the pursuit of it is fast condemning them to isolation and poverty.

Thus, apart from its interest in giving a purely formal study of the structure and genesis of truths – the conditions of their emergence, the effects that they generate – Badiou's philosophy has another aim: that of developing an ethic that will enable individuals to cultivate the courage necessary to continue the pursuit of a truth procedure, making faithful subjectivity more viable, and reactionary and obscurantist subjectivity less tempting. Philosophy's task then is "to produce, in the world such as it is, new forms for the reception of the arrogance of the inhuman" (LM 16). This is why I will argue in this book that Badiou's work remains very close to the project proposed by his teacher, Louis Althusser, who advocated a fusion of theoretical anti-humanism and practical humanism. In Badiou's work, we have a philosophical defense of the human as a practical possibility, as a possible way of living; a defense that is enabled by a theoretical account of the *inhuman* structures and conditions in which human beings are what they are. Plus, Badiou makes the strong suggestion that it is perhaps not possible to encourage the former without the latter as a framework. Why this should be so is one of the mysteries I hope to clear up through the course of this book.

Philosophy is supposed to elaborate on "the ways of saying 'yes!' to the previously unknown thoughts that hesitate to become the truths that they are" (LM 11). The reference to hesitation here is as important as the emphasis on truth itself. Philosophy, Badiou is saying, should be able to carve out a space for a type of practice that much in the contemporary world tends to disallow. Our reigning ideology holds that there is nothing better than the creature comforts we hold dear, the pursuit of an individual happiness that frustrates and eludes us so much, the pursuit of a wealth that never seems to be enough, and that there is nothing worse than daring to live the kind of life only a human being can live – a life dedicated to an eternal truth. Such a life may well come at great individual expense (although it does not *have* to), and it may well come at the price of happiness (although it does not *have* to either). Nevertheless, Badiou thinks such a way of being is a truly human life.

Chapter outline

Is there a fundamental principle for Badiou's work, in the manner of those German Idealists who found it necessary to begin their systems with an incontrovertible truth, from which everything else about their systems could be somehow derived? If there is, it would probably be the claim that "the one is not," and its (seemingly contradictory) companion claim "there is something of the one." I am not convinced that everything about Badiou's philosophy can be derived from these claims, but they do condition quite a bit of it. Therefore, I begin my treatment of Badiou's philosophy proper with what I have been referring to in this introduction as the structural and formal side of his philosophy: with a study of his claims about ontology, being, multiples, sets, situations, and finally evental sites and events themselves.

There is some risk involved in this way of presenting Badiou's work, for one may get the mistaken impression that such discussions are what Badiou's philosophy is primarily about. This is not the case. Badiou is far more concerned with promoting things such as the notion of a faithful subject procedure, or the idea of a generic truth. And by spending roughly half of this book discussing the structural aspects of his philosophy, I am afraid that I may give the reader precisely this altogether inaccurate impression. Yet, to see how Badiou's positions on ethics and politics are grounded on philosophical principles, the systemic part of his work needs to be given a certain amount of attention.

Chapter 1 is something like an introductory chapter again, although it looks at Badiou's philosophical background, his activism, and some events in his life that have been central to the development of his philosophy. My argument in this chapter is that Badiou, initially inclined to develop what I call a philosophical Maoism, has long been interested in developing a materialist theory of the subject, first within the framework of a dialectical philosophy, and then within the framework of a philosophy informed by the insights of set theory. I do not mean to suggest any incompatibility between these two projects. Bruno Bosteels argues convincingly that the model of dialectics is not at all supplanted by the turn to set theory in *Being and Event* – a claim that is borne out by Badiou's recent use of the phrase "dialectical materialism" to describe his position in *Logics of Worlds* (Bosteels 2004: 150–64). I conclude this chapter with brief descriptions of Badiou's major works, details of which are explored in subsequent chapters.

Chapter 2 focuses on some of the main theses of *Being and Event*, which promotes the view that mathematics, and set theory in particular, is ontology. I consider here the two key claims I just mentioned: that the one is not, and that there is something of the one, or a one-effect, after all. This sets up the basic idea that being is subtracted from presentation. The nature of a situation is discussed here, and I consider some of the lessons Badiou draws from the axioms of Zermelo-Fraenkel set theory. Why Badiou uses set theory at all, and whether he really needs to, is a question with which I conclude the chapter.

A discussion of further axioms from set theory used by *Being and Event* occurs in chapter 3, and this chapter also addresses some of the more complex matters raised by *Being and Event* such as the distinction between belonging and inclusion, between a situation and a state, the different types of multiples in a situation (normal, excrescent, and singular), and finally the notion of an evental site. These are difficult matters, but a discussion of them is required in order to appreciate the importance that events and evental sites have for Badiou's philosophy. I also introduce here Badiou's claim that events are multiples that contain themselves as members: this seems to be their most significant property, and their most perplexing one.

In chapter 4 I consider the modifications Badiou makes to the theory of the event in *Logics of Worlds*. There are some terminological changes in this text too, and the overall task of *Logics* is to do something different, and supplementary, to the task in *Being and Event*, but the implications for the status of the event itself are clear. Badiou is explicit about the fact that he thinks he has in *Logics of Worlds* come up with a better theory of the event by focusing on the status of its effects in a situation, rather than on an event's intrinsic properties. According to the theory developed in *Logics of Worlds* events are changes in a world that involve changes in the very manner in which appearances in that world are ordered (by what he calls a transcendental). He describes his method in this work as an objective phenomenology, and I explore how this constitutes a refutation of philosophical idealism, while also being an important part of his theoretical anti-humanism.

After an account of Badiou's views on infinity and truth, chapter 5 considers the concepts in *Being and Event* that address how inhabitants of historical situations (human individuals) handle events. Foremost among these concepts is the notion of an intervention, but the issue of naming an event, and the status of that name in a situation is also discussed, as well as the forcing of a subject. These are notions which start to raise questions about the rigor of Badiou's theoretical anti-humanism. To what extent is Badiou really avoiding aspects of the idealist tradition? To what extent can his philosophy do without references to a human consciousness that constitutes situations and worlds? I use this chapter, then, to set up the issues that are treated by Badiou's theory of the subject.

In chapter 6 I present my interpretation of Badiou's theory of the subject. My thesis is that the subject is his term for the real presence of change in a situation or world. I explore the anti-Cartesian and anti-phenomenological aspects of this theory, and consider whether his subject is active or passive (or both or neither). I also consider whether there are one or many subjects. I argue that there is really one type of subject in Badiou's philosophy until the publication of *Logics of Worlds*, which pluralizes the subject's forms. The significance of this is discussed in chapter 7. In the conclusion to chapter 6, I consider the problems raised by some of Badiou's terminology which often suggests the kind of philosophy of the subject that he wishes to avoid – especially when he writes about decisions, choices, interventions, beliefs, and the like.

Chapter 7 continues filling in the picture of the subject in Badiou's work, yet it does so from a slightly different perspective by focusing not on the subject as such but on the different styles, deviations, tendencies, or forms that subjects take on. I chose to approach this from the perspective of ethics and affects. As anti-humanist as his theory of the subject is, his philosophy is still a philosophy about what it means to be human. With an important terminological distinction, Badiou posits that individuals or "someones" or "inhabitants of situations" are distinct from subjects, and are the ones who are affected by events and by truth procedures, and react to them in various ways – including carrying them out, continuing with them, covering them up, or reacting against them. With this distinction, the practical import – the ethic – of Badiou's philosophy can be considered. I also include in this chapter discussions of the fields in which truth procedures occur – particularly art, love, and science.

Badiou's views on politics I deemed worthy of a separate chapter, given the importance of his views on politics for so many other aspects of his work. In chapter 8 I address the constant themes found in his writings on this topic, such as the presence of communist universals or invariants in history and his suspicion of parliamentary politics, party politics, and even voting itself. I also track his shift away from what he calls the insurrectionary paradigm in politics and from the theme of destruction, which is replaced by the idea of subtraction. Also, I consider in this chapter what is living and what is dead about Marx for Badiou.

Finally, in my conclusion, I discuss again the link between Badiou's theoretical anti-humanism and his practical humanism. Unlike the theoretical anti-humanism of the 1960s (found in Althusser, Foucault, and Lacan), Badiou's is not working out the "death of Man" – hence my exergue for this introduction, "neither god nor man." His work entails instead an ironic resurrection of the concept of the human, and an ironic return to themes from the religious tradition – such as immortality, infinity, and, of course, fidelity. This has led him recently to develop an intriguing theory of what it means to live, and of how a human life differs from other animal lives.

1
Badiou's Philosophical Background

Alain Badiou was born in Morocco in 1937, which was at the time a protectorate of France. His parents were well educated, and were French citizens – both, in fact, graduates of the prestigious École Normale Supérieure (ENS) in Paris. His mother graduated with a degree in literature, his father in math. In a recent biographical sketch, Badiou sees his own work as a convergence of the two different studies his parents pursued: "I am an alumnus of the École normale supérieure and agrégé, but agrégé of what? Of philosophy. That is to say, probably, the only possible way to assume the double filiation and circulate freely between the literary maternity and the mathematical paternity" (PB). Involved in the resistance during World War II, his father became a math professor and then mayor of Toulouse on the Socialist Party ticket after the war.

When he entered the École normale himself in the late 1950s, Badiou says that he was a Sartre enthusiast; he writes that one of his professors at the time thought he was quite talented, but that he wasted his time imitating Sartre's *Being and Nothingness* (LM 580)! Sartre was probably the most prominent public intellectual in France at the time, combining philosophy with works in theater, novels, and activism. This seems to have been Badiou's model: he did some journalism, covering a strike in Belgium in 1960, and he was teaching philosophy at Reims in 1966–7 until he took a post at the newly created University of Paris VIII, in Vincennes, in 1969.

And, like Sartre, Badiou actually did enter publishing through literature. His first publication, in 1964, was with the reputable avant-garde press *Éditions du Seuil*. Entitled *Almagestes* – a reference to the book that contains Ptolemy's views on astronomy – it can be described kindly as a very experimental work of fiction. The same is true for its sequel, *Portulans*, published in 1967. A Sartrean influence can be detected in these novels, insofar as each character seems to stand for a certain philosophical orientation, and it seems as if Badiou is trying to use these works of literature to present philosophical, political, and sexual/romantic problems. (These two were to be part of a trilogy, to be completed by a book called *Bestiaires* which has not yet appeared. Badiou did publish another novel, *Calme bloc ici-bas*, three decades later in 1997. They have not yet been published in English; nor have any of his plays.)

But Badiou's major accomplishments were not to occur in the world of letters, at least not of this kind. In the mid-1960s Badiou remained active with a group of students affiliated with the ENS, calling themselves the "epistemology circle," who put out a journal called *Les cahiers pour l'analyse*. These students were united by their shared interests in mathematics, structuralism, Marxism, psychoanalysis, and language. The journal published essays by students in the circle as well as some of the leading thinkers of the day, such as Jacques Lacan, Michel Foucault, Jacques Derrida, Louis Althusser, Claude Lévi-Strauss, and Georges Canguilhem. Badiou himself contributed two essays to the journal, and these count among his first philosophical publications: one called "Infinitesimal Subversion" (1968), the other entitled "Mark and Lack: On Zero" (1969). The mathematical orientation of these early works, suggested by the titles, should be noted. Badiou's interest in combining formalism and dialectics had already started to manifest itself in these works in the late 1960s, and would converge strongly in the publication of his first book, *The Concept of Model*, in 1969.

Badiou's Maoist May

Badiou has called his experience of May 1968 his "road to Damascus." It is often said that May 1968 served, on the level of theory, at least, as a refutation of structuralism, or that it forced structuralism to mutate into something different called post-structuralism: scrawled on one professor's blackboard at the time was the slogan "structures don't march in the streets"! Yet it is also notoriously difficult to give clear expression to what the differences between structuralism and post-structuralism are supposed to be, and how May would have refuted the former. Furthermore, there are probably no self-identified "post-structuralists" in France – this is largely a creation of anglophone scholarship. It would be quite a stretch to say that any of these theories were factors in the student and workers' movements anyway, and the effect of May 1968 on Badiou's thinking has little to do with debates about structuralism.

When he describes that period as his "road to Damascus," then, what does he mean? The phrase refers to the site of St Paul's famous conversion to Christianity. Given Badiou's early and long-standing interest in Marxism, as well as in activism, one might wonder why he would describe the events of May 1968 in terms of conversion. For, unlike St Paul's experience, there does not seem to have been much of a conversion required. Paul had been a Jew and a Roman citizen, tasked with the persecution of Christians. When he fell off his horse on the way to Damascus and had a vision of Christ, one can see how that would count as a proper conversion. Badiou was a student of Louis Althusser, one of the foremost Marxist scholars of the time; he had already written about issues in Marxism himself; he was a longtime critic of colonialism and protested the Algerian war very early on; and so he would not at all have been opposed, one would think, to the kind of radicalism that came to a head in that month of May. But something about the events of May clearly surprised him, and was responsible for shaping the thinker and activist he would become.

For him, the significant encounter – one that he could well speak of in terms of conversion – was with Maoism. The decisive event seems to have actually occurred in the fall of 1969, not spring 1968 – it was the founding of the UCFML. His interest in and involvement in this group (which stands, when translated, for the Marxist-Leninist French Communist Union) really defined his work through the 1970s. According to the historian A. Belden Fields, Badiou himself founded the UCFML in 1970 while he was on the faculty of Vincennes. According to the group's regular publication *Le Marxiste-Léninste*, the foundation was in 1969, and I have found no reference to Badiou having founded the group.

Describing it as "probably the third largest Maoist organization in France" at the time, Fields notes that the group was keenly aware of its absence of a "mass base" and of the fact that it could not really claim to be either a party or a union (Fields 1988: 98). It stood out from some other far-left groups for its emphasis on the plight of immigrant workers: "in its very first year of existence it directed its efforts at trying to assist the immigrant workers who were still locked into the shantytowns" (ibid.: 98). Also, its "strictly non-electoral" posture was noteworthy: it refused to post candidates for election (ibid.: 99). Described by Fields as a "hierarchical" Maoist group (as opposed to the more anarchic, terror-inclined groups such as the outlawed Gauche prolétarienne), it also was not a supporter of the Chinese on political and global affairs (ibid.: 129). In a text published by the UCFML in 1981 (anonymous but perhaps written, at least in part, by Badiou), the group explains its position this way:

> Some, hearing the word "Maoism," believe that we march with the Chinese. This is a complete error. Unlike other groups (the PCML) we owe absolutely nothing to the Chinese state, and we have never had any contact with them. China has never been for us a model to follow. What founds our judgment is rooted in our own experience.
>
> Our own experience – that is, the creative application of Marxism-Leninism-Maoism to the concrete conditions of the revolution in France. Of course, we live off of the universal lessons of the Cultural Revolution. In this sense, we have educated ourselves from the Chinese proletariat and its historical directors. (*Le marxiste-leniniste* (spring 1981), special issue)

The reference to the Chinese Cultural Revolution of 1966–7 is significant here, because it explains the interest many young French political activists had in Maoism. When Mao asked "where is the bourgeoisie in China? It's in the communist party!" many Marxists in France could look at their own situation and see something similar happening. For many of them, the PCF (French Communist Party) was just such a party becoming "bourgeois." Also, what Mao was saying was clearly a rejoinder to the USSR, and can be taken as an attempt to prevent the bureaucratization that occurred there from happening in China. This was music to the ears of the anti-Stalinist and anti-Soviet youth in France. Furthermore, the Cultural Revolution's ambition to smash social barriers, to fuse intellectual and worker, for example, expressed an anti-elitism that had a certain appeal. Add to this Mao's pro-third world and anti-colonial views, and the appeal is perhaps not so hard to see.

Still, much about Maoism is not so different from the Marxism Badiou had long been familiar with. Why speak of a conversion then? Practical and not just theoretical matters account for this, I believe. In *The Century*, Badiou described May 68 as a time in which his life was profoundly uprooted, in a manner that thoroughly surprised him:

> I myself underwent a definitive experience of this correlation between transgression and submission. It took place in May 1968 and the years that followed. I felt that the uprooting of my prior existence (that of a minor provincial civil servant, a married father, with no other vision of Salvation besides the one provided by the writing of books), the departure towards a life submitted, ardently submitted, to the obligations of militancy in hitherto unknown places (workers' hostels, factories, markets in the *banlieues*), the clashes with the police, the early morning arrests, the trials – that all of this originated, not from a lucid decision, but from a special form of passivity, form a total abandonment to what was taking place. (C 125–6)

This claim about a "special form of passivity" that is present in a momentous, life-altering occasion such as this constitutes a very important part of Badiou's theoretical anti-humanism, one that I will be paying close attention to in this book. Clearly, this passage indicates that what made May into a "road to Damascus" for Badiou was his sudden possession by activism, without knowing clearly what he was doing, and without really having willed it.

Badiou's Maoist May also had a philosophical side, and that will be my focus for the rest of this discussion. Throughout the 1970s, Badiou wrote a series of short texts aimed at explicating the Maoist contribution to dialectical theory, and discussions of mathematics and the kind of formalism found in his first book *The Concept of Model* do not return until *Theory of the Subject*, published in 1982. Nevertheless, Badiou puts his encounter with Maoism on the level of theory this way:

> Maoism, in the end, has been the proof for me that in the actual space of effective politics, and not just in political philosophy, a close knot could be tied between the most uncompromising formalism and the most radical subjectivism. That was the whole point. In Maoism, I found something that made it possible for there to be no antinomy between whatever mathematics is capable of transmitting in terms of formal and structural transparency, on the one hand, and on the other, the protocols by which a subject is constituted. These two questions were no longer incompatible. (Quoted in Bosteels 2005: 611)

In what follows, I wish to track Badiou's pursuit of formalism and a theory of the subject in his most significant publications.

A philosophical Maoism: *Theory of the Subject* (1982)

As the political situation in France settled down, and with the rise of reaction and the *nouveaux philosophes* I discussed in the introduction, Badiou continued to pursue his work in relative obscurity, and significant shifts in his thinking were occurring. At a time when academics from anglophone countries were taking an interest in many of the new theories coming from France (usually described as postmodernist, post-structuralist, or deconstructive), Badiou's work was neglected. For some obvious reasons: the work that he was doing in the 1970s and 1980s does not fit into any of the categories or schools I just mentioned, and his work evidently did not contain much that was of interest to anglophone academics at the time. It is curious, though, that anglophone Marxist thinkers did not take note of Badiou's work either.

Theory of the Subject, published in 1982, is the culmination of the work Badiou had been doing in a number of short texts in the 1970s. But other things are going on in it too. For example, his interest in mathematics returns. He discusses the history of philosophy, Christianity, and Marxism, the poet Mallarmé, psychoanalysis, and Greek tragedians as well. All of these discussions play a role in an attempt to deliver on what he calls in the book the "black sheep" of the dialectical materialism he had long been advocating – a theory of the subject, precisely (TS 196).

Why is a theory of the subject the "black sheep" of dialectical materialism? *Historical* materialism can do without a classical theory of the subject in its approach to history. The subject in philosophy always had something to do with the consciousness of individuals; historical materialism, however, explains the movement of history not in terms of what people think and know about their situation, but in terms of the development of supra-individual economic, social, and political forces, with labor power and technological innovations being key to their changes. From the perspective of historical materialism, it is productive activity that is the true motor force of a society, a nation, and international capital, ultimately developing to the point at which class antagonism no longer needs to be a definitive feature of society (communism).

Badiou describes his orientation in *Theory of the Subject* as a "structural dialectics" that juxtaposes force with place (TS 88). The strength of a structural dialectics over an idealist one and a vulgar materialist one, Badiou argues, is that it gives an account of a "spiral-development" instead of a strictly causal historical development. In an earlier text, Badiou called this a Chinese (by which he means, no doubt, Maoist) idea, and, indeed, the basic orientation of *Theory of the Subject* is consistent with the philosophical Maoism he was developing in the 1970s. A structural dialectics in this fashion envisions "the development-through-splitting of the new" – this is actually how the earlier *Theory of Contradiction*, published in 1975, put it (TC 69).

As a reading of history and a theory of social conflict and change, how does this pan out? A vulgar materialist dialectics would find the ultimate cause of historical change in economic and technological developments. Different historical periods have different prime movers: in Feudal Europe, the revolutionary class was the emerging bourgeoisie, not the peasants; in capitalism, the industrial working class is the prime mover of the next revolution. But such classes are also not the *ultimate* sources of revolution: the source would have to be the political economy itself. History, from this perspective, then, is simply a history of conflict and opposition. One group takes power and does what it can to preserve its position, while a new group emerges on the basis of developing technologies and other shifts, eventually overtaking the old, all guided by the invisible hand of economics (at least until class antagonism ends). The subject that Badiou theorizes, the black sheep he is trying to describe, is located right in the midst of a "development-through-splitting." Neither force (revolutionary agent) nor place (the group that is in power), which are the key terms of Badiou's dialectical analysis of history and society, are identical to what he posits as the subject. But when the two intersect, oppose each other, and change each other, then we have the appearance of a subject.

The key terms and positions maintained by Badiou in *Theory of the Subject* are discussed in more detail in chapters 6 and 7. It is worth reiterating at this point, though, that the subject, as Badiou thinks it, is not an aspect of consciousness, and is not even the same as an individual, as it is in most philosophies that have a theory of the subject. This is a point that is absolutely central to Badiou's philosophy. The subject – which, I claim in chapter 6, can be thought of as the real presence of change in a given situation – is thought of in *Theory of the Subject* under two aspects. It consists of a subjectivation and a subject-process. A subjectivation refers to a moment when force interrupts the order of places, when a structural order is threatened with chaos, rearrangement, and so on. A subject-process refers to the continuation, within a structure, of the disruption that begins with a subjectivation. Without becoming a process, a subjectivation would just be a moment of sheer destruction. The subject as such is conceived of as a knotting together of these two things – an instant of subjectivation together with a process of continuation. Or a moment of destruction and negation, followed by a period of reconstruction.

In *Theory of the Subject*, the subject is also thought of in exclusively political and collective terms: as a political party, Badiou thinks, and it is probably not a stretch to say his own UCFML was a model for it. As such, we can already see how a subject for Badiou would be something more than any individual, yet still less than a nation, or the entire human race, or what Hegel would call Spirit.

A pivotal work: *Can Politics Be Thought?* (1985)

Theory of the Subject is Badiou's first grand treatise, and it employs a philosophical Maoism to arrive at a theory of the subject, which is itself a theory of revolutions. As such, its concerns are primarily political, even though there are readings of many other matters given there. Furthermore, an ethics is developed at the end of the work, which I discuss in chapter 7.

Just a few years after *Theory of the Subject*, he published another work on politics called *Can Politics Be Thought?* This text was close in spirit to the texts he wrote in the seventies for its interest in making sense of the current political situation in France (characterized, Badiou thinks, by the rise of reaction). But the work is significantly different from the earlier ones because it contains many views that could be called post-Marxist and even post-Maoist. Badiou does not, he writes, want to add his voice to the post-Marxists of the day, but he does argue that a Marxism of a certain type – even of the type he pursued in the UCFML – is dead. In 1985, his own UCFML had disbanded, and Badiou and others started a group called the *Organisation Politique*. Central among its views is the claim that the figure of "the worker" in French politics, which had already lost much of its currency and political efficacy, needs to be reworked into the figure of the "immigrant worker." But equally significant is the organization's refusal to be anything like a political party. The UCFML had already been opposed to participating in elections: the OP would not even try to be either a union or a party.

The text of *Can Politics Be Thought?* explains this shift, and it also exemplifies something about the kind of fidelity and faithful subjectivity that Badiou spells out in his later philosophy: a kind of fidelity that he thinks is more true to its cause than strict doctrinal adherence. Reinventing or redoing Marx for the 1980s, an era of advanced and increasingly triumphant global capitalism, entailed, he argued, discovering and advocating for a different revolutionary agent. Marx's great claim was that the industrial proletariat was the revolutionary class of the nineteenth century, the class that would usher in the end of class conflict. Badiou wants to claim that it is non-citizen, undocumented workers (perhaps not even constituting a class) who play a role analogous to the role the industrial proletariat played in Marx's day. And, in a significant infidelity to Marx, no end to class conflict seems to be projected either. Badiou even arrives at the conclusion that the nation-state should not be the addressee of political activity; in other words, political activity is not to be aimed at taking over the state. This entails a withdrawal from the party-form in politics altogether.

In this respect, *Can Politics Be Thought?* is a text that marks a change not only in Badiou's political activity, but also a break with the theoretical centrality of politics in his work. With this text, he begins to develop a framework that he can apply to far more than just social and political situations. Something like a philosophical liberation from politics takes place for Badiou at this point, and when his work turns even more strongly to formalization, via set theory (although still never abandoning dialectics), he is able to take the insights he gained from his political activity and reflections and use them to develop a more general philosophical system that can be used to study non-political situations as well.

The major system: *Being and Event* (1988)

Theoretically, *Can Politics Be Thought?* continues to use some of the terminology from *Theory of the Subject*, such as dialectics, force, destruction, and reconstruction; but it also uses some terms and concepts that will dominate *Being and Event* a few years later, such as event, fidelity, situation, and intervention (PP 76–7). *Being and Event* will be studied closely in subsequent chapters, since it remains to this day Badiou's major and most influential work, and I will not have much to say about it in this chapter. It is a culmination of what he had been doing for the previous twenty years (since

1968) as well as a step beyond it, or an expansion of it. An interest in formalization and novelty, in structure and change, is signaled in the title of the book itself, which could be rephrased as "The Old and the New" or "The Continuous and the Discontinuous."

Being and Event is where Badiou makes some of his most significant claims. Foremost among them is the claim that mathematics is the discipline that studies being qua being, and one branch of mathematics in particular – set theory – happens to delineate the very laws of being itself, by which is meant the laws that pertain to the formation and organization of any group, any multiple, no matter what it is made of. In fact, being – "what is" – is a thoroughgoing multiplicity, but it cannot be said to be a multiple "of" anything in particular. I will start unpacking this idea in chapter 2. This orientation goes against two of the main trends of twentieth-century philosophy, one of which holds that in order to study being one needs some kind of theory of consciousness, since being only appears to a perceiver (this is phenomenology, and much of continental philosophy); the other holds that the hard sciences (physics and chemistry) are in the best position to describe the "laws of being," if they can even be called that; perhaps, this tradition would hold, philosophers are better off avoiding a topic like being qua being altogether.

Accompanying the position on mathematics and being is the claim that events, truths, and subjects do exist somehow, even though they are otherwise than being. As such, another discipline – not mathematics – is required for their study. This will be philosophy, as it happens. Badiou will also claim in this text that events happen only in historical situations, of which there are precisely four – love, politics, art, and science. Natural situations are not susceptible to events, in Badiou's strict sense of the term. This does not, of course, mean that nothing happens in nature: it only means that a certain kind of change does not occur in the natural sphere.

After *Being and Event*

Through the course of the 1990s Badiou's work became increasingly read, responded to, written about, and puzzled over. By the end of the decade two very different things were true at the same time: Badiou was both an established figure in French philosophy and an emerging new voice. In the handful of English-language surveys of twentieth-century French philosophy published around this time, Badiou was not given any significant attention, for perfectly valid reasons.

The flurry of texts published by Badiou after *Being and Event* will be given just a brief overview here. Most significant was the appearance of *Ethics: An Essay on the Understanding of Evil* in 1993: sharply critical of many current trends, intended for a general audience and thus perhaps more accessible than the other texts he had written, it was a remarkable success, especially among those who were ready to start entertaining arguments against identity politics (partly affiliated with the legacy of deconstruction), arguments about the nature of the multiple itself (involving Heidegger and Deleuze), and arguments against the ethical and religious turn in continental philosophy (in Levinas, phenomenology, and again deconstruction). *Ethics* was also one of the first books by Badiou translated into English (in 1999), and it served for many as an introduction to Badiou's work. And, just as that was happening, more publications began to appear in which Badiou expanded on and ultimately transformed some of the main theses of *Being and Event*.

The publications in the 1990s can be grouped as follows. To one group belong the texts that address the four types of truth procedures posited in *Being and Event* in more detail: politics was covered in *Metapolitics* (1998), art in *Handbook of Inaesthetics* (1998), science (math, at least) in *Number and Numbers* (1990), and, while love did not receive a book-length treatment, there is a good-sized chapter devoted to it in *Conditions* (1992). To this list should be added *Manifesto for Philosophy*: although it is not about a truth procedure, it is closely related to the work he was doing in *Being and Event*.

To another group of publications belong studies of individual thinkers and figures: *Beckett* (1995), *Gilles Deleuze* (1997), and *Saint Paul* (1997). And to yet another group belong a series of interventions on current events, and political and social issues in general. These were published in a series entitled *Circumstances*, which comprises now four volumes (published in one volume in English as *Polemics*, with volume four, *The Meaning of Sarkozy*, published separately). Two other significant works since 2000 are *The Century*, 2005, and *Logics of Worlds*, 2006, which is the second volume to *Being and Event*. Badiou has projected a third volume that will be devoted to the theory of the subject. I will be discussing these works in detail in subsequent chapters too. I turn now to a discussion of the main theses of *Being and Event*.

What I hope has become clear from this survey is that there is a remarkable unity to Badiou's philosophy, despite the presence of two different ways of approaching his main topic, which is a theory of the subject – one through dialectics, the other through mathematics or set theory. As I claimed in the introduction, Badiou is trying to bring together a formalism and a theory of change (an "intelligence of change"). The purpose of this is to enable an ethic that would support the continuation of a faithful subject procedure. After discussing the architecture of Badiou's philosophical system in *Being and Event* and *Logics of Worlds* (the topics of chapters 2 through 5), I will return to this theme in chapter 6.

2
Being and Event

Especially since the publication of a book on Sarkozy in 2008, entitled *The Meaning of Sarkozy*, Badiou has become a well-known figure in French intellectual life. But, apart from his political orientation, and some of his positions on current affairs (such as calling for the union of France and Germany, calling for a one-state solution to the Israeli–Palestinian conflict), what is known about Badiou's philosophy? If it is famous for anything at the moment, it may be for its claim that mathematics *is* ontology, one of the central tenets of *Being and Event*, and a claim that was not present in any of his earlier works (BE 4). This chapter will be devoted to exploring that claim.

What does one really need to know about mathematics in order to understand the nature of this claim about ontology? For one thing, there is nothing mathematical about making the claim. That is, there is a difference between making claims about what ontological practice is – or about which discipline does ontology – and actually *doing* ontology. A philosopher making this claim does not need to practice ontology; and, insofar as she remains a philosopher, she may not even do ontology at all. A mathematician may be doing ontology without knowing it, if Badiou is right; and, of course, any working mathematician may still not *agree* that she is doing ontology, if Badiou is right. The claim that mathematics does ontology is a philosophical claim, not a mathematical claim. It is philosophy that claims mathematics does ontology, after all, and not mathematicians themselves. So, to understand the philosophical sense of this claim about mathematics, one does not have to do any mathematics.

Nevertheless, an exploration of set theory – since that is the sub-discipline of mathematics Badiou relies on – is required because the *results* of the claim that mathematics is ontology have significant effects on the rest of Badiou's philosophy. Set theory is in the privileged position of articulating what he calls in *Number and Numbers* (a very helpful supplement to the key arguments in *Being and Event*) the very "laws of Being" (NN 63). This turn to set theory allows a certain type of metaphysics to be curtailed – what Badiou describes at different times as a metaphysics of presence, a metaphysics of the one, or a metaphysics of identity. (Badiou even sees his equation of mathematics and ontology as a continuation of the Nietzschean proclamation on the death of God.) At the same time, a certain type of thinking about the multiple becomes possible with the equation. With it, a space for philosophy is opened up in which philosophy can focus on what is not being, on what is other to being (events, truths, and subjects), which allows us to gain access to what Badiou is really after – an "intelligence of change" (LM 103).

But how can an activity that would seem to involve numbers, calculations, maybe writing symbols on paper or typing them on a screen, be said to be doing anything at all like ontology, wittingly or not? How could something like *mathematics* be a study of being? There has even been a longstanding and widespread suspicion among philosophers about the ability of mathematics to do anything like ontology.

It may be helpful to keep in mind that Badiou's claim that math is ontology is, as he puts it, a decision. This means that he admits he cannot offer a proof that mathematics does ontology. But this does not mean there are no reasons for this decision. The decision can still be justified and explained, and Badiou does this mainly by pointing out the beneficial consequences of the decision he makes, some of which I have already mentioned (avoiding a certain kind of metaphysics, in particular a metaphysics of identity and the one).

Badiou's return to Plato: being is neither one, nor multiple

Ontology is normally considered a sub-discipline in philosophy that is tasked with studying the nature of being. (Metaphysics, by slight contrast, might be said to be about the nature of reality in general: ontology would focus more narrowly on the nature of being itself.) This assignment has always made it a bit obscure. What is it, precisely, about *being* that ontology is supposed to study? Physics studies nature or matter; biology studies living things; geology studies interactions among rocks, wind, water, and so on. Every science can be said to have a particular region of being as its object of study. Ontology is supposed to be the area of philosophy that studies being in general.

But still, what about being can it study? What it is? Its nature? Its laws? How it works or how it presents itself? Is there even any such thing as being *itself* or "being qua being," as it is so often put in ontology? Could any branch of philosophy be more abstract and currently irrelevant, rendered outmoded by the development of the hard sciences?

Many have thought that such questions cannot be answered in a way that leaves ontology with anything to do any more, and they have therefore consigned ontology to the historical dustbin, along with such things as alchemy and astrology. Badiou, like many continental thinkers, thinks that the position a philosophy takes on ontology still decides or determines nearly everything else about that philosophy, even when a philosopher wants to avoid doing ontology altogether. Thus, ontology still has an important role to play in philosophy – but for Badiou, unlike many continental thinkers in the wake of Heidegger, and more like many Anglo-American "analytic" philosophers, the role ontology plays in philosophy will be a thoroughly negative one. That is, philosophy will not be tasked with doing ontology (in strong contrast to Heidegger's claim that this should be the primary occupation of philosophy), but is simply able to name the discipline that does study being qua being – mathematics. On this point Badiou also differs quite strongly from the recent Anglo-American tradition.

Badiou thinks that many contemporary philosophers reduce mathematics to logic: according to them, mathematics works by following basic logical rules, and so logic is the meta-language for mathematics. Badiou sees another status for mathematics, and by fusing mathematics to ontology Badiou concedes that he is making a basically Platonic gesture. A place is still held for Platonists in contemporary books about the philosophy of mathematics, but it is a very lonely place; practically nobody adheres to it. This is because mathematical objects are taken by classical Platonism to be real objects, or really existing, distinct things – a rather difficult position to defend, and this is not the position Badiou wishes to adopt. Instead, what he finds valuable about Plato's position is simply the fact that it gave mathematics an ontological bearing – which is what he wishes to do as well. His own position on mathematics is so close to Plato's that he goes ahead and embraces the label "Platonist" – although, crucially, he adds that what he is working on is a "Platonism of the multiple" (C 165–6; M 104).

This addition – "of the multiple" – is actually a significant departure from Plato because of the status that multiplicity had for the Greek. There are actually two ways in which multiplicity is present and functional in Plato. What was genuinely real for Plato was not to be found in the many material things that we perceive with our senses (already itself a multiplicity, one should note), but in what could be called intellectual objects, or, ultimately, in concepts themselves, independent of human minds. Multiplicity is ontologically degraded in Plato's work – the many things we perceive are trying to be like other things, things (forms) that are really real, and in some way more real than what we perceive and occasionally bump into. Plato does admit that there are multiple forms, and thus different types of beings, just as there is a multiplicity of appearances; but even these depend in some sense on a fundamental form for their being (what Plato called "the Good").

So multiplicity is present at both levels of Plato's ontology; at the level of appearances and at the level of forms, or true being. Plato does not argue that all is really one, for example, as his predecessor Parmenides did. According to Parmenides, the famous monist, "what *presents* itself is essentially multiple; *what* presents itself is essentially one," as Badiou puts it (BE 23). The same could be said for Spinoza (and, Badiou argues, secretly for recent thinkers of radical difference such as Gilles Deleuze also). Classical Platonism may avoid a monistic position on being, but it still cannot be said to be "of the multiple" in the sense Badiou is looking for. This is because for a philosophy to give the multiple priority – for it to maintain that what is, is primarily a multiplicity – it is not enough for it to acknowledge that appearance is multiple, and it does not suffice to grant that there are multiple forms (as many forms, presumably, as there are types of things). What separates Badiou's position on ontology from Plato's, ultimately, is not just the rejection of the idea that being is one, but also the rejection of the idea that being consists of a *series* of ones.

What is meant by this? Consider what a contemporary type of materialism might hold on this question. Many of us may call ourselves materialists because of our belief that the fundamental building blocks of reality are being studied by contemporary physics: what things "really are" would be atoms or strings or whatever the current view holds is the minimal unit of stuff. Contemporary atomists and materialists might want to say that everything is really composed out of the same stuff; but this does not mean that we must conclude, with Parmenides and others, that "all is one." There are, instead, many different and discrete individual cases of the same primary stuff. All is far from being one, in this case: the real is multiple, and what is is a multiplicity of (perhaps the same) tiny units of stuff.

Badiou's position on ontology needs to be contrasted to this currently popular materialist position on multiplicity too. So his view is different from classical Platonism, Parmenidean monism, and a common form of contemporary materialism (call it atomism) all at the same time. For him, the starting point for ontology is the claim that "the one *is not*" (BE 23). And what makes Badiou's claim that the one is not distinct from other attempts to give multiplicity pride of place in ontology is its simultaneous (and paradoxical) denial of the idea that being is many. Strikingly, Badiou denies both sides of what looks like an exclusive disjunction: he holds that being "is neither one ... nor multiple" (BE 24).

What can being be, then, if it is neither one nor many? Badiou will call it a multiple of multiples. But how can multiples not ultimately, at some point, be "of the one" or at least "of something" in some sense? How can a radical multiplicity not consist of a multiple bunch of ones? Gilles Deleuze claimed that "difference is behind everything, but behind difference there is nothing" (Deleuze 1994: 57). This is close to what Badiou is going to argue. (Although Badiou's take on Deleuze's position on ontology leads him to conclude that even though Deleuze wished to think a multiplicity prior to the one, he did not succeed in sufficiently thinking of being without one.) Badiou maintains that what is required for the full flourishing of an ontology based on the thesis that the one is not, is the equation of being qua being with nothing – with the void (BE 58).

So there are some glaring oddities in Badiou's claims about being. On the one hand being is multiple, radically multiple, while on the other hand it needs to be called "void." This is due to Badiou's intuition that being itself is foreclosed from presentation – that is, being is not at all able to be presented as such (BE 27). This leads him to endorse a "subtractive ontology" – an ontology in which being is subtracted from presentation, and never presents anything of itself. The atomism I discussed earlier might hold that despite the fact that we do not, strictly speaking, see atoms, what we see are large groups of them, and they are thus somehow present in what we perceive, even if we do not see them individually. Atoms make up the material objects of our surroundings, and even if they are never presented as such, they are present in what we see. The same cannot be said for being in Badiou's philosophy. Being does not present itself as such, ever; it does not somehow shine through the many things of presentation. Thus, the proper name of being needs to be "void."

On presentation

To gain some clarity on this juxtaposition of the "multiple qua multiple" (as Badiou also calls being qua being) with the void, we need to consider more carefully the role that presentation plays in Badiou's philosophy. Although the one is ruled out ontologically, the one does occur, or happen, or appear, and this is always the result of something that Badiou refers to, with a bit of obscurity, as an operation (BE 24). Any "one," any distinct being (*a* being, rather than being itself) is derived, and is an effect of some type of operation on the pure multiple.

There is, therefore, really nothing for ontology to study about the pure multiple apart from how that multiple is counted, or operated on; ontology studies the different ways in which counting and operating can happen. There is an important distinction, then, between presentation, or "what is *presented*," and the pure multiple itself, and it is a distinction not unlike Heidegger's famous ontological difference. Being is not a being, Heidegger claimed, suggesting that while everything that *is* necessarily has some relation to being qua being, being itself is never encountered without, or apart from, particular beings. Yet Heidegger's ontology could not be called subtractive like Badiou's. For Heidegger, being still presents itself *in and through* beings. Thus, Heidegger's is an ontology of presentation, in which being is transcendent to every particular thing, but also immanent in things somehow. Whereas Badiou's is a strict ontology of subtraction, or "im-presentation," in which nothing of being qua being is ever rendered present.

So, any claim about the way in which the pure multiple is operated on is necessarily always going to be made from a perspective in which the pure multiple is not and cannot be presented. Ontology can only study *how* being is presented, in other words, and has no direct purchase on the pure multiple itself. Although being is radically subtracted and absent from any order of presentation, this does not mean that a negative theology of being is the best we can do. Just because being qua being defies our ability to think about it, just because it exceeds any name, etc., does not mean we have to be silent about it. Ontology is still a study of being qua being, even though ontology is not able to obtain a direct grasp of the inconsistent multiple that is being itself. What does ontology do, then, and how does it do it? What is there for it to actually study?

If there cannot be *a* presentation *of* being because being occurs in every presentation – and this is why it does not present *itself* – then there is one solution left for us: that the ontological situation be *the presentation of presentation*. If, in fact, this is the case, then it is quite possible that what is at stake in such a situation is being qua being, insofar as no access to being is offered to us except presentations.

By studying the nature of presentation itself, Badiou maintains that ontology actually *is* able to make claims about the pure multiple, even while it is doing the only thing it is able to do – studying the nature or structure of presentation, from which being is subtracted. Ontology, by studying the various ways in which orders of presentation order the multiple qua multiple differently, is actually after all studying being.

On situations

The order of presentation – in Heideggerian terms, the "ontic," or beings, as opposed to being itself – is called by Badiou a consistent multiplicity, which is quite different from the inconsistent multiplicity that he holds characterizes being qua being. Moreover, presentation is always described by Badiou as the result of a count or an operation – the multiple ones that are found in presentation are always a product, a result, of a count, or some kind of organizing activity (BE 90).

These structures are called by Badiou situations, and a typology of situations is possible. These will be discussed in chapter 3. Presentation (of multiple-ones, of distinct beings) is always in, or of, or according to, a situation. There is no presentation (of multiples) without a situation in which that presentation is contained. And there is no situation that does not entail presentation.

So there are actually two main ideas at the heart of Badiou's ontology, and they can both be considered decisions or axioms because there are not really any arguments given to demonstrate them (and, Badiou holds, there cannot be, although there are arguments for why it is better to start with them). First and foremost is the claim that the one is not. And then there is the claim that, after all, there is "something of the one," or, there are one-effects, or multiple-ones. This second thesis expresses a suspicion about the manifold of what is present: it does not let the presence of many different and distinct things tempt the philosopher to give any ground on the status of the one. There are many things – this is evident. But still, despite appearances, the one does not exist, is not really real, and these many things are not themselves really "ones" nor are they even made up of discrete "ones." Badiou does call them "multiple-ones" but that is still not enough: what they really are, of course, are results of a structuring of the pure multiple, which is also to say that they are something like abstractions from the pure multiple. Any situation establishes, then, in its own particular way, a multiplicity of ones, or one-effects. And any situation rids itself of any remnants of the pure, inconsistent multiple, which thus never appears and can always be said to not be.

Badiou writes, in fact, that "there is nothing apart from situations" (BE 25). What there is, what is *presented*, is always some collection of ones, or more precisely multiple-ones. These multiple-ones are always in situations, and there are in fact multiple situations existing simultaneously – as individuals, for example, we inhabit multiple situations at any given time. A situation is defined, in the glossary contained in *Being and Event*, in a perhaps deceptively simple manner: a situation is said to be "any consistent presented multiplicity, thus: a multiple, and a regime of the count-as-one, or structure" (BE 522). One might think that "any presented consistent multiplicity" might include within it everything from a litter of kittens to a nation-state. Are such diverse things to be considered situations? Yes. If we consider the definition of a situation in *Being and Event* more closely, paying attention to the second part of it, with its reference to a "regime of the count-as-one, or structure," it is possible to gain some clarity on the nature of a situation. This part of the definition gets at what is probably the more crucial feature of a situation, which is the fact that it is a system of organization, a way of counting and structuring the pure multiple without one. Insofar as anything is presented, then – be it a litter of kittens, a group of militants, a chess game, etc. – it is in a situation, or is situational.

Ontology – a doctrine on being – is also a situation by presenting theses on the multiple and laws of being. But it is a situation unlike others in some important ways. For one thing, ontology is called by Badiou "the situation of situations," and is said to involve the "presentation of presentation." Ontology presents us with the rules for the formation of any ordered multiples out of the inconsistent and pure multiple that is being qua being. As I argued above, this does not mean that ontology has no purchase on being qua being. As far as Badiou is concerned, ontology is the study of the features shared by any order of presentation whatsoever, which amounts to the same thing as saying that it studies the conversion of what there is of pure being into something consistent and structured – an order of multiple-ones, rather than an order (or lack thereof – chaos) of the pure multiple. And so ontology is about the different ways in which the pure multiple can be counted, and that is all there ever is to study. This is why set theory is so important to Badiou; because it is about ways of counting.

On being as void

We already know that Badiou describes his ontology as subtractive – being is not presented, it is absent from situations. But to go one step further and say that the proper name of being is "void" may still seem to be unwarranted. And how can this be reconciled with the simultaneous claim that being is a multiple of multiples anyway?

Badiou's argument for this point (and there can be an argument for this, since it is not an axiom) seems to go something like this: since presentation is always situational – there is never any presentation of any multiple apart from and outside of a situation – all we can ever do is name being, and think of being (what *is* presented), from within a situation. A typical situation (a non-ontological one, one that is not doing ontology) won't even bother having a name for being, since being qua being is never presented in it, and is not able to be presented: so why bother. But an ontology names and presents what other situations do not need to name and present, because ontology is *about* presentation itself, it is a study of presentation; while other, non-ontological situations (all others, those that are not doing ontology) do not do this. (I am referring to Badiou's theory of naming in situations here, which is very important, but I will not address it in detail here. I will in chapter 5.)

Indeed, what makes a situation ontological is this very property: ontology is a distinct situation because it takes note of how any regime of presentation operates on something prior to it, prior to presentation. In other words, ontology takes note of the operation being performed on the pure multiple, an activity to which the situation created by the operation is itself blind. It is like the difference between counting (which Badiou claims is a way of thinking about what any situation does to the multiple) and noticing that a count is happening – counting the count, as it were. These are two distinct activities (to some extent mutually exclusive activities: doing one means you are not doing the other), and Badiou is saying that ontology pays attention to the latter, and it thus presents counting itself, the count as count.

Ontology can then tell us about the status of this pure multiple for any situation – and its status is presupposed, but excluded and absent. Hence, void works as the proper name for being, provided we recall that this is a proper name always within a situation (BE 56). So, from the perspective of any (non-ontological) situation whatsoever, what there is, is always a plenitude of multiplicity. There is not nothing. Furthermore, this plenitude of multiplicity is able to be subject to the situation's system of counting beings – nothing escapes a situation's ability to count and organize multiples.

Consider how, in a political situation such as a modern nation-state, the state can fairly easily determine which people are members (citizens) of it and which ones aren't: one is either documented or not. It is equally easy to tell which multiples belong to a particular litter of kittens and which ones don't (the dog lying next to them isn't in it, the rug isn't in it, etc.). The individuals who are not citizens are excluded from the situation of the nation-state, but are not literally "nothing" either, quite obviously. They are multiples counted by the situation, only to be deemed as not belonging to the situation. The same point can be made about any natural situation – certain multiples will belong to Central Park, and others won't, and it is fairly easy to determine which are which. It seems as if there is no multiple about which a situation could not decide whether it belongs to the situation or not. (This is what ontology tells us, anyway. Philosophy, based on a theory of the event, will have something quite different to say about this matter.)

So, strictly speaking, there is nothing entirely other to a situation. Outside of a situation (as far as the situation is concerned) there is a void. This negative relation to the void is even foundational, according to Badiou. Any situation is founded on, and can be said to start with and presuppose, *the exclusion of the void*. This exclusion does leave a trace in the situation – only it is a trace that the situation itself cannot account for, or does not notice and take into account. Ontology, by contrast, does take this trace of exclusion into account, and accounting for the void's exclusion from presentation becomes one of ontology's primary features.

Set theory's contribution to ontology

At this point we can start to consider what particular role set theory plays for Badiou. The claim that this void, presupposed by any situation and also subtracted from any situation, coincides with being qua being still needs to be justified better, and it is only by looking at what Badiou learns from set theory that this can be done. For Badiou, being qua being is a pure multiple upon which certain operations happen, which create situations that are characterized by their construction and organization of a bunch of multiple-ones. Ontology can be said to study the laws of composition for any organized multiple – that is, any multiple that is not strictly identical to the pure multiple. (Yet ontology can never become a study of any particular situation in its particularity. This would more properly be described as a study of appearance, or existence, and Badiou assigns this task to logic – a "logic of worlds" or a logic of appearance, the title of the second volume of *Being and Event*, which will be covered in chapter 4.)

If ontology is going to study the ways in which a multiplicity that is without one gets composed into a series of ones (which are still, themselves, going to also always be multiples – hence, multiple-ones) what type of discipline can ontology be? We know that the answer is going to be mathematics, and specifically set theory. But is there no other way to study such a thing? Intuition (human experience, human perception) is not going to be up to the task, Badiou argues. True, what we perceive is always a multiplicity of objects, but this is not identical to the kind of pure multiple Badiou posits. What about dialectics? For a long time, Badiou considered this approach to be the proper way to study multiplicity. During the period of what I refer to as his "philosophical Maoism," best expressed in *Theory of the Subject*, he expressed skepticism about the possibility of any "ontology of the multiple" precisely because he felt that such an ontology would never fail to be a "veiled metaphysics" that "presupposes the One as substance" (TS 40). By contrast, he felt at the time that dialectics would be better able to respect the idea "that there is Two," and would be better able to reveal that any "one" is a construction, a derivative of the multiple.

Badiou claims, in *Being and Event*, that it was his continued reflection on logical problems that allowed him to revise his views on the possibility of an ontology of the multiple (BE 5–6). He was drawn to set theory for a number of reasons, but foremost among them was set theory's complete detachment from an intuitionist account of number. This anti-intuitionism seems to be the key to set theory's ability to think radical multiplicity, and in a manner that can have ontological bearing.

Set theory is a theory about the construction of orders (sets) without any requirements on what it is that is being ordered. It does not rely on objects of perception. Set theory's indifference to what it counts allows it to avoid the philosophical idealism that has been a default position for much of philosophy when it comes to ontology. Idealism, basically, would think of being from the perspective of a subject who constructs its experience and posits a variety of theses about what it is that appears. In idealism, the subject is active in what it experiences; the subject operates on the raw material that being qua being presents to it. By turning ontology over to set theory, Badiou can argue that there is a possible study of being in which what human subjects experience and perceive does not matter. The distinct strength of set theory, then, is that it does not require any definition of the multiples being collected. It "excludes any explicit definition of the multiple" and is indifferent to what is being composed into a set (BE 60). So, in *Number and Numbers*, which contains some of his best discussions of set theory and its relevance for his work, "a set," Badiou writes, "is 'made out of elements,' is the 'collection' (in my language, the count-for-one) of its elements" (NN 62). The nature of the elements does not matter.

There are different versions of set theory, and some of them differ quite a bit from the one Badiou designates as having an ontological bearing. But the one he uses – called "Zermelo-Fraenkel set theory" after two of the mathematicians who articulated its axioms – is commonly seen to be the best. The axioms of Zermelo-

Fraenkel set theory define a set simply in terms of the relation of belonging: a set is a collection of elements. Such sets are called transitive and not intuitive sets because they are not limited to collections of well-defined objects, such as cats, people, apples, numbers, and so on. They may contain anything whatsoever; the elements may be as diverse and scattered as you like.

And, in fact, "in Zermelo and Fraenkel's stabilized elaboration, there is no other non-defined primitive term or value possible for the variables apart from sets. Hence, every element of a set is itself a set. This accomplishes the idea that every multiple is a multiple of multiples, with no reference to units of any kind" (B 41). All elements of such a set are also considered to be parts of the set – that is, they are themselves sets or, rather, subsets (NN 64). A subset is a part of a set that happens to contain members of its own, which may in turn be distinct from those of the original set. Technically, such a subset is said to be included in a set, rather than to be belonging to it. Consider how this plays out in the following example from *Number and Numbers*:

> Suppose for example that V is the set of living beings. My cat belongs to this set. But a cat is composed of cells, which one might say are themselves all living beings. So, my cat is at once *a* living being and *a set* of living beings. He belongs to V (qua one, *this* living cat), and he is a part of V – he is included in V (qua group of living cells). (NN 62–3)

Badiou's cat is an element in the set of all living beings, but because the cat is also itself a collection (a set) of living things (cells) this set has a particular property, which set theory tries to capture by saying that the cat not only belongs to the set of living beings, but is also *included* in that set. The distinction between belonging and including may not sound as if it means very much, but it is a crucial terminological difference, and it will also have profound ontological consequences, according to Badiou. Elements belong, subsets are included; and in Zermelo-Fraenkel set theory, all elements of a set are actually subsets. If his cat both belongs to and is included in the set of living beings this is because the cat is itself a multiple, a multiple composed of elements that also belong to the set of living beings.

The philosophical interest of this distinction becomes clearer with the following consideration: it is entirely possible to have a set that contains subsets that do *not* themselves contain elements that are members of the initial set in question. Badiou uses the same kind of example to illustrate this:

> Let's return to the example of my cat. It is an element of the set of living beings, and it is composed of cells that are in turn elements of this set, if one grants that they are living organisms. But if we decompose a cell into molecules, then into atoms, we eventually reach purely physical elements that don't belong to the set of living beings. There is a certain term (perhaps the cell, in fact) which belongs to the set of living beings, but none of whose elements belongs to the set of living beings, because those elements all involve only "inert" physico-chemical materiality. (NN 71)

The cat's cells could be considered minimal elements in the set of living beings: but the cells themselves are also multiples (and sets) consisting of elements too, and some of these elements (the chemicals, for example) would not be members of the set of living beings. We can imagine other, similar cases. Consider a nation-state as a set, composed of its citizens (and perhaps other relevant terms). Any citizen can be considered also to be a set consisting of elements that do belong to the nation-state (whatever it takes to be a citizen, for example: ID cards, tax numbers, parentage, oaths, etc.) and also of elements that do not belong to the nation-state (limbs, clothing, hobbies, etc.). Or, again, consider what belongs to an artwork, considered as a set: form, color, shape, perhaps ... but at some point, there is an element of the artwork (the brushstroke) that is minimal, and whose elements (pigment, chemicals) would not be considered to belong to the set in question (the painting).

Set theory's axioms as "laws of being"

Since set theory is tasked with doing ontology, it must somehow express "laws of being," rules that would pertain to the composition of any multiple whatsoever (NN 63, 71). The examples used above actually articulate one of these laws, expressed in what is called the axiom of foundation. This states that for any set, there is an element of that set to which no other element belonging to the set belongs. This means that there is, for any set, a sort of minimal defining element. In a helpful discussion of this issue in *Number and Numbers*, Badiou writes:

> Of this term, which belongs to the set, but none of whose elements belongs to it, we can say that it grounds the set, or that it is a fun-

damental term of the set. "Fundamental" meaning that on one side of the term, we break through that which it constitutes; we leave the original set, we exceed its presentative capacity. (NN 71)

The reference to presentation is important here. Badiou thinks of the members of a set as things that are present in the set, and the set itself defines what is presented by it. Now, the minimal, foundational elements of any set are always going to be composed of elements that are not present in the set in question. In the example considered earlier the chemicals making up the cat's cells are not presented in the set of living beings (because they are not living beings); the habits and some of the possessions making up the citizens of a nation are not presented in the nation-state; the chemicals making up a brushstroke are not presented in the painting considered as an artwork.

There is something strange about this, since it would seem reasonable to hold that in some sense, after all, of course the chemicals or atoms making up a brushstroke are presented in the painting! And consider the status of DNA in an organism. Is DNA not presented in a living body, even if it is questionable whether it is itself alive? Is it not presented in the citizen of a nation-state? Or consider something like a park: would there be any foundational subsets for a natural object like this? What subsets of a park could possibly contain something that would not be also part of or presented in a natural set such as this?

One thing that is going on here is that Badiou's set-theory approach to ontology requires us to make a distinction between sets, on the one hand, and objects of experience and perception on the other, which would just be one type of set. In fact, one of the reasons why Badiou wants to give ontology over to set theory is exactly because set theory does not limit us to considerations of natural objects and objects of experience; it allows for a far more expansive, indeed non-human, take on the multiple. Thus, we can just arbitrarily designate a set – such as the set of living beings, this particular painting, this particular cat – and hold that strictly speaking, then, what is presented in these sets would only be what the set ascribes to itself; even if, in terms of what we perceive and experience, we would also want to say that the chemicals making up those beings are somehow present too. Again, from the point of view of perception, of course the chemicals making up a brushstroke are presented in the painting, along with everything else about it, all at the same time. But considered as a set, the painting defines itself, and the axiom of foundation assigns to the painting a sort of minimal meaningful unit – the foundational element, which in this case would be the brushstroke, perhaps, but not the chemicals that compose it.

Badiou holds that all of the axioms of Zermelo-Fraenkel set theory are laws of being, and I have only brought one up so far: the axiom of foundation. I will not discuss them all here, only a few more. We already know that the axiom of foundation designates a minimal element for any set. When translated into ontological terms, Badiou puts the axiom of foundation this way: "within an existing one-multiple, there always exists a multiple presented by it such that this multiple is on the edge of the void relative to the initial multiple" (BE 185). Why describe this minimal element as something that is on the edge of the void? Void, we have seen, is the name of being qua being, and a key feature of being qua being, or the pure multiple, is that it does not actually present itself: what is presented is always an ordered multiple, a group of elements counted-as-ones, or, to Badiou's way of thinking, something like a set. To justify the claim that the minimal, foundational unit of a set is at the edge of the void we need to turn to another one of the axioms of Zermelo-Fraenkel set theory.

Badiou takes the assertion of the empty set in set theory as an affirmation that the unpresentable exists (BE 67). The empty set is, then, the way in which the unpresentable can be put into a language, as it were (BE 67). For what the empty set is – a set with no members, no elements, and thus a set that contains nothing – cannot really be said to ever be "presented" in any meaningful sense. Yet at the same time, the empty set has a position within any set, and within any regime of presentation, at least as a mark or symbol or "proper name" (ø). The axiom of the empty set is of special ontological interest, then, because it is presented by Badiou as a significant existential claim made by set theory. (It is, however, not the only existential claim: there is also an axiom of infinity claiming that infinite sets exist. The role of infinity in Badiou's philosophy is discussed in chapter 5.) Most other axioms can be treated simply as rules for the composition and transformations of sets: none of them requires the existence of any sets, and none of them asserts that there *is* a set at all (BE 62). With the axiom of the empty set, however, we do have a claim about existence – the axiom claims that there exists a set, a multiple, to which nothing belongs (BE 67).

Interestingly, the axiom of the empty set is phrased in terms of a negation: it usually goes something like "there exists β such that there does not exist any α which belongs to it" (BE 68). Remember that mere belonging is the basic property upon which set theory is based. The axiom of the empty set can be understood as the simple negation of the relation of belonging itself: there is a set to which nothing belongs, and this is the empty set. The empty set has been explained in terms of an empty sack: it is not that the empty set *is* nothing (which would be absurd); rather, it contains nothing. As a set, then, it is actually distinct from nothing; just as a bag full of nothing, so to speak, nevertheless exists, as an empty bag.

Badiou takes this axiom to be preserving a place, among all the sets that will ever come to be, for what is not presented, and the equivalence between being qua being and the void in Badiou's work can be understood on its basis. Badiou wanted to make this equation in order to go as far as possible with the thesis that the one is not. The empty set is, precisely, a "multiple of nothing" – like being itself would have to be for any order of presentation, for any situation, and so on. Thus, the empty set works as a place holder, within any multiple, for being itself – which is, of course, excluded, in an exclusion that Badiou deems to be foundational for every order of presentation. For this reason, the idea of a minimal or founding set can be said to be situated at the edge of the void. It is the minimal space between presented being and nothing at all.

Conclusion

There are some important claims in Badiou's work on ontology and set theory that seem to be going without argument. For example, there is no argument offered for the claim that the one is not, and there is no argument for why set theory rather than anything else does ontology. With respect to his rejection of a metaphysics of the one, Badiou writes that it is "vain to want to deduce the existence or inexistence of the one – one must decide and assume the consequences" (Con 108). An absence of arguments for fundamental positions might be considered disastrous for a philosophy: without arguments, it seems that Badiou cannot do much to convince anyone who adheres to a contrary philosophy to abandon her position. Badiou gives much in his philosophy the status of axioms, and, like Gilles Deleuze, he does not seem to believe that philosophy consists of a grand conversation in which big questions are debated. Deleuze claims that philosophers are rather bad at such conversations: when there is disagreement about fundamentals (such as, is being one or many? is there a God or not?) there is just not much to talk about. There is no strong way to argue for axioms: they are, precisely, presuppositions.

Yet this is not to say that Badiou's decision for the claim that the one is not is without reasons. It is perhaps not yet clear what these reasons are, but they concern his interest in giving both a theoretical and ethical defense of the continuation of truth procedures, and the faithful subjects associated with them. When he presents the different perspectives that can be held on the status of an event in a situation, these reasons become clearer – these topics will be introduced in the next chapter.

Some further questions could be raised about the status of set theory in Badiou's philosophy. Is it not possible to take the same positions as he does on the multiple without the support of set theory? It is hard to see why not: nothing about the view that the one is not requires one to embrace anything about set theory, for example. Could not the basic theses of Badiou's philosophy be entirely independent of set theory's axioms? This brings up the following concern. Does his use of set theory make him into one of those French philosophers who tries to give his philosophy scientific and objective airs that it does not deserve? Does he include set theory in his work to make it seem like it has all already been established, that there is some external basis for his ontological views other than his own peculiar taste? Several years back, two authors published a book accusing many recent French philosophers of just such a practice. Badiou is mentioned in this book only in passing, and is accused of making an unjustified leap from mathematics to politics in *Theory of the Subject*. The basic thesis of *Being and Event* might have been more fertile ground for these critics, one would think, yet it is not mentioned.

Addressing this issue requires a careful consideration of the status of Badiou's use of set theory. Is it simply an aide for thinking about multiples, or does it go deeper than that? (We can rule out any sort of number mysticism on Badiou's part: he is not a classical Platonist, and he does not think the nature of being *is* mathematical.) In *Being and Event*, Badiou has the following to say about a demonstration made by the mathematician P. J. Cohen: "the question of the being of truth has only been resolved at a *de jure* level quite recently (in 1963, Cohen's discovery)" (BE 341). He takes Cohen's work to have demonstrated that truths (in Badiou's sense – generic procedures, which I begin to discuss in chapter 5) exist: implying that, without Cohen's work, we would not have that demonstration and would only be taking on faith the existence of this kind of truth. This passage indicates that set theory is not something he thinks one can just do without. It indicates that what set theoreticians are doing is quite essential to Badiou's position, and is not mere window-dressing. Set theory, he claims, has contributed something significant to the understanding of being itself, and set theoreticians – some of them, anyway – have actually solved some ontological questions, even if they did not know they were doing so. It still seems possible that Badiou, or someone else, could have arrived at his theses on being and the multiple without set theory. In this sense, there remains something accidental about the status that set theory has for Badiou. For him, an encounter with set theory was, as we have seen, required to even consider the possibility that an ontology of multiplicity could be done. For others, such an encounter may not be required at all, and similar theses could be maintained about multiplicity, the void, and being without any reference to set theory.

But again, work being done in set theory has, Badiou thinks, actually *established* some (not all) of the theses he is interested in supporting philosophically. That is why he can say to philosophers that they should take more of an interest in set theory, because some of the problems they are working on are already handled and, he thinks, settled, by it – especially concerning the nature of truth procedures, as we have seen.

3

Situations and Events

It seems to be the case that ontology, for Badiou, is not just a study of being itself but also of how being is composed into semblances of ones, or into particular multiple-beings. Something happens to being qua being (the pure, inconsistent multiple) such that it is operated upon and rendered into an order of consistent multiplicities. So we can consider any presented order of things (multiples all) to be derived from something else, from something prior to it: the chaos of the inconsistent multiple, which is what really is.

The claim that mathematics is ontology is made by Badiou not because he thinks numbers are the really real, but because a foundational branch of mathematics – set theory – tells us how to compose multiples into ordered collections, more properly known as sets; and this is exactly the kind of method needed to explain the relation between the pure multiple and the multiple-ones that are presented in situations. Set theory articulates rules for the composition of multiples without making any requirements about what a multiple is, or what is being composed: in a sense, set theory is agnostic about the nature of being. Badiou does think, however, that it rules out the presence of any foundational "one" (other than the empty set, which is, precisely, a multiple of nothing, to which no "one" belongs).

I already noted in chapter 2 that part of what makes this approach interesting is that it does not privilege objects and beings that are of any particular concern to human perception and consciousness. This take on ontology strips human intuition, human consciousness, and the human perspective generally, of any privilege. This is an aspect of what I refer to, after Althusser, as Badiou's theoretical anti-humanism. This consequence is intentional on Badiou's part, and he thinks it is one of the most important consequences of his work. His approach to ontology is supposed to work with our intuitions too, of course; but it also exceeds them. The point is, set theory is ultimately indifferent to the way in which we perceive and carve up the world conceptually or linguistically. It allows being qua being to be carved up in all sorts of different ways that have nothing to do with what we perceive and how we need to organize our experience.

Set theory does impose some conditions on the multiples it composes, however. Two of these conditions (found in the axioms, the laws of being) were discussed in the previous chapter, and other relevant ones will be discussed here. The major distinction between being qua being, as an inconsistent multiplicity, akin to Chaos, and any number of different situations that order this multiple in particular ways, is the key first point. Chapter 2 described this distinction. This chapter will address the relations between the two orders, and also something else about the nature of the ordered multiples themselves that Badiou calls situations. On top of the laws of being found in set theory, Badiou also thinks it is possible to discern on their basis a *typology* of situations, some of which will contain properties that take us beyond ontology.

More on the empty set and the void

To arrive at the rest of Badiou's philosophy, we need to consider the difference between including and belonging once again. Being qua being is an inconsistent multiplicity, yet Badiou holds that the proper name of being is "void." This means that "void" is how being is named within situations. It so happens that the void is, as such, never actually presented in any situation or any set – it is only present in name, as it were – and the empty set is this name in any particular situation, acting like a place-holder for the void. For every situation, ontology is able to assert that there is this name, "void," acting as a place-holder for being qua being in the situation.

Now, it would be incorrect to say that the void is an *element* of every set (or situation, for that matter), because elements are, properly speaking, what belong to sets, and the empty set contains no elements. The empty set is better seen as the "place" in any set at which the void is marked or named but, also, then excluded and barred from presentation. Thus, the empty set does not properly speaking belong to anything. (Recall that "belong" is a technical term here, referring to the status of elements in a set.) Furthermore, Badiou associates the set-theoretical notion of belonging with presentation. There is, of course, in the case of the empty set no question of presentation either – there is nothing presented in the empty set, and nothing *of* it to present.

If such a set is not presented anywhere and cannot be said to be an element of other sets (since nothing belongs to it), what is the empty set's status for sets? To account for this another order or structure, or way of counting, seems to be required. Badiou refers to this as a metastructure, as the state of a situation. In order to account for why the void as such, or the inconsistent multiple as such, or the chaos of pure being, is never presented, Badiou appeals to this idea of a metastructure governing any ordered multiplicity. There do not seem to be any intrinsic reasons why the chaos of the pure multiple could *not* be presented as such. He puts the same point in a slightly different way when he writes that the consistency of any order of presentation is "merely a result of the action of structure" (BE 93). Thus, one of the accomplishments of any order of presentation is a prohibition on the void's presentation. The catastrophe that would be a presentation of being itself must be prohibited because without the prohibition the order itself, the organizing of the multiple, would dissolve.

So, this prohibiting action performed by a metastructure proper to situations is something Badiou feels that ontology must also address. Ontology, then, is not just a description of the way in which multiples are ordered, but will also account for this prohibition on the void ever being presented in situations and sets. And this leads ontology to distinguish between two orders, a distinction that Badiou claims is marked in set theory by the difference between the terms "belonging" and "inclusion." In fact, Badiou writes that his "entire edifice" – his entire philosophy, I take it – is based on this distinction (BE 97). It is true that what I have been referring to as the rest of Badiou's work – which should really be considered the majority of his work, built around the notion of the event – comes from the consequences of what Badiou calls the theorem of the point of excess, which spells out the main consequence of this distinction between belonging and inclusion (BE 97).

On presentation and representation

Why is this distinction so important? Recall that elements are said to *belong* to sets, while subsets are said to be *included* in sets. This becomes interesting because of the way in which Badiou has linked belonging to presentation. Something that belongs to a set is said by Badiou to be present in it. Can the same thing be said for subsets? Are they always presented in the sets in which they are included? The answer is no: subsets are not necessarily presented in their sets (BE 62).

Subsets are parts of sets that are themselves composed of elements. As we saw in chapter 2, when a living cat is considered from this perspective we can say that its minimal living elements – cells (and I add "living," because that is the restriction the set "living cat" imposes) – themselves contain elements (mere chemicals) that could not be considered present in a set of living things. A living cat does not present itself as a chemical soup, for example. That is because chemicals are not living things – cells are, however. So, we could say that a living cat does present itself as a collection of living cells. Badiou writes: "no element of the cell (no chemical molecule as such) is an element of the cat, since every element of the living multiplicity 'cat' is a cell" (TW 100). The minimal, foundational elements (cells) of the cat as a living thing should in fact be considered *subsets* (since they are themselves composed of discrete elements); and these subsets are clearly composed of elements that do not belong to the set "cat as a living thing" and are, therefore, said to be not presented in it.

So subsets can have a strange status within their sets. Badiou is going to say that while some may not be *presented*, they may nevertheless be *represented* in a set – and it is a different order, a different count, that accounts for the representation of subsets in a set. The metastructure of a situation, or what Badiou calls the state of a situation, is what does this work. So there are, then, two different orders or structures governing situations – one that accounts for the composition of elements into a set in the first place (this covers presentation) and another that takes a different perspective on those elements, considers them as subsets, and then includes them in the situation or not (this covers what Badiou calls representation).

The power-set axiom and the point of excess

What is called the power-set axiom in Zermelo-Fraenkel set theory draws out one of the important consequences of this distinction between belonging and inclusion. It allows the following claim to be made: the subsets of any set can be treated as a set themselves (BE 62). We can take all of the subsets of a set and make them into a new set: this is called the power-set of the set. Something called the theorem of the point of excess adds that this power-set is necessarily distinct from the set of which it is the power-set. Badiou says it "exceeds" its initial set, and he will want to claim that the excess is, in some cases, immeasurable: one cannot determine, in the case of certain types of sets at least, by how much, by what number, the power-set of that set exceeds its set.

This is not always so. Consider a simple example of a set – say, a family of three. Call this set X. The power-set axiom tells us that the number of the set of subsets in this family is different from the number of elements of the family (three). Let's say that you would have individuals A, B, and C as elements of the family: the possible subsets – different groupings of the elements – would be AB, AC, and BC, which, in addition to A, and B, and C themselves (which are also by definition subsets because they have their own elements distinct from the set of which they are members), and then also the group ABC itself, makes for a total of eight subsets. The number of the "set" of subsets (8) thus exceeds the number of elements in the set (3). The formula for figuring out the power-set of a set is 2 to the power of n, where n is the number of elements in the set. In the case of our family of three, we have 2 to the power of 3, or 8.

So why does Badiou say that for some sets the measure of the power-set's excess cannot be determined? The complete answer as to why the difference between the power-set of a set and the set itself is not able to be measured requires a discussion of Badiou's claims about infinite sets, which I have not addressed yet. I will address this in chapter 5: for now, I will just state that in an infinite set, the power-set axiom is still functional, and the difference in number between the power-set of an infinite set and the infinite set itself is what cannot be measured.

The power-set axiom also shows us something about how every set is subject to a double count: on the level of belonging (elements) and on the level of inclusion (subsets). Badiou writes:

belonging is an ontological function of *presentation*, indicating *that which* is presented in the count-for-one of a multiple. Inclusion is the ontological function of *representation*, indicating multiples re-counted as parts in the framework of a representation. A most important problem (the problem of the *state of a situation*) is determined by the relation between presentation and representation. (NN 65)

Terms like presentation, structure, belonging, and element are to be considered as terms pertinent to a situation, while terms such as representation, inclusion, subset, and part are terms pertinent to the state of a situation (BE 103).

Another theorem – the theorem of the point of excess – leads us to something that is otherwise than being altogether: the event. Badiou spells out the theorem as follows: "there is always – whatever a is – at least one element (here y) of $p(a)$ which is not an element of a" (BE 85). This means that there is something in any order of presentation that exceeds, and is other than and different from, what is itself counted and represented in the ordered set. This establishes fairly well, Badiou thinks, that there is a significant gap between presentation and representation, between a situation and its state or metastructure. (Although, again, to say that it is immeasurable really requires a consideration of infinite sets, not finite ones.)

Types of multiples in situations: normal, excrescent, and singular

It would seem natural to say that a set is a more basic thing than a situation, and that a situation is a large collection of sets. Remember that Badiou defines a situation as a consistent presented multiplicity, which, because it is consistent, implies some kind of structure (BE 522). And he also claims that to exist means "*to belong to* a situation" (BE 372). So, a situation seems to be something more than just a mere set, not simply because it is larger but because there is something else going on in it: a double count, or a doubling of structure such that the distinction between subsets and elements is relevant or accounted for within it. It will turn out to be the case that in Badiou's philosophy every situation is infinite, while obviously not every set is infinite: "every situation is ontologically infinite" (Meta 143 and TW 159). The difference between a situation and a set is therefore important to uphold.

What I want to note now is how Badiou develops a typology of situations on the basis of the theorem of the point of excess, a typology that is based on the different possible relations between a situation and its state. This will ultimately lead to the concept of the evental site: a situation will be event-prone, or not, depending on the relation between presentation and representation in it.

If a multiple, counted (presented) in a situation, is also counted (represented) by the situation's metastructure, this multiple is said to be normal. The theorem of the point of excess tells us that there are also multiples that are included (represented) in a situation but not properly presented in it. Badiou calls these multiples excrescences for their situations. And, finally, there are presented multiples that are not represented – these are described by Badiou as immediate and not a part of the situation. They are singular. Singular multiples have the quality of being of their situation, while what composes them is something *not* presented in the situation, but rather something that functions in a separated manner (BE 99). (As a last possibility, there are multiples that are neither presented nor represented in a situation: these are, of course, members of the void itself (BE 108). So, within a situation there are really only three types of possible multiples available: normal, singular, and excrescent ones.)

There are many ways to illustrate these multiples. One of the most intuitive given by Badiou is an example of a situation that happens to contain all three types of multiples. For a Marxist conception of a capitalist nation-state, Badiou claims that the bourgeoisie would be a normal multiple, obviously present and represented in the state, while the proletariat would be a singular multiple, because although it is present in the capitalist situation it is not represented (BE 109). The state, in this conception, would be an excrescent multiple.

The elements of such a capitalist nation-state would be multiples like individual citizens, private property, laws, governmental institutions, markets, and so on. The distinction made by Badiou between this situation and its state or metastructure (which, recall, "counts the count" made by the situation, as it were) allows the following remarks to be made: there can be some elements presented in the situation but not represented in it, some that are represented without being presented, and some that are both presented and represented. The trickiest one to figure out may be the notion of excrescence. But the Marxist example Badiou gives makes this fairly clear: in a Marxist analysis of a bourgeois state, the state

Situations and Events

itself is said to be an excrescence because the state is a thing of pure representation with no real grounding in the multiples that are present in the situation (the state is itself an unfounded excess, as it were). The nation-state, like the state of any situation, is actually a separate order, a separate count, not necessarily grounded on anything intrinsic to what is presented in the situation. Hence Badiou's use of a term like excrescence for it, which suggests something like an excessive outgrowth.

The state of a situation, remember, counts the subsets of the situation rather than elements of the situation. Thus, a different type of multiple is present (or, rather, to use Badiou's terminology consistently, "represented") for it. From the state's point of view, individuals in a bourgeois society would be subsets consisting only of one thing: themselves – the point being that what individuals are for the state, insofar as they are represented in it, is quite different from what individuals are as genuine multiple-beings, with their diverse traits and interests and characteristics present in their communities. Only certain things about them count as far as the state of a situation is concerned – what Badiou here calls their unicity (as individuals identified by a number or name) (BE 107).

So the state itself in a bourgeois nation-state is an excrescence because "the state is less a result of the consistency of presentation than of the danger of inconsistency" (BE 109). This is related to Badiou's claims about the need for a situation to prohibit the presentation of the void. This prohibition is, in a sense, arbitrary, but also completely essential for the consistency of a situation.

The nation-state situation's singular multiples – in this case, the proletariat – act, by contrast, as what Badiou describes as emblems of that situation's void (BE 109). Why should this be the case? Since they are presented, after all, what do they have to do with the void? His point seems to be that multiples like this serve as a reminder of the contingency of the state's way of counting the situation's multiples: the proletariat marks the possibility of an entirely different way of organizing society.

Singular multiples and eventsl sites

The discussion so far has tried to show how ontology is able to give us a "typology of being" (BE 93). This is distinct from ontology's articulation of the "laws of being" (NN 63). The typology is of particular importance for philosophy, and not just ontology, because philosophical practice will focus on those situations in which a particular type of multiple occurs, one that Badiou describes as abnormal. And it is on the basis of this type of multiple that something other than being occurs.

How can there be something other than being, which is a phrase Badiou uses often in his discussions of events? We know that Badiou equates being qua being with the void, or pure chaos – that which is not able ever to be presented as such – and then, within situations, there are beings, or multiples, that are like pseudo-ones. Can an area for something other than being be found in this ontological framework if we look more closely at the notion of singular multiples, introduced in the previous section? A singular multiple was one that was present in a situation without being represented in it, or counted in it. Consider again the role the proletariat plays in a Marxist analysis of capitalist nation-states. For Marx, this multiple was the revolutionary class, the class present in its situation without representation in it, strictly speaking: the class, therefore, that possessed the seed of a new order. Clearly, though, the proletariat must be considered *of* its situation somehow: it is a multiple, it is presented after all. It simply may not count for much within the bourgeois nation-state.

Such a singular multiple would not be otherwise than being at all. The theory of the event, to which this discussion is building up, requires a different type of multiple. Badiou considers another situation to see again how notions like singularity and excrescence and normalcy work, this time using a family as an example. He writes of a family who might be considered both a presented multiple and a represented multiple in the French national situation. They are presented, because they live together, go out together, and so forth; and they are represented in that situation if they are citizens whose papers are in order, and so on. Badiou claims that if there were a member of that family who lived with them but was illegal, undocumented, and thus only went out in disguise or with fake ID or something (or never went out), this member would make the family into a singular multiple (BE 174). That is because, while the family, with its clandestine, undocumented member, remains presented in the situation, it is no longer represented (because one of its members is not counted).

And, in this case, the multiple who is the hidden family member cannot be said to be presented in the situation either. This multiple is, therefore, neither singular nor an excrescence (and, obviously, it is not going to be normal either). Remember that multiples like this were also discussed in the example of the living cat in the previous chapter, whose chemical make-up was said to be not presented at all in the cat as a living creature. Such a multiple – the chemistry of a living cell – is also neither singular, nor excrescent, nor, obviously, normal, for the situation of the living cat. It is a multiple of a different sort altogether.

Now, if we were to take all multiples like this – the multiples in a situation that are not presented – and make them into a set, what would the status of this set be for the situation in which these elements are not presented? Would this *set* of non-presented multiples be present or not? Badiou calls this an abnormal set, and he also calls it an "evental site." He claims that such a set itself is present in its situation, even though its members are not:

> I will term *evental site* an entirely abnormal multiple; that is, a multiple such that none of its elements are presented in the situation. The site, itself, is presented, but "beneath" it nothing from which it is composed is presented. As such, the site is not a part of the situation. I will also say of such a multiple that it is *on the edge of the void*, or *foundational*. (BE 175)

An evental site is not a part of the situation, which means that it is not represented in the situation; but as a set it is presented, even though none of its elements is presented. This is rather strange. An evental site would seem to have all the qualifications of being what has already been described as a singular multiple. What Badiou claims, however, is that an evental site is a multiple that is "totally singular: it is presented, but none of its elements are presented" (BE 507). So an evental site entails somewhat more than what is found in a singular multiple, as indicated by Badiou's description of it as totally singular. What distinguishes an evental site from other singular multiples is the fact that the *elements* of this site are not presented in the situation in question, while the set itself *is* present, and is an element for the situation. Not all singular multiples are like this. For example, the elements of the proletariat, which Badiou describes as a singular multiple, would for the most part be present in the situation of the bourgeois nation-state, as the proletariat as a whole certainly is (even if there are problems with its representation in the state).

In the other type of social situation discussed above, where there was a family presented in the situation one of whose members was not present – thus making the entire family not *represented* – the family was said to be a singular multiple. A family would, by contrast, be an evental site if it were "a concrete family, *all* of whose members were clandestine or non-declared, and which presents itself (manifests itself publicly) *uniquely* in the group form of family outings" (BE 175). How is this to be understood? What is a multiple "solely presented as the multiple-that-it-is"? This suggests a kind of anonymity. The multiple in question is presented as a family, although none of the individuals are counted socially, because we are dealing with a case in which the family is a unit of social *representation*. A family of illegal immigrants is presented in the social space of a nation-state as a family, even though none of its individuals are official members of that space.

For the situations in which they are present, such evental sites can be said to be at the edge of the void and foundational because just beneath them, so to speak, as far as the situation is concerned, would be the pure multiple itself. An evental site is certainly not identical to the void, or being qua being, since it is, after all, a composed multiple and not chaotic. But it is a multiple composed of nothing presented or represented in the situation. Since "within the situation, this multiple is, but *that of which* it is multiple is not," the evental site is like the first multiple of a situation, or its minimal unit, and can therefore be considered foundational for the situation (BE 175).

Another example of a situation with an evental site comes, perhaps surprisingly, from the example of the cat as a living creature. Badiou argues that the living cat too has an evental site. Of what does this consist? And how would this evental site be present in the living cat without any of its elements being present? The cat's organs, for example, would not qualify as evental sites, because these – which could certainly be considered subsets of the cat, since they are composed of elements (cells and their parts, etc.) – contain elements that are presented in the cat as living thing. But the individual cells of the cat would, by contrast, qualify as evental sites.

> A cell can be considered as a site, because the molecules that compose it are not "organic" in the same sense as the liver may be said to be organic. A chemically determined molecule is no longer "alive" in the sense that the cat can be said to be alive. Even if it is "objectively" a part of the cat, a simple aggregate of molecules is not a vital component in the same sense as the liver. We could say that with this aggregate we have reached the material edge of the cat's vitality. This is why such an aggregate will be said to be "on the edge of the void"; that is, on the edge of what separates the cat, as a singular

multiple-situation, from its pure indistinct being, which is the void proper to life (and the void proper to life, as death shows, is matter). (TW 99)

The cat's cells are clearly presented, yet they are subsets that contain elements not themselves presented in the situation. This is exactly the characteristic of an evental site.

Situations and evental sites

Not all situations have evental sites. For what Badiou calls a natural situation, there is no evental site. This is because in any natural situation (which would seem to be non-living aggregates such as a clump of matter, a national park, the planet Neptune, and the like), there could not be any elements of the situation's subsets that would not also be considered present in the situation if it is natural. That is, if to count in a natural situation means "being part of nature," there is no component of a natural thing that would not also be itself a natural thing. Badiou's views here seem to echo Spinoza's claim that whatever exists, exists in nature. Badiou devotes a chapter of *Being and Event* to his differences with Spinoza, and this is placed amid his discussion of the distinction between situations and states. His view is that, while Spinoza is sensitive to multiplicity, the claim that whatever is, is in nature, ultimately means that for Spinoza all situations are natural, and they all have the same state (BE 112). Badiou calls this view circular: presentation and representation are wound together in such a case. Any element composing a natural multiple is also going to be present in that multiple. In other words, everything presented is also represented in a natural situation, and vice versa.

What Badiou calls a natural situation is, then, one in which a condition he calls normalcy reigns: all multiples in a natural situation are normal (BE 128). This makes some intuitive sense. Natural situations would not have any excresences and singularities. An important implication of Badiou's claim about the characteristics of natural situations is that there are no events in nature. This does not mean that nothing changes in nature, of course. The claim that there are no events in nature really just means that nothing happens to nature from outside of nature.

A *historical* situation, however, is one in which there is an evental site – and this is why the living cat would have to be considered a historical situation and not simply a natural one: it has at least one evental site, as we have seen (BE 177). This means that something like an event can occur for the living cat. As Badiou mentioned, this would be death, the return of its elements to mere matter. (Consider, by contrast, how nothing can possibly be done to a natural set that would make it unnatural!)

There are also, it should be added, neutral situations, distinct from both natural and historical ones (BE 515). It is difficult to find specific examples of such situations in Badiou's work. It seems that there are no evental sites in such a situation either, but surprisingly, also, there are no natural multiples in it (BE 177). These might be things like arbitrary collections of objects that have nothing to do with each other, but still would not be entirely, or exclusively, considered from the perspective of nature: such as a set containing a glance, a bookshelf, light, and a memory, each miles and miles apart.

On an event as a violation of the laws of being

Setting aside the case of neutral situations, we have a major distinction between two types of situations, and this is important for Badiou's general philosophy, because it turns out that ontology – mathematics – cannot give a theory of the historical situations that contain events, because it cannot give a doctrine of the event (BE 184). This concept – the event – is what will take us to the rest of Badiou's philosophy.

An evental site is an abnormal multiple, a set that contains elements that are not presented in the situation, but that is still itself present in the situation. What makes these sites evental and thus of philosophical importance is the claim that there is a special type of multiple that belongs to them. This multiple is the event itself, which Badiou defines as a multiple composed partly of elements of the evental site itself, and partly of something else.

What could this something else be? From what else could the event, as a multiple, draw its resources or elements? We have two possibilities to consider: if an event is partly composed of elements from the evental site, the remaining material for its composition would have to come either from being qua being itself or from elsewhere in the situation that the evental site is in. Badiou will say, however, that neither is the case. If what composes the event came from being qua being itself, then the event would be just like any other multiple. It would be the result of an operation on being qua being, and would be presenting the inconsistent multiple in some form or another. Now, as an element of an evental site, the event, like all elements of that site, should be presenting precisely *nothing* for its situation. The other option is that the event is composed of elements already in the situation itself. But this clearly cannot work either, since if that were the case the event would not be part of the evental site, whose very condition requires that it consist of elements not themselves presented in the situation.

What are we left with then? And what is it that is driving Badiou to theorize such a strange thing anyway? What Badiou ends up claiming about the event is this: it is *"a multiple such that it is composed of, on the one hand, elements of the site, and on the other hand, itself"* (BE 179). It is the important claim that an event is *a multiple that contains itself as a member* that requires our attention first.

One of the axioms of Zermelo-Fraenkel set theory (called "the axiom schema of separation" or "the axiom schema of specification") states that a set *cannot* contain itself as a member. This is made into an axiom of set theory in order to avoid what is known as Russell's paradox (after the philosopher Bertrand Russell). What is this about?

The set of all objects containing the color red certainly is not itself red. Similarly for many other kinds of sets: the set of all squares is not itself a square; the set of all humans is not itself human. Such sets – collections of objects with something in common, let's say – can be said not to contain themselves, and they are called, within set theory, *normal* sets. Now, there can be some sets that do contain themselves as members: the set of non-red things is itself non-red, and thus would include itself as a member. The set of non-square things is itself non-square, and would include itself too. These are called *abnormal* sets.

Russell's paradox emerges when we ask a sort of higher-order question about normal sets. Let's say we collect all the normal sets together into one set. The question is this: is our collection of normal sets itself normal or not? Does it contain itself as a member or not? If we want to say that it is normal, this must be because it does not contain itself as a member. But it is supposed to be a collection of all normal sets, so it *should* include itself! But then, if it does include itself as a member, that makes it abnormal. And so we end up creating a scenario in which there is a real contradiction – a set has been created that seems to be neither normal nor abnormal, when these are the only two possibilities going. Zermelo-Fraenkel set theory's way out of this is to simply rule out the construction of abnormal sets. No set can contain itself as a member, as a matter of principle.

So why does a violation of that axiom appear in Badiou's theory of the event? This is a question about what is driving Badiou's claim about events: why does he want to say that there are such things?

As was the case with the decision that set theory does ontology, Badiou claims that this is simply a decision on his part – again, one with motivations and some justification, but one without perhaps any proper argument in support of it. Prior to explaining his theory of the event, Badiou suggests that some kind of a leap is required, since the move is difficult to justify with arguments (BE 179). Perhaps in contrast to his decision that set theory does ontology, though, with his theory of the event he is able to make some appeals to experience in support of it.

Remember that historical situations are the ones that are going to contain evental sites, and thus at least the capacity for events. So Badiou considers a historical situation like France in the eighteenth century, and an event within that situation, the French Revolution. If the French Revolution is going to be the event, the evental site within the situation of eighteenth-century France would, of course, have to be some multiple presented in the situation without the elements that compose that multiple itself being presented. Badiou writes that the evental site for eighteenth-century France was a multiple composed of a variety of elements that played a key role in the French Revolution (BE 180). It seems odd to state that these elements are not properly presented as such within the situation of eighteenth-century France. Is it only the case that they are presented insofar as they are unified by an evental site? Or is it rather something about their status in the situation that remains ambiguous? Are they really present in France, elements of that situation, or are they aberrations, deviations, and so on? Do they really have a place within that situation?

Badiou claims, we know, that an event partly consists of elements from the evental site, and partly of itself. What he will claim for this example is that the event, "the French Revolution," is self-referential. This means that key among the elements that compose the French Revolution is the thing itself, the French Revolution. Why? This amounts to saying something like the French Revolution was an issue for itself: Badiou refers to St-Just's famous line in

1794 about the revolution being frozen (BE 180). But, presumably, other writings and comments would make a similar point: part of the French Revolution was a concern about its own status – its status, precisely, for the situation of eighteenth-century France. Does it count in that situation or not? Is it an element of eighteenth-century France, or not? Does it belong to a different situation?

Badiou claims that the evental site is present for a situation, but the event itself is, perhaps, not. In fact, the event's status – whether the event proper is presented in the situation or not – turns out to be undecidable, and Badiou considers this to be somehow the foundation of his philosophy (BE 181). The belonging of an event *"to the situation of its site is undecidable from the standpoint of the situation itself"* (BE 181). Here, we can say that the event itself would be this thing called "the French Revolution" while the evental site would be the happenings, the organizations, the writings, the turmoil, and so on – all of which, considered together, are certainly present in eighteenth-century France, perhaps falling under a signifier like "troubled times." What is not clear is whether the thing being trumpeted as a "Revolution" by some elements of the troubles is or not.

Thus, the question is whether this event called the "French Revolution" belongs to and is presented in the situation of eighteenth-century France. Badiou's claim is that such a question is undecidable from the situation itself, and this is true for any instance of an event. If an event is an element of an evental site (which, again, contains elements not presented in the situation but is, as a site, or set, present), why is Badiou even asking this question? The answer would seem to be obvious: of course an event (as an element of an evental site) is not going to be present in the situation! This was just one of the conditions for being an element of an evental site! But here is why Badiou is not content with this answer. If the event does not belong to the situation, then it presents nothing in the situation and is not at all for it. This implies that the situation would remain undisturbed by it. An event, then, would make nothing happen in the situation. And this does not seem to fit with our intuition about how historical situations work. Badiou does argue that one of the functions of the state of any historical situation is to prohibit events: the title of one of the chapters of *Being and Event* reads "Being's Prohibition of the Event," which could equally well read "ontology's prohibition of the event" (BE 184). In this case, if an event simply does not belong to its situation, and simply presents nothing in that situation, that is like saying that the French Revolution is just an empty phrase used by its partisans and enemies alike, with no real referent (BE 182).

This leads us back to why Badiou wishes to claim that an event violates one of the axioms of set theory. Badiou wants this to mean that the event takes us outside of the realm of ontology altogether. The event "belongs to that-which-is-not-being-qua-being" (BE 189). Yet Badiou can also claim that the event is very close to being qua being itself. As Badiou says, it connotes the void for a situation (BE 182). We are already familiar with the idea that there are sets that are foundational for a situation and at the edge of the void – these are evental sites. What Badiou is claiming about an event proper is that it somehow reveals the radical contingency of any way of ordering the multiple. The event is, nevertheless, separated from both the void itself and any situation . . . and what does the separating, or what makes it separated, is nothing other than the event itself (BE 182). The event is, then, not just at the edge of the void, like the evental site to which it belongs, but "*between the void and itself*" (BE 182). An event is the "being of non-being" – and, thinking of what kind of presence an event might be said to have, Badiou will describe it as a vanishing (BE 183).

Another example Badiou uses in this context comes from Arnold Schoenberg's invention of twelve-tone music. The relevant situation would be, let's say, musical composition in Europe in the early twentieth century. There would be all sorts of composers and compositions that would be presented in this situation and represented in it: the canon at the time, for example, as well as living composers, and certain kinds of dominant and acceptable styles (say, Viennese Romanticism). We could say that Schoenberg's invention consists of a series of compositions characterized by a trait – atonality – that sets them apart from other compositions. If Schoenberg's works make up an evental site, Badiou would need to hold that the compositions themselves are not properly presented in the musical situation of their day. It is, however, the case that this thing called "twelve-tone music" is presented as a whole (maligned by some, celebrated by others). But the compositions themselves, if they are elements of an evental site, cannot be held to be presented in the situation.

An evental site marks, therefore, a kind of division within the situation. Such a site is a subset, it contains its own elements, but these elements are not properly part of the situation in which the site itself is presented. The evental site has one foot in its situation, and one foot out, as it were. And it also, crucially, contains a strange thing called an *event* whose status – whether it is presented or not in the situation – is actually undecidable. (This is not the case for any other element of an eventual site: note that these would be decidedly *not* presented in the situation.)

Conclusion

At the opening of this chapter there was a major difference between being qua being and being-in-situations. Now there are also evental sites, which Badiou situates at the edge of the void, which means that they are between being qua being and situational or situated being. And there are also events themselves, which seem to be neither fish nor flesh: "trans-beings," as Badiou calls them, or the very "being of non-being" (BE 183).

With the theory of the event it seems that the major difference in Badiou's philosophy, between being qua being and situations, is somehow collapsed into and repeated in a difference within the evental site itself. The evental site is, one presumes, composed of typical multiples with one significant and transgressive exception – the event, which violates one of the axioms of Zermelo-Fraenkel set theory, one of the laws of being itself. A potential problem here is that it is this exception that seems to make the evental site into what it is – evental at all, rather than just a singular multiple (a set present in its situation, whose elements are not presented). If that is the case, why is an event an element of an evental site? Why is it not something that occurs on its own? Why does an event need to be grouped with other elements that are somehow associated with it? For a situation, an evental site is of course presented, but unlike the rest of the elements of an evental site an event proper has an undecidable status for the situation (precisely because of its self-belonging, its violation of a law of being). The state of the situation would require the event's exclusion for this very reason – it presents nothing, after all. So why is an event something that is grouped with other elements in a situation? The key feature of an event is its status as a multiple that belongs to itself, that is in some respect self-referential. We saw that when Badiou fleshes this idea out with examples, they concern moments during which, within a situation, something is going on whose status – let's say, whose correctness – cannot be decided upon. This would seem to allow anyone to claim that something is an event: in other words, if the only condition for an event is self-belonging, all sorts of things could be considered this way. The problem that arises, then, is that there may be a distinction between events proper and pseudo-events. How are we supposed to be able to tell the difference? I will argue that this is not really a problem for Badiou's philosophy when I discuss his ethics in chapter 7. But I will consider, in the next chapter, how he moves away from this recognition problem in the sequel to *Being and Event*, *Logics of Worlds*.

4

Logics of Worlds

The discussion of set theory and ontology so far in Badiou's work threatens to miss the forest for the trees, for Badiou's main philosophical interest is not to be found in doing ontology. Philosophy, he claims, is concerned with what is otherwise than being. What Badiou has in mind by this – in large part, the notion of the event – was introduced in the last chapter. Clearly, the event is on his account a violation of ontological principles. An event is therefore not a being, and it is not identical to being qua being either.

According to *Being and Event*, the defining feature of an event is that it is a multiple characterized by self-belonging. This is Badiou's way of expressing what is a distinctive feature of events in human history: there is no objective way to decide on their status, to decide on whether they really belong to the situations they challenge or not. Some kind of leap or choice or decision is required with respect to them – and it is a leap either way, whether it is a leap *for* the view that the event belongs to the situation, or *against* it. There are several key ideas in Badiou's philosophy surrounding this notion of a leap – what he calls an intervention on behalf of the event, as well as a naming, a forcing, a truth procedure, and ultimately a subject – but before discussing these (starting in this chapter and continuing in chapter 5), I want to consider first how Badiou has developed a more nuanced theory of the event through his account of a "logic of appearance" or a "logic of worlds." It is worth considering this before going on to the rest of Badiou's work because this addition has led Badiou to develop a more complex theory of change, and accordingly a more complex theory of the subject.

In *Being and Event*, the event's status in a situation seems to be an unaccountable mystery, and readers can be forgiven for detecting a kind of religiosity in Badiou's philosophy, a messianic structure, because the event seems to emerge spontaneously, descending from the sky like a miracle. An event is, after all, a violation of the very "laws of being." In *Being and Event*, we are presented with a theory that posits a pure multiplicity on one side (being), and a unit of absolute change and non-being on the other (event). (Perhaps Badiou could have simply borrowed a title from Jean-Paul Sartre, and named his book *Being and Nothingness* instead of *Being and Event* . . .) The problem with *Being and Event* is in this ultimately flawed (Badiou himself comes to feel) attempt to bring the two together with the conglomerate notion of an "evental site": a notion that seems to be something like Badiou's version of the Cartesian pituitary gland, that impossible object in which two radically distinct substances – the body and the immaterial soul – were supposed to meet and interact.

In *Logics of Worlds* Badiou accounts for what he calls the *value* of an evental site's existence, or appearance, in a manner that seems to resolve the problem of interaction between being and event – not because it bridges the gap between being and event in a more effective way (the gap remains), but because its account of change pays more attention to what is internal to situations (which are now called worlds). Doing this manages to make an event less absolutely other to its situation than it seemed. The status of an event can now be accounted for better: what makes for an event is not just a unique property of the event itself (in *Being and Event*, this was self-belonging, and in *Logics of Worlds* it is roughly similar), but its consequences in its situation or world. An event is now a term for the far end of a scale of changes that an evental site brings about in a situation. In other words, an event is one type of change that situations or worlds undergo, among others. And, therefore, an event is measured as much by its consequences on its situation or world as it is by any properties that are intrinsic to it.

Logic as a study of transcendentals

So, *Logics of Worlds* should be read as Badiou's attempt to provide a philosophical framework for the revamping of the notion of an evental site from *Being and Event* – even though the text seems to be mainly concerned with doing something else. The bulk of *Logics of Worlds* is concerned with presenting what he calls a Grand Logic, covering how "multiple-being can be thought in a world, and not only in its being as such" (LM 103). Ontology thinks of multiples from the perspective of their being, and is not interested in how they appear, and what relations these multiples might have to each other in the situations in which they occur. Another way of putting this is to say that ontology does not really study what is internal to situations in any detail – it studies the laws of being that must hold for whatever ends up appearing in a situation. Or ontology considers how multiples are and can be *composed*, and what properties such multiples can have. What Badiou calls logic in *Logics of Worlds* considers multiples from the perspective of their appearing or existence in what Badiou calls now a world rather than a situation – but the two are meant to be synonymous (LM 45). And in *Logics of Worlds* he studies what he calls existence or "being-there" instead of presentation.

Logic is, then, a study of appearance, where this means a study of how a multiple actually takes form in real situations and real worlds. And since there are always situations and only ever situations (everything that *is* is in a situation) being's essence is, Badiou says, to appear: "it is of the essence of being to appear" (TW 15). And what appearance, for its part, requires is some account of relation: the essence of being is to appear, and the essence of appearing is relation (B 162). The reason why appearing requires an account of relation is because what appears is always a being-situated, as it were. Any being, in order to be, must be presented: which is to say, it is located with respect to other appearances. This means that its appearance is always situational, and is in some place, some *there*, some "localization" (B 161). Thus, any appearing being or multiple contains or expresses a relation between that thing's being (as a multiple), and some structure that places that being with respect to others. What Badiou calls logic is the study of such structures, which he calls transcendentals (plural, because there are different types of them).

Kant used the term transcendental for the structuring activity that the human mind performed on raw sense-data. There was, Kant held, a kind of mental apparatus that would filter this raw data into categories such as space, time, cause, and substance. Thus, the term *transcendental* in Kant's work refers to the conditions for our experience itself: it was structurally necessary, for example, that objects of human experience appear in space, in time, as effects of causes. The phenomenologist Edmund Husserl also used the term transcendental to describe an aspect of his phenomenological method: a "transcendental phenomenology" would study the basic structures of conscious experience.

Badiou has made it clear that in his systematic philosophy he wants to do without any reference to a subject who has and constructs its experiences, and the structures of conscious life are not his focus. So his use of the term transcendental is risky since it evokes precisely those aspects of the philosophical tradition he wants to avoid. Notice that a similar problem occurred in *Being and Event* with his use of terms like operation and even presentation. A situation in *Being and Event* was said to be some kind of organizing or counting of the pure multiple, leaving one with a question about who or what does the organizing or counting. Badiou's view is that this organizing is simultaneous with the situation, or embedded in it somehow: he wrote that "the operation is the situation itself. The operation is not distinct from the multiplicity in itself. There is no presentation of multiplicity *and* the operation. The operation *is* the same thing as the presentation" (IT 127). Similarly, the transcendental structure of a world does not precede the beings that appear in it. Badiou's point must be that it is simultaneous with them, and that is why he believes his view can avoid the subjectivism of philosophers such as Kant and Husserl. A transcendental is the measure of an existing being's relation to others in its world, and, as such, a world's transcendental does not have to be considered something separate from its world – Badiou calls it a subset of the world, even.

Since a logic of worlds is going to study the rules or properties intrinsic to worlds, and since these are about appearances and relations among them, the notion of a transcendental is one of the most important concepts of the book (LM 618). It is on the basis of this notion of a transcendental that any multiple that appears can then be said to be "more or less different from another being that belongs to the same world" (LM 128). So, the transcendental of a world does not govern *what* appears, but measures, rather, the "degrees of identity or difference among a multiple and itself, or between a being-there and other beings" (LM 112–13). A transcendental contains or consists of a scale of degrees of resemblances and differences among appearances, and every appearance in a world is going to have a transcendental indexation – it is going to fit somewhere on the transcendental's scale. No being exists in a world without being indexed to the transcendental of that world (LM 129).

The theory of objects, and Badiou's refutation of idealism

In a sense, what the logic of worlds needs to do is rather simple: it just needs to describe the basic structure of transcendentals. But this is not all Badiou is interested in doing in *Logics of Worlds*, and there is actually much more that needs to be covered, because worlds are actually composite things in Badiou's philosophy. They are able to be studied from an ontological perspective as well as from this logical perspective, and their basic components – objects – express this duality. Badiou's notion of an object is something that bridges ontology and logic.

A distinct discussion of objects is required because a transcendental on its own does not make anything appear – being itself must be involved in appearances somehow. Hence the need for a hybrid notion like an object. This also gives Badiou another chance to continue his break from idealism and assert his style of materialism. Kant's transcendental idealism argued that there had to be some kind of receptivity on the part of anyone having experiences: the structure of the human mind contributes to perception, but the mind also needs to be given some raw material (sense-data) to work up into something that can be called an experience. Kantian idealism, then, is an idealism not because ideas are what are most real, but because the mind makes perception or experience, although it does not, strictly speaking, make a thing be. A strong idealism in philosophy (one that Kant himself tried to refute) would be one that holds that an object does not exist unless it is perceived – consider Bishop Berkeley's famous claim that "to be is to be perceived." Such a view raises questions about the existence of a world distinct from perceivers. Kant's brand of idealism is able to claim that there is such a world, only we don't have an unfiltered access to it.

Badiou's materialism – even though it retains the notion of a transcendental, and even though it uses a method that he describes as *phenomenological*, as we shall see – also holds that a transcendental (which is not at all the possession of anything like a subject, and is also not some kind of activity distinct from worlds, an activity that makes worlds be) does not suffice to make anything appear. To be is *not* to be perceived: to be, for Badiou, is: (1) to be an organized multiple; and (2) to be indexed by a transcendental, located in a world, and so forth. So, instead of having to insist that there really is a world distinct from a perceiver, Badiou's refutation of idealism can say that any existing, appearing being must be an organized multiple, drawn from the reservoir of the multiple qua multiple or being itself, as well as indexed to a world's transcendental (LM 206).

An object on this account is precisely "the couple formed by a multiple and a transcendental indexation of this multiple" (LM 233). By describing an object this way, Badiou thinks he can avoid an understanding of objects that relies too heavily on a notion of substance, and also one that avoids an account according to which objects are fictional, mere constructions in a mind (LM 234). Clearly, Badiou's theory of objects is not idealist. And, though he is a materialist, objects are still not reducible to the multiple that composes them. To be what they are – which means, to appear, to exist in a world – requires an assessment of their relation to other appearances (and this is not anything that belongs intrinsically to the multiple that the object is).

The basic structure of a transcendental

To begin setting up some illustrations of how this works, consider for example something like a library-world, whose basic objects would be books, which, as objects, are not just collections of pages and words, but are also placed according to some system of classification. This cataloging system, for the purposes of this example, would be like the library's transcendental. Of course, a transcendental in Badiou's philosophy is supposed to do more, and something other, than this: it also assigns degrees of appearance and existence, as well as degrees of resemblance and difference, to objects. Consider an even simpler world – not the entire library, but just one book in it. Objects in this world would be the pages of the book: ontologically, each is distinct, each page is a separate organization of the pure multiple. But, considered from the perspective Badiou calls logical, we can say that some pages are similar to each other, close to each other, far from each other, and so on. We can even say that some pages do not exist (such as page 721 in a 700-page book) (LM 134).

A *complete* logic of worlds is a formal study of such things as transcendentals, objects, existence, and appearance. Here, I will discuss what the basic structure of a transcendental is like. There is in any transcendental a minimum, a maximum, and a range of values of appearance in between. So, in the world of Badiou's house in the country in autumn, he would say that certain things will exist or appear close to maximally in it – the house itself, the foliage perhaps – while certain other things appear minimally, such as hard to see things, hard to notice things, perhaps, or barely present things. And there would be a large range of in-between degrees.

A complete logic of worlds describes the types of relations that appearances have with each other. Badiou uses terms like conjunction, disjunction, synthesis, dependence, inversion, and envelope to describe these. Conjunction refers to the connectedness of appearances: one appearance can be an identifying part of another, such as the red leaves on the vine crawling up the house's wall, which just present themselves as a group. Also, two beings can relate to and depend on a third being that is more evident than the two themselves: Badiou refers to the country house on which the vine and its leaves are growing in this case. Badiou also considers anomalies such as what happens when, sitting in the garden of his country house, the sound of a motorcycle in the distance suddenly intrudes on the peaceful setting. This sound certainly appears in this world but it is a case of what he calls a null-value of conjunction, and so, a disjunction (LM 139). The sound of the motorcycle has nothing to do with all the other appearances of that world: the red leaves, the house, the walls, the road, as he puts it. The possibility of disjunction in the structure of a world leads Badiou to develop the notion of an envelope of a world, which is able to account for the stability of worlds, rather like the way in which a horizon in a landscape might be the trait that allows all things within it to be considered together.

Badiou calls his extended example in *Logics of Worlds*, of the country house in this context, allegorical. This is because an example like this is potentially misleading, since it is a description from the point of view of how a human being would perceive the world in question. It should be possible to discuss the organization of beings in a world in a manner that does not rely on what a human consciousness would notice, and how a human consciousness carves up beings: just as the organizations of the multiple in ontology were not limited to organizations based on resemblances among elements, or on the objects that present themselves to human experience.

Objective phenomenology

To make matters worse, though, Badiou even calls the method he uses in his logic a phenomenology – although he adds that it is an *objective* phenomenology because it is about the existence of objects in a world and the relations that obtain among these objects, the degrees of identity and difference among objects in a world. By objective phenomenology he means that

> one lets come the consistency of that of which one speaks (an opera, a painting, a countryside, a novel, a scientific construction, a political "episode") while neutralizing, not at all, as Husserl did, its real existence, but on the contrary its intentional or "lived experience" dimension. One "experiences" the equivalence between appearing and logic by a pure description, a description without subject. (LM 48)

How can this work? A phenomenologist might argue for some version of the view that 'to be is to be perceived': we cannot philosophize about appearances without implicitly supposing there to be a perceiver of the appearance. And, of course, in all of Badiou's examples it is always someone, a human consciousness in particular, going through the example, imagining the appearances, and so on. Is there ever an appearance apart from a consciousness?

To say no to this question would be to surrender too much to idealism, Badiou claims; a position Badiou has been arguing against since his earliest books. Even when idealism tries not to go so far as to claim that consciousness or thought makes beings into what they are – a weak form of idealism might hold just that the mind contributes to how being appears – it still implies that we cannot, in philosophy, get beyond or outside of human consciousness. Thus, for idealism, what being is would remain mysterious, some kind of inaccessible X.

In *Logics of Worlds*, when Badiou is explaining why a study of appearance requires a logic and some kind of phenomenology, he claims that "every world pronounces degrees of identity and difference without there being any receivable reason to believe that these degrees, as intelligible as they are, depend on any 'subject' whatsoever or on the existence of the human animal" (LM 129). Referring to Quentin Meillassoux's "argument from fossils" in support of a refutation of idealism, Badiou claims that paleontology provides ample evidence that a world existed and presented a consistent order of appearance before the emergence of any consciousness whatsoever:

> We know, from a sure source, that such and such a world preceded the existence of our species, and that, as in "our" worlds, it stipulated identities and differences and had the power to deploy the appearance of innumerable beings. This is what Quentin Meillassoux calls "the fossil argument": the irrefutable materialist argument that interrupts the idealist (and empiricist) apparatus of "consciousness" and the "object". The world of the dinosaurs existed, it deployed the infinite multiplicity of the being-there of beings millions of years before there could be any question of a consciousness or a subject, whether empirical or transcendental. To deny this point is to indulge in a recklessly idealist axiomatic. We can be certain that there is no need of a consciousness in order to testify that beings are obliged to appear – to be there – under the logic of a world. (TW 198)

Badiou's point might be more effectively made if he had referred to a period in the fossil record even before dinosaurs, which are creatures to whom one might be willing to attribute some kind of conscious experience, after all. Even the record from the earliest days of life on Earth (and before!) would show that, before the emergence of anything like consciousness at all, what appeared on Earth was organized and consistent. Geology would demonstrate this too. To illustrate this same point, Badiou could also have mentioned the way in which we are able to know something about the appearance of objects we never really perceive: black holes, neutron stars, and the like, which are also used as examples in *Logics of Worlds* (LM 339).

Badiou is arguing that for any world, no matter how inhuman, the same principles of organization (the same "logics") adhere: there is a transcendental for that world, there are minimal and maximal degrees of appearing in it, there are relations of dependence, synthesis, and so on that can all be formalized. When Hegel wrote his famous *Logic*, he claimed that he was describing the laws of being before God created the universe. Badiou may not put what he is doing in such grandiose (and idealist, and theological) terms: but there is nevertheless a similarity between the two projects. And this represents a strong break from the phenomenological tradition of the twentieth century, which proposed for itself the more humble task of describing the structure of human consciousness. This study shows yet again how Badiou is following through with his attempt to develop a theoretical anti-humanism.

On phenomenon and existence

The "Greater Logic" part of *Logics of Worlds* starts with a study of the basic structure of any transcendental. This study only needs to describe the relations of appearances to each other in terms of appearances themselves: that is, it does not need to say anything about the being of the appearances, or the elements that compose them. In subsequent parts, Badiou studies what it is that a "transcendental regime" ranks or orders or indexes. And, for that, notions such as object, phenomenon, and existence are used, because these are all mixtures of beings and appearances – they all refer to appearing beings.

The examples, the "worlds," Badiou uses in this context are a protest rally in the Place de la République in Paris and a painting by the eighteenth-century Frenchman Hubert Robert. According to Badiou, an *ontological* (not logical) study of a protest rally would describe a rather indistinct multiple – a bunch of people in groups, their banners, their cries, some people handing things out, other people trying to sell things. Such a study would not be able to say anything about what is actually appearing at the rally (LM 211). From the perspective of his (objective) phenomenology, important differences among the multiples at the rally are discernible, as well as resemblances and near-identities among individuals and groups (LM 211). A purely ontological perspective levels differences and ignores resemblances, and would therefore not be able to measure degrees of appearance and degrees of existence.

In these studies in the Greater Logic, Badiou identifies what he calls an appearance function proper to worlds. This refers to a world's ability to measure the degrees (Badiou calls it a p-degree) of identity and differences among the multiples it contains. There is a minimum (at which the two multiples would be "entirely different"), a maximum (at which two multiples would be "absolutely identical"), and a range in between (LM 212). For example, at the protest rally, say there is a group of anarchists and a group of Kurds standing close to each other. Their identity would fall somewhere between the maximum and the minimum: one group stands under a red banner, the other under black flags, but both groups might be dressed similarly (LM 213). In the world of my office, for example, two books on my shelf would have a higher p-degree of identity than either of the books would to the floor or the computer.

On the basis of a p-degree, an identity-degree in worlds, Badiou defines *phenomenon* and *existence*. A phenomenon in a world is the totality of a being's p-degrees with respect to the other beings in the world, or its identity and difference to all others of its world considered as a totality (LM 213). Thus, a phenomenon is a measure of a being's total relations, its total status in a world (to what extent does it stick out in comparison to other things, for example, or seem to matter more than others?). By contrast, a thing's *existence* in a world is a measure of a thing's identity to itself, excluding any consideration of its relation to others (LM 220). This view of existence allows existence to be a matter of degree: the higher a thing's identity to itself, the more forcefully Badiou claims that it exists in its world. This is quite striking, as we are accustomed to thinking of existence as an all-or-nothing affair: a thing either exists or it does not, and my laptop cannot be said to exist less than a redwood just because it is smaller and likely not to last as long. But we say such things because we tend to think of existence as an ontological category, as something that refers to the components of an object. Badiou claims that existence is a category of *appearing*, not of *being*: thus, some things can exist more or less in a world than others, depending on their place in the world's transcendental (LM 220).

How can a thing be more or less identical to itself? Badiou's idea is that there is an indistinctness to some things: in the painting he refers to by Hubert Robert there are some trees in it, and some pillars of a temple, that are barely discernible. The fact that some of these trees and pillars are so blurry and indistinct tells us something about the force of their being-there in this world: they do not appear as intensely as the bathing nudes, as the columns in the foreground, and as some of the other trees. That Badiou thinks of this vagueness as a deficiency in the things' self-identity is curious, but compelling: it is as if some things in a world may be more strongly defined by their belonging to a group, or to a vague background, than by what they are in themselves.

Against phenomenology

With these two interesting positions on phenomenon and existence, some further important traits of Badiou's objective phenomenology emerge. A phenomenon is not a temporal notion for Badiou, as it would be for what he calls an intentional or subjective phenomenology. With respect to the example of the Kurds and the anarchists at the rally, Badiou says that a classical phenomenological orientation's account of the difference between the two groups would happen in terms of the time it takes to apprehend each group: there is a perception now of one, now of the other. Our gaze, for example, has to go back and forth between them. Thus, despite resemblances among the groups, they are always going to be perceived as distinct groups because of a consciousness that must move from one to the other to assess and compare them (LM 214). Badiou's objective phenomenology suspends this reference to time and consciousness, and to a situated perspective or embodied consciousness at all, by claiming that the identity-degree of the groups is inscribed in the world's transcendental structure itself. Thus, resemblances and differences are there, inscribed in the groups themselves and their way of appearing, and are not merely subjective things.

With respect to existence, a phenomenological orientation would argue that, in perception, certain objects seem to jump out at us more than others, partly due to something about the perceptual field itself, perhaps, but certainly due to the interests and desires we bring to our world at any given moment. But this does not tell us anything about the thing's existence. Indeed, for most phenomenologists, questions and claims about existence are suspended as a matter of principle. A computer screen could be said to draw the attention of a human consciousness more than other objects in an office would – more than the bookshelf behind it or the floor underneath the desk. But this is purely a function of the interests that a human consciousness brings with it to the office, and says nothing about what actually exists in the office or not. Jean-Paul Sartre was able to claim that when he went to the café to meet his friend Pierre, who did not show up, Pierre's absence was perceived, as if his absence were an object even more important to his perception of the world of the café than the people who were actually present in the café at the time. Unlike this type of phenomenology, Badiou's objective phenomenology does entitle itself to make claims about what exists in worlds, and even to make claims about degrees of existence. What exists, and how much it exists, is packed in to the structures of worlds themselves, and is not a function of human consciousness.

Practical effects of a logic

A world bestows maximal and minimal degrees of existence. Badiou's analysis of the Battle of Gaugamela in 331 BC, fought between the armies of Alexander the Great and Darius III of Persia, tries to drive this point home. The battle is noteworthy for a daring tactical move Alexander made with his cavalry, which managed to break the Persian front lines. Badiou argues that the success of the move, which many describe as an act of military genius, was just as much a result of a "genius of transcendental functions" and a "genius of appearing" (LM 304). His point is that both the very possibility of the move and the conditions for its success were rooted in something intrinsic to the structure of that particular battle-world itself. It was not a matter of mere luck, or of entirely subjective or contingent factors on the part of Alexander.

Badiou's analysis of this battle is significant, because it links his formal study of worlds to what he is trying to accomplish practically through his philosophy. Recall the gentleman from the Paris Commune, mentioned in the introduction, who knew not what to do in a moment of crisis. Now that much of Badiou's formalism has been considered, we can begin to see the practical payoff such a study is supposed to have. Badiou is trying to develop a philosophy that will allow one to read situations, worlds, or whatever, accurately, such that weak points, strong points, impasses, possibilities, and so on will emerge clearly. In this manner, Badiou's brand of theoretical anti-humanism is tied to a desire to enable a practical humanism. However, as a theory, this formalized anti-humanism does not require, expect, or privilege any particular type of practice at all. In this sense, it is breaking with a trend among many continental thinkers who try to derive some kind of ethic of authenticity from an ontological or metaphysical thesis: holding that if being is a certain way, we must therefore act in such-and-such a manner. There are no ethical obligations that are similarly built in to Badiou's positions on ontology and appearance (an ontology and a logic of worlds do not endorse any sort of action whatsoever); but he does develop an ethic on their basis that I will discuss in chapter 7.

What inexists

In his analysis of relations among objects in a world, one of the most important points concerns the notion of the inexistent. This is important, because it provides an opening for a theory of change and a revised theory of the event. Badiou describes the inexistent as a trace or remainder of the contingency of being-there, of the fact that what appears could just as well not appear, or could appear in another world (LM 318/338). There are two important ideas here: one concerning contingency (any appearing object could also *not* appear in its world), and one concerning the difference between being and appearing (the same collection of elements can appear in multiple worlds, although it will appear differently and may have a different status in each one). As a result, every object can be said to contain a "reserve of being" – take this to be part of the object's pure multiplicity – that is withdrawn from that object's appearance in any given world. This reserve is what Badiou calls the inexistent of the object. It is an element of an object's multiple that has a minimal existence-value for a given world (LM 340).

Yet there is also an inexistent not just for objects in a world but for an entire world. In the painting by Hubert Robert, Badiou argues that the masculine sex inexists in the painting (LM 222). While it is true that no men appear in the painting, they are not absent from it in the same way in which, say, elephants or computers are also absent from the painting. The masculine sex is an inexistent proper to painting because, although no men appear in it, the painting very clearly supposes, structurally, and can be said to include, a reference to a male gaze (observing the bathing women): the painting is clearly an erotically charged *display* of femininity for a supposed male perceiver who is not portrayed in the painting. What inexists to, or in, a world, therefore, is not simply something that is absent from that world but something that plays a particular role for the world from which it is absent. It is an absence somehow built in to the world in question, in the manner of a founding exclusion.

The revised theory of events: on changes and modifications

My opening claim in this chapter was that in *Logics* Badiou is trying to correct what he perceived to be a flaw in his earlier conception of the event – a flaw that involved an event's intrinsic properties and how one could account for an event's relation to situations. The problem seemed to be that there was too much of a difference between events and situations: an event seemed to be so entirely different from anything else in a situation (it entails a violation of ontological rules, even, with its self-belonging) that it was difficult to account for how it could affect situations at all. With the discussion of worlds and appearances, he is able to give a more nuanced account of the changes that occur in worlds (as well as a more nuanced study of subjects, as we shall see), one that includes an account of their manner of presentation in what he calls bodies.

Logics of Worlds continues to use the term "site" for the broad category of what happens when being subverts or upends an order of appearing (LM 383). But now Badiou notes that there are various types of changes that worlds undergo, and an event is only one of them. An event is what occurs when the inexistent of a world appears maximally in its world, bringing about a radical change in the transcendental ordering of the world in question: that is, a change in all the other appearances and degrees of existence. Consider, given the example I just discussed, what would happen if the inexistent of the Robert painting, a male gaze, *were* included in the painting. It is fair to say that some of the appearances in the painting – the bathing women in particular – would be charged differently, would have different degrees of existence, and so forth. And the whole painting itself would be, in fact, a different world, a vastly different painting, in a way in which it would not be so different maybe if an elephant were added to it, or some trees were changed, and so on.

Ontologically, what defined an eventful site in *Being and Event* was its possession of a multiple that contained itself – the event. In other words, every site was eventful, at least ontologically. Because the event violates a basic ontological rule (the one against self-belonging, stipulated in order to avoid Russell's paradox), the event was, by definition, never anything presented in a situation. It was characterized by disappearance, which is something Badiou still claims (LM 389). The eventful site as a set was presented in its situation, according to the account in *Being and Event*, but it contained an element that could not be presented in the situation. The theory of sites and events in *Logics of Worlds* is coming from another orientation – it thinks about both eventful sites and their events from the point of view of worlds, and not from an ontological point of view, not from the perspective of what constitutes them (LM 389). What Badiou describes as a logic of sites in *Logics of Worlds* addresses "the distribution of intensities around this disappeared point that is the site" in a world (LM 391). So an event is considered not in terms of its constitution but as a sub-category of a site's possible consequences in its world.

Badiou claims that from the logical, not ontological, perspective, a site involves some kind of change for its world, and this type of change is different from what Badiou calls a mere modification of a world. So the first major distinction to consider is one between modifications of a world and changes. What a modification affects is not the transcendental structure of its world, but rather only the appearances in it (LM 379). A modification is something that happens to a being that exists "there" through time. Worlds, as orders of appearing being, would contain what he refers to as becoming, but this is still not what he has in mind by change (LM 378). A branch that falls into the garden after a wind-storm might change the view from the window: there is now a different arrangement of appearances in the world of my yard, but nothing about the transcendental organization of that world itself has changed. The style of the world persists through such modifications. The same would be true if renegade landscapers came and did a radical reorganizing of my yard overnight, though. The face on a coin gets gradually worn down as it is handled in transactions: nothing about this process entails a discontinuity in the coin's being. Thus, what Badiou calls the appearing of a being would include all of the modifications of that being throughout the course of its consistency: the fading of its color, the deterioration of its edges, changes in place. All of this is different from what Badiou wants to call a proper change, which is the term he will use for what happens when the transcendental of a world itself is affected by an eventual site.

Such a site still involves an element that belongs to itself, as it did in *Being and Event*. In *Logics of Worlds*, though, a site is described additionally as an object that "falls under its own transcendental indexation, in such a way that it attributes to its being an existence-value" (LM 617). Ontologically, a site contains a multiple (the event) that belongs to itself; logically considered, however, a site is an object in a world that, in addition to this, assigns to itself its own existence-value. Where an event entailed a violation of a basic ontological principle, a site in a similar fashion brings with it its own alternative transcendental, one different from the world the site appears in. Thus, one has with change a subversion of appearing by being.

While a site is said to give itself its own existence-value, that value has varying degrees, and it is not the site itself that is ultimately responsible for the *degree* of its existence. A site's existence-value is determined by the consequences it has on the world it appears in. The degree may be maximal, minimal, and anything in between, as is the case for any object. Badiou calls a site with a non-maximal existence a fact, and one with a maximal existence is called a singularity. It is under the heading of strong singularities that Badiou will place events. A strong singularity is an event and a non-maximal singularity is a weak singularity (LM 395).

What determines the difference between a strong and weak singularity is the site's effect on the inexistent of a world. When a singularity affects the inexistent of an object, it is a strong singularity, because when this occurs something from being itself upends the order of appearing: Badiou writes that in this case where "the inexistence was transcendentally evaluated as minimum, it is now, in its post-evental figure, evaluated as maximum" (LM 416).

One of Badiou's examples of an event is provided, not surprisingly, by the Paris Commune of 1871. He takes the relevant world to be "Paris in the Spring of 1871," and takes one object in this world – the date March 18 – as his example of an evental site. What makes March 18 such a site for this world? This is usually taken to be the date at which the Commune started. What happened, according to Badiou, was that on that date something that had inexisted in that world – the figure of a worker who had a role to play in politics and government – suddenly asserted itself, and appeared no longer minimally but maximally (LM 385). Badiou writes that from the point of view of the political world in Paris and the way in which it regulated appearances, such a figure was ruled out – and workers themselves bought into this (LM 386). And then, on the day of March 18, 1871, even when acknowledging the fact that they did not have a mandate to govern, the central committee of the National Guard authorized itself into existence by not following orders from Versailles to turn over the cannons stationed in Paris after an armistice had been signed with Prussia. But none of this was entirely clear on the day in question. On the next day, March 19, March 18 itself became the key reference point for the new Commune's authority. Accordingly, Badiou sees "March 18th" as a site because of its "subversion of the rules of political appearance" (LM 386).

The key feature of an event in *Being and Event* was its self-belonging. This is a property that now seems to be expanded into a quality of the evental site itself. The site is an event once it has a maximal presence in its world, which is registered by the split the site introduces in the world: within one and the same world, there are suddenly competing orders of transcendental evaluation. And a site becomes something maximally existing, depending on whether anyone in a world is doing anything with it.

Conclusion

The theory of the event in *Logics of Worlds* sounds far less mystical than the theory given in *Being and Event*. It is no longer some mysterious property of an event that makes an event happen or not happen for a situation. Instead, whether a site has maximally existing consequences or not, and thus whether it even constitutes an event or not, is now due to how it is handled in its world. This ultimately means that events are not primarily things *to come* and need not be awaited at all. As he had already written in *Saint Paul*: "but if everything depends on an event, must we wait? Certainly not. Many events, even very distant ones, still require us to be faithful to them" (SP 111). He does go on to describe the coming of an event there in the following terms: "for it is of the essence of the event not to be preceded by any sign, and to catch us unawares with its grace, regardless of our vigilance. [. . .] Nietzsche says that true events arrive on dove's feet, that they surprise us in the moment of greatest silence" (SP 111). Yet this does not go against what I am arguing here. What Badiou is doing in this passage is describing something like the phenomenology of an event – what it is like for an individual when an event seizes her, and not whether there is an event or not for a situation.

Ontologically, there could be an event for a situation that is a dead letter. Yet nothing in Badiou's discussion of events prevents us from thinking that events are already factors for *every* historical situation. The lesson of *Logics of Worlds* is that what needs to be considered is not whether events happen or not, whether events are or not, but rather what is being done with them. What is measured and judged or decided on is not whether there is an event, then, but whether the consequences of an eventual site are such that their force is bringing about a radical shift and reordering in a situation. Thus, again, it is not a matter of waiting for an event. That an event has consequences in a world is now an entirely practical matter, a function of what the inhabitants of a world or situation are doing with what an event is doing to them and their situation. The next chapter, therefore, is devoted to a discussion of the relation between events and the inhabitants of situations.

5
Infinity and Truth

The previous chapter discussed Badiou's objective phenomenology and how it differs from traditional (what we could well call subjective) phenomenology. The main point was that Badiou's phenomenological approach does not presuppose or require a consciousness that constitutes objects and bestows meaning and value on its world. As an objective phenomenology, it should circumvent references to the subject and simply describe the way in which worlds and situations are structured. Thus, such a phenomenology makes up part of Badiou's attempt to avoid philosophical idealism, and it is also a central part of his theoretical anti-humanism.

This chapter will continue to explore aspects of Badiou's theoretical anti-humanism, starting with the topics of infinity and truth. The former is an important property of situations or worlds that has not yet been addressed in this work. The theory of truth pertains to events and their consequences in worlds, and it is closely linked to Badiou's theory of the subject, which will be the topic of the next chapter. This chapter, then, addresses what could be described as the contact point where Badiou's theoretical anti-humanism starts to meet his practical humanism.

On infinity

Badiou believes that his philosophical investigations require an important shift in the way that human beings understand themselves and their worlds or situations. Arguing that modernity has been dominated by the view that human beings are finite and mortal creatures, he believes that ontology and logic now require us to take a different view of finitude, because ontology and logic show us that there is nothing mystical or divine about infinity. Infinity is, rather, banal, since worlds and situations are all infinite multiples: "far from being a predicate whose force is that of the sacred, the infinite is a *banal* determination of being" (NN 56). Echoing a remark he made about difference itself, Badiou writes that "infinite alterity is quite simply *what there is*" (E 25).

Rendering the infinite banal has important philosophical consequences, because it should affect our understanding of being human. Views on what it means to be human have always been influenced by an understanding of infinity. By thinking of us as finite creatures for whom the infinite is an inaccessible beyond, modernity has tended to emphasize the idea that the species is error-prone and fragile. But, if the infinite is simply *"what there is,"* then this view of human beings as finite and mortal creatures may represent some kind of bad faith or mere prejudice. In light of this, Badiou comes up with a critical definition of being human in *Being and Event*: "a human is that being which prefers to represent itself within finitude, whose sign is death, rather than knowing itself to be entirely traversed and encircled by the omnipresence of infinity" (BE 149). But if we come to acknowledge the infinite's banality, what precise effect is this supposed to have on us? I have been arguing that it should enable some sort of practical humanism. The consequences are perhaps clearest in the theory of truth that Badiou develops, which I will discuss later in this chapter, but a few words can be said about the importance of the infinite apart from that.

Since the infinite is usually understood to exceed our experience and be more than we can grasp, and more than we can think, it is no wonder that the infinite has been associated with the divine. But, in the wake of Immanuel Kant's philosophy, claims about the infinity either of God or the world have been avoided by many philosophers. Kant wanted to figure out what can legitimately be claimed about human experience, and drew a line separating what we can possibly know from what we cannot possibly know. This line would be based on what it is possible for us to experience. What we cannot possibly experience is something we should not make any claims about at all. What we can experience will, in turn, form the basis for our knowledge of the world. This move was so important because it curtailed classical metaphysics. From Kant's perspective, any claim about the nature of being, of God, of the soul – claims as to whether the world is infinite or finite, for example – would be illegitimate, in part because we simply do not and cannot experience the objects in question, like infinity itself.

Set theory's treatment of infinity as actual and, indeed, as multiple (there are multiple infinities – indeed, infinitely many) forces a reconsideration of this influential Kantian position, Badiou argues; and set theory's take on infinity can be seen as yet another way in which it is able to exorcize the ghost of the one from ontology. Usually, infinity is understood to be an endless series of units or ones. Given this understanding, questions about the existence of an actual infinity might well arise: isn't it always only a possible or potential thing? Can we really ever know if there is an actual infinity of things? How could this ever be confirmed? And, even if it is somehow demonstrated that infinity is actual, other questions arise: wouldn't there have to be an infinite series of odd numbers as well as an infinite series of natural whole numbers? Can one infinity be larger than another?

One of the axioms of Zermelo-Fraenkel set theory asserts that there is an infinite natural multiplicity, as Badiou has it (BE 148). This does not mean we are entitled to claim that nature is infinite or that the universe is infinite. Such claims would be incorrectly thinking of infinity as a closed totality. Being is infinitely infinite, or a multiple infinity. Badiou calls this the thesis of the infinity of being (BE 148). This view entails a rejection of the infinite as a possible totality (think of this as an all-encompassing set, a final or total set) and it is linked to Badiou's desire to eliminate the one from his philosophy.

As we saw in chapter 2, if there is no "one," that means that being can be equated with a void, and is a multiple "of nothing"; there is no "one" at the bottom of things, as it were, no ultimate ontological unit. Badiou also claims that there is no "one" at the top either, no possible overarching totality or unity of things: no big, all-embracing infinity, as a set of all things. Another way of putting this is to say that there is an infinite series all the way down and all the way up. In fact, there is an infinity of infinities.

To see how infinity is not simply totality or some kind of end point, I will very briefly present the set-theory account of infinity. The axiom of infinity in Zermelo-Fraenkel set theory posits that there is something called a limit ordinal. This means that the entire successive series that begins with the counting of the empty set can itself be treated as a set. The entire series of natural whole numbers would be contained within the limit ordinal, but the limit ordinal itself is not contained within the series (in accordance with another one of Zermelo-Fraenkel's axioms). The limit ordinal itself is outside the series of natural whole numbers. Cantor assigned to this limit ordinal the symbol *aleph-null*.

By containing the entire series of natural whole numbers within itself, the limit-ordinal *aleph-null* is a set just like any other, except it has an infinite number of elements and can itself be considered the starting point for another series of sets. That is, *aleph-null* is like the empty set for another series, another count – this time of infinities.

One of Badiou's goals is to base his philosophy on an ontology that carries the claim that the one is not as far as it can go. Notice that both the empty set and *aleph-null* allow for this thesis to be maintained as strongly as it possibly can be. The empty set rules out the existence of a one at the bottom of a multiple, so to speak, and set theory's take on infinity (that there are infinite infinities) rules out the one as a whole or at the top of multiples, as it were. And these points are linked together: because of the absence or subtraction of the pure multiple, we can have the build up of actual infinities, and an infinite number of them as well.

This theory of infinity is important not just for numbers but for Badiou's approach to situations and worlds. Badiou writes that "every situation [. . .] is a multiple composed of an infinity of elements" (E 25). This assertion that worlds are infinite is an anti-humanist move in theory, because it is saying that any situation human beings might live in exceeds their ability to count, or to intuit and catalog, the objects or elements of that world. The transcendental of a world takes care of this organization of the infinite, without a human mind having to do any of the work.

Some basic points about truth in Badiou's philosophy

Perhaps the most surprising twist this anti-humanist thinking takes in Badiou's philosophy occurs with his position on truth. Badiou even describes truth as "an experience of the inhuman" (LM 80). Truth and infinity – which is a similarly inhuman thing – are linked to each other because it turns out that truth involves the construction of an infinite set (BE 524). Badiou is trying to establish with this point that truth is something that exceeds human experience: but at the same time it is unique to us, because truths only pertain to what Badiou calls historical situations, situations in which there are events (art, love, science, and politics).

The claim that there can only be truth in historical situations is counterintuitive. One would be more inclined to think that truth is available and accessible in natural situations especially, where there is a stable set of facts that can be hit upon with the appropriate theory. When it comes to human and historical situations, we tend to be content to let much be a matter of opinion. Concerning things such as taste in music, what counts as love between two individuals, political principles and preferences, it seems quite a stretch to say that there is anything like truth involved in them; yet this is exactly what Badiou is claiming.

What he is naming truth is something that happens to humans in their historical situations (love, politics, art, and science) sometimes, and it is a phenomenon in which something possesses them, seizes them. This phenomenon will be addressed more directly in subsequent chapters. None of this means that a truth is a merely subjective thing, a matter of subjective conviction: a truth alters the very situations humans are in, and in this manner truths exceed humans. A truth is a name for a certain type of happening, with a certain type of force – and it often appears in Badiou's work with the term procedure or process after it, highlighting the fact that a truth is something that develops and is neither static (dogmatic) nor anything like a flash of insight. It should also be noted that on this theory a truth will be necessarily divisive, risky, and difficult to ground or justify.

But the one thing that does the most to make Badiou's theory of truth so counterintuitive is the fact that a truth for him is not a property that may or may not belong to statements about the way the world is. Wittgenstein claimed that truths do not pertain to the world, or are not of the world (the set of facts, the order of whatever is): truth, rather, is a property of some *propositions* about the world (propositions that are, of course, true). In other words, from Wittgenstein's point of view, statements about the world may be true or false, but objects, and the world itself, cannot sensibly be said to be either true or false: things just are.

This notion of truth, according to which it is a property of propositions and statements, is just not what Badiou means by truth. He calls the propositional take on truth veracity or the veridical; and he is not critical of it or against it in any sense. He is just trying to describe something else with his own theory of truth. Badiou's understanding of truth may be closer to the philosopher Martin

Heidegger's than to Wittgenstein's. According to Heidegger, we inhabit truth, we live in truth, and the statements we use to describe the world depend on (and often distort) this original truth that we inhabit. Badiou will disagree with much about Heidegger's view, but in a basic sense his use of the term truth is closer to Heidegger's since it is not about propositions matching up to things more or less well. In fact, one of the hallmarks of a truth is a crisis in an ability to determine whether statements match up to things.

Ways of thinking about situations and states: on names and encyclopedias

Although Badiou's theory of truth is not about propositional truth, a discussion of language and naming is nevertheless an important part of it. To explain why a theory of naming occurs in *Being and Event* at all, we need to consider something brought up earlier in chapter 3, during my discussion of the state of a situation. The state of a situation is a sort of meta-order for the situation: it is the "count of the count," and is able to account for what is presented as well as represented in a situation. A situation's state is distinct from the situation of which it is the state. More precisely, Badiou claims that a state is *in excess* of the situation (BE 280). One of the important accomplishments of set theory as ontology is that it can establish the existence of this gap between a presented multiplicity and its organization. Badiou calls meta-ontological a variety of basically philosophical attempts to articulate the nature of this gap. In short, different theories hold that the gap is either significant or insignificant. There are three basic types Badiou discusses.

One of them, called constructivist, attempts to develop a language for the situation that can clearly discern what is part of the situation and what is not (BE 282). According to this orientation in thought, the state determines what exists and it tries to obliterate the gap between the situation and itself (BE 288). For the constructivist orientation, what cannot be expressed in its language just does not exist. And since, ideally, any multiple can be given a name – even an entirely arbitrary one – there is nothing outside the state according to this orientation (BE 283). All can be named – both what is presented and what is not: there is then nothing that is not nameable.

There are two other orientations or ways of thinking about this issue that Badiou mentions – the transcendent and the generic.

Infinity and Truth 91

The latter is of special interest to Badiou, and plays a role in his theory of truth. Where the constructivist orientation is made out to sound like a conservative or reactionary ideology, the generic will sound leftist and militant, and the transcendent orientation will sound like a kind of mysticism or obscurantism (BE 524).

Badiou has little to say about the transcendent orientation on this issue in *Being and Event*. The constructivist orientation, however, receives quite a bit of attention, in part because he feels that it is a prevalent orientation, the dominant one, in most historical situations (BE 328). Because of the constructivist orientation Badiou claims that every situation has a special language for classifying and discerning its multiples, which leads to the development of what Badiou calls an *encyclopedia* for the situation. The existence of such an encyclopedia may be only virtual, never actually written and published by anyone. What Badiou is talking about, again, is an orientation in thought – something like a philosophical persuasion – that would maintain that a total language *can* be developed in principle for a situation, or within a situation, such that nothing is unnamable (BE 331).

Since truth in Badiou's philosophy does not pertain to the relation between statements and things (multiples), the stuff of truth is going to be very different from whatever the contents of a situation's encyclopedia would be. And so the contents of a situation's encyclopedia are not called true by Badiou, but, instead, veridical (BE 331). And while the veridical does have a contrary – i.e., the false, the erroneous – truth in Badiou's philosophy does not (BE 525). This has significant implications for a truth's status in a situation.

Consider Badiou's description of one of his philosophical enemies in the later text, *Logics of Worlds*, which he calls democratic materialism. (More will be said about Badiou's understanding of this in chapter 7.) Democratic materialism embraces the view that "there are only bodies and languages"; there are just multiples and ways of speaking about multiples (LM 9). He actually agrees with this, but for him the shortcoming of democratic materialism is that it stops there. If there are only bodies and languages, then a kind of relativism is practically required when it comes to the assessment of historical situations. Democratic materialism is Badiou's way of describing the reigning ideology of liberal democracies. An increasingly plural society benefits from an ethic of tolerance that requires that no one get too militant about anything. Thus, "there are only bodies and languages" means there are many different ways of being human, and many different ways to describe the world. Different strokes for different folks; live and let live.

Badiou wishes to claim instead that bodies and languages are not *all* there is. There are also truths. What makes the truths Badiou posits so unpalatable to the advocates of democratic materialism? Badiou would say it is their universality, their indifference to opinion, or what he also calls their generic nature. But it is certainly not only this: from the point of view of democratic materialism, what is unpleasant about truths is that they are always partial or partisan. Even though, in any situation, "difference is what there is," a truth might be described as indifferent to difference: it cuts across differences, it unifies, it compels, it addresses all; it is universal and generic. Interestingly, then, one of the most significant characteristics of a truth for Badiou is that it is as divisive as it is generic: in fact, its generic nature is a large part of what makes it so divisive, as we shall see.

Interventions, names for the event, and the divisiveness of truths

A truth procedure – the process in which a truth is developed in a situation or world – begins with what Badiou calls an intervention, which is a decision to recognize a certain multiple within a situation as an event (BE 202). Thus, truths and events are linked, and this has led some commentators on Badiou's work to use a phrase for this such as truth-event, even though it seems that truth and event should be held apart from each other, for reasons that I think will become clear.

We know that an event's belonging to a situation is supposed to be undecidable. An intervention is Badiou's term for a decision on behalf of an event, or *for* an event: that an event *does* belong to its situation. This decision is expressed in a naming of the event, an act by means of which something of the event itself ends up being presented in the situation. Badiou even claims that "the act of nomination of the event is what constitutes it" (BE 203). This is a strong way of putting it. How does a name for an event *constitute* an event? Was an event not supposed to be constituted by its self-belonging, by its violation of a basic ontological principle?

Badiou's claim about the nomination of an event is not supposed to mean that *naming* an event is what makes an event happen: we will see that this is the nature of what Badiou describes as a leftist

Infinity and Truth

theoretical deviation, and it is one that he tries to avoid. Rather, the point is that naming an event constitutes the event *for* the situation, or as far as the situation is concerned. By being named, an event attains some efficacy, something like presence, some sort of being in a situation. It is as if the name becomes the trace of the event in the situation, and is even the only way for the event to have any consequences on the multiples of a situation (remember that an event is never presented as such: it cannot be, it is entirely other to presentation).

The notion of intervention thus plays a very important role in *Being and Event*, since it is what is able to make a bridge between the non-being of an event and a situation as an order of presentation. This theory is perhaps flawed in a manner similar to the way in which the theory of the event itself was, because Badiou runs into problems when he tries to give an account of where the name for the event might come from. Must it not always come from a term within the situation itself? But if it does, why would there be any controversy about whether an event belongs to a situation? The situation's encyclopedia would always be able to determine this without problem. On the other hand, if the name of an event does *not* come from the situation, from where else can it come? The evental site? But in that case the problem is the same: it would again be easy to determine that the event does not belong to the situation – it is just not present in the situation if it is an element of the evental site . . .

Badiou holds, in *Being and Event* at least, that neither alternative is the case. He recognizes that, because of his description of the situation and the evental site, the name for an event cannot come from either one. So he claims that the name for an event comes from the void itself (BE 204). But what kind of name can be pulled from the void, where this void must be the pure multiple itself? Must it not always be the case that the name an intervention decides on for the event is already a name that belongs to the situation? Or how could a name not already be part of a situation's encyclopedia, part of the language for a situation? How could there be a word or name that would be utterly new, one that a language could not recognize and employ? The issues surrounding the topic of intervention in Badiou's philosophy are indeed, I think, about novelty in language: can there be any room in a situation, or in the language of a situation, for a new way of speaking (and thinking)?

When Badiou claims in *Being and Event* that the name for the event must be drawn from the void itself, he is saying something similar to the psychoanalyst Jacques Lacan's words about the status of the unconscious for conscious life. Lacan said it this way: "the truth makes holes in knowledge." Badiou makes use of this phrase often, and it expresses exactly the way in which he envisions the relation between a truth and a situation. The Freudian notion of repression might allow one to say that there is a truth about what an individual desires, or that there is some truth (a trauma, for example) about an individual's past that, when covered up, when blocked from memory and conscious access, ends up manifesting itself in other ways: in things like symptoms or fantasies or slips of the tongue and the like. These types of behavior may present themselves as mysteries to the individual, leading her to wonder – "Why do I do this? Why do I think of this? Why does this keep happening to me?" In such cases we can say that there is a truth about the individual that is creating problems for what the individual knows about herself. In other words, a truth is "making holes" – exposing gaps – in her self-knowledge.

Notice that this does not mean that the truth simply fills in the gaps in knowledge. Lacan did compare the unconscious to the blank pages in a person's biography, the idea being that there is much that we can remember about our pasts, but much that is gone. The unconscious might be thought of as the place where the rest of the story is recorded. But the claim that the truth makes holes in knowledge is saying something different. It is not that there is some truth outside memory, outside knowledge, that when included in my story about myself would finally complete my self-knowledge. The relationship between truth and knowledge in Lacanian theory is more conflicted than that. The kinds of truths about the self that psychoanalysis is interested in are truths that create a real crisis for self-understanding. In other words, there is something about the reason for a symptom's emergence and development, for example, that does not fit with an individual's story about himself. This is similar to the effect that a truth has on a situation in Badiou's philosophy.

When Badiou says that a truth is *of* its situation, and that the truth has something to do with the very being of the situation, this is supposed to mean that a truth exposes something about a knowledge's (a situation's) foundations that the situation actually needs to exclude in order to be what it is. And this is why it is important to ask a question about the status of the name that an intervention on behalf of an event can use, and why the situation's encyclopedia cannot decide on the propriety of this intervention. Once again,

Number and Numbers is maybe more helpful here than *Being and Event*:

> A truth supposes that the situation of which it is truth attains non-self-identity: this non-self-identity is indicated by the situation's being supplemented by an "extra" multiple, one whose belonging or non-belonging to the situation is, however, intrinsically undecidable. I have named this supplement "event", and it is always from an event that a truth-process originates. (NN 27)

For the situation, the event itself is not present, and the evental site is presented but not represented in the situation. An intervention, then, because it uses a name for the event that is said to come "from the void" of the situation, thus evoking something of the status of the pure multiple itself, can be said to split a situation in two. And the splitting of the situation seems to be coming from a splitting – or, rather, a doubling – intrinsic to the event itself. Badiou indeed claims in *Being and Event* that there is always a doubling of the event: there is the event itself, which is never presented and is always disappeared or subtracted, and then the *naming* of the event, which is like a repetition of the event, only this time a repetition of the event for the situation, or within the situation, bringing about its presentation therein, at least as a (problematic) name.

The problem of deviations, and other problems

There is a significant problem that Badiou is trying to avoid by asserting that there is a doubling of the event – once as a multiple that belongs to itself, and once as a name in a language. His concern is that if the event on its own served as the basis for the possibility of an intervention, an intervention would be superfluous. It would be as if the event already were enough to cause decisions and interventions on its own behalf. This would also remove any need for talk of the kind of fidelity Badiou's philosophy is ultimately interested in defending. Instead of having to think about fidelity, what we would have in this case is the possibility of certainty about events, and there would even be, in this case, evidence *for* an event's belonging to a situation.

However, if there is no event without an intervention, if an event somehow *depended* on decisions being made for it and people advocating for it, it would seem that in this case it is the event itself that is superfluous. In other words, there would be no need for references to some kind of extra-situational event whose status is problematic for a situation: there would simply be a division within a situation, with different claims being made. This would be some kind of voluntarism or decisionism: that is, an event boils down to the decisions by interveners that an event has happened.

What we have here are two perspectives (both of them "deviations" according to Badiou): one makes the intervention superfluous (all is due to the event itself and its scrambling of a situation) and the other makes the event superfluous (all is due to interveners who simply decide to scramble their own situations, on no other basis than their ability to do so). By doubling the event with an intervention, and by emphasizing the separation or difference between an event and an intervention, Badiou is trying to avoid both of these positions.

Where does he end up? The intervention turns out to depend on what Badiou calls a recurrence, by which he means another, earlier, event (BE 209). At first glance, this hardly seems satisfactory, and seems to open up an infinite regress, especially since this other event is also described as simply *an earlier intervention with respect to an event*! Why would Badiou need a theory of the event at all, if there are only ever a series of interventions? If every intervention depends not on an event but on an earlier intervention on behalf of an event, and so on and so on, what status does an event ultimately have? Has the difference between event and intervention become so large in Badiou's philosophy that an event never really is the basis of the latter: interventions are always based on earlier interventions, *ad infinitum*?

Badiou's central claim that an event is never presented in a situation turns out to be even more significant than it seemed at first. There is an absolute difference between situations and events; events are, after all, otherwise than being, while all (presented) being is situational.

The solution: fidelity and the generic

Once the decision for a name of an event has been made (such as "yes, atonality is music too," or, "yes, I am in love with her"), what is there? Badiou's position on the relation between events and interventions entails that an intervention creates a split in a situation, a split rooted in the claim that an event has occurred, and that this event is outside of the situation's purview even though the event also somehow pertains to the situation. After the intervention, the traces of the event address the situation and render the situation volatile.

It is not clear that the name of an event should be said to be present in a situation: the name's status in a situation is also an issue. If it can be said to be present, it is only as a pretender or something: its status or legitimacy is still up in the air. For example, the situation of eighteenth-century France would have assigned a certain status to this thing being called by some the "French Revolution" – perhaps a denial that it is happening, or a condemnation of its partisans as enthusiasts. Partisans of that revolution, obviously, consider that in light of the name "French Revolution" the situation of eighteenth-century France is no longer what it was, and is no longer adequate to contain a whole host of new multiples, and a new way of ordering already familiar and well-established multiples.

With the naming of an event (which is what an intervention is all about), what happens is that the difference between the state of the situation and what the partisans of the event are doing becomes ever more important. These partisans (if they have not fallen into either a leftist or rightist deviation) are engaged in what Badiou calls a fidelity procedure: they are looking at the multiples of the situation they are in and considering which ones are affected by the event and which ones are not. This is why Badiou describes fidelity as an operation, a task, and a process, rather than a state of mind. Fidelity is not something one can stay still with, as if one could say "I've had my conversion, I know what's what, and now I'm done." What fidelity requires in Badiou's philosophy is the performance of a series of decisions about the elements of the situation in question, asking whether each one is modified by the event or not. Given the fact that every situation is infinite, there is no end to a fidelity procedure: the series of decisions is going to be endless. What individual human beings can accomplish, however, is what Badiou calls an "enquiry" – a term with a legacy in Maoist thought – which is a finite slice of the infinite series that the fidelity procedure must be.

Hopefully, it is easy to see now how such a procedure suggests something different from what happens in the deviations that Badiou wishes to avoid. One of the deviations, which he describes as leftist, envisions a total destruction or reorganization of absolutely every multiple in the situation, based on nothing but the correctness of the insight of the militants. Another deviation, which he calls rightist, claims that there is nothing new under the sun, and every other possibility is negative, destructive, and terror prone. For this point of view, there are no events. This is like expressing a wish that all situations are natural or neutral: that there are no historical situations. A fidelity procedure avoids both of these deviations.

Badiou describes a fidelity procedure as an operator that "separates out, within the set of presented multiples, those which depend upon an event" (BE 232). What a fidelity procedure gathers together is a multiple, a series, that is a truth: thus, a truth *"groups together all the terms of the situation which are positively connected to the event"* (BE 335). The following passage explains quite well the effect this truth-series has on a situation and its language or encyclopedia:

> The names with which a subject surrounds itself are not indiscernible. But the external witness, noting that for the most part these names lack a referent inside the situation such as it is, considers that they make up an arbitrary and content-free language. Hence, any revolutionary politics is considered to maintain a utopian (or non-realistic) discourse; a scientific revolution is received with skepticism, or held to be an abstraction without a base in experiments; and lovers' babble is dismissed as infantile foolishness by the wise. These witnesses, in a certain sense, are right. The names generated – or rather, composed – by a subject are suspended, with respect to their signification, from the "to-come" of a truth. (BE 398)

Because of the intervention's link to an event, the encyclopedia of the situation does not necessarily say the intervention is wrong or erroneous. Rather, Badiou wants to claim that a situation's encyclopedia cannot assess or place the intervention. (This is similar to the claim about an event's status being undecidable.) What comes after the intervention then – the fidelity procedure – would have something like the status of an unrecognizable utterance in a language. The encyclopedia cannot decide whether the utterances in question make sense, which also means it cannot simply dismiss them as nonsensical. What it can say is that there is clearly something illegitimate about them ("illegal" is the term Badiou likes to use in this context).

For this reason, the multiple constructed by a fidelity procedure is not only a finite part of a truth but is also generic. The encyclopedia of a situation, of course, gives a place to, or can account for and give a name for, every part or subset in the situation. But a fidelity procedure is putting together a series of multiples under a new heading, as it were: in other words, this series, these multiples that are deemed to be affected by an event, escape determination by the encyclopedia. Generic is thus a good name for them, and keeping this qualifier in mind is helpful for distinguishing a fidelity procedure from its rightist and leftist deviations. One of the key features of names in a fidelity procedure is that they do not have referents in their situation (BE 398). Instead, they designate terms that "'will have been' presented in a *new* situation: the one which results from the addition to the situation of a truth (an indiscernible) of that situation" (BE 398). So every truth is a novelty, or every truth is new (Con 189; TS 139). And the novelty of a truth's language is what makes its status so difficult for a situation or world. Hence, a truth creates a split in a situation. It creates holes in knowledge.

Forcing and some problems

So it is not enough to say that a situation finds the multiples of a generic procedure indiscernible; it also cannot determine their correctness, their veracity, for a future, revised situation, and this reference to an alternative situation is a crucial part of the procedure. Badiou claims, for example, that the ability to decide whether Galileo's new concepts were correct or not did not come until the new scientific process launched by them had gone on for a while and established the criteria for verification: until, effectively, Galileo (and others) had created a new situation for science (BE 401).

Badiou uses the set theoretical notion of forcing to address this matter. He claims that the twentieth-century mathematician P. J. Cohen was able to articulate how the indiscernible and the undecidable are related with the idea of forcing, which is about linking generic multiples (which are indiscernible) to statements (demonstrable or not) (BE 410). The main idea is actually quite straightforward: the multiples involved in a truth procedure would be indiscernible for a situation – not presented. And what would be undecidable is whether the *statements* about (or a language for) these multiples and their status are correct or not (for, being indiscernible, how would we ever know?). Forcing addresses how the undecidable can be decided upon after all, and Cohen's accomplishment was to show that such a decision can be legitimate. This is why Badiou thinks Cohen's work is so significant. For him,

Cohen's insight amounts to the assertion that truth, in the form of a truth procedure, anyway, *does* exist, that what is going on in a truth procedure has some ontological status even if the event still does not, and even if we are not able to "know" the truth. This is why, at the end of chapter 2, I claimed that set theory is not just window dressing for Badiou's philosophical claims.

The fact that events *are not* is important to remember here, because what a truth procedure is doing is making statements based on something not present at all. There are no multiples that correspond to the names being used in a truth procedure, and even the people using such names can do no better than believe in them (BE 427). Cohen's work on forcing shows that "it is possible [...] to determine under what conditions such or such a statement is veridical in the generic extension obtained by the addition of an indiscernible part of the situation" (BE 410). The names being used in a truth procedure amount to additions to a situation, and their correctness can be settled in a future anterior tense (BE 401). According to Badiou, the ontological version of this law is what was formulated by Cohen, and that is what is called forcing. A statement that is undecidable in one situation may be veridical (or demonstrably false) in a new one (BE 509).

While this does not give anyone certainty about the use of such terms in any present situation, the notion of forcing does render inapt a certain type of critique of a truth procedure, and I think this is where its true importance for Badiou's work is to be found. The language being used by any truth procedure, as far as the situation and its encyclopedia are concerned, could always be dismissed as just so much gibberish. Imagine how many of the utterances of early Christians must have sounded like insane ranting to most Romans: consider how the languages of many political movements, artistic movements, and couples in love have a similar status. Badiou writes that "the external witness, the man of knowledge, necessarily declares that these statements are devoid of sense ('the obscurity of a poetic language,' 'propaganda' for a political procedure, etc.). Signifiers without any signified. Sliding without quilting point" (BE 400). Yet forcing shows that the use of such terms cannot be summarily dispensed with: the terms are indeed undecidable in the current situation, but not for a future one.

What is the relation between forcing and the subject itself? What Badiou calls subjectivation is an act that brings a name for the event into the situation. This sounds exactly like an intervention, yet the two are different. The name still has a peculiar status, and something must be done with it; subjectivation handles this. Issues arise because the name is the name for an event, which "is not"; the name has no referent. This leads to the kinds of legitimacy problems being discussed here. Remember that the encyclopedia of a situation should have a name for every multiple of the situation. So, strictly speaking, there cannot be a new name as far as the encyclopedia is concerned, and forcing still leaves the inhabitant of a situation in a state of risk, a state in which faith is all the inhabitant has to go on. And so, while forcing does not give certainty, it does give a space within which to work, and a possible confidence in the truth procedure. Forcing, then, is a term that has an ethical punch to it: despite the apparent nonsense of what a truth procedure is doing, forcing establishes that it is legitimate to carry on with it. Subjectivation is one of the consequences of this.

Conclusion

One of Badiou's examples of forcing in *Being and Event* is clear, but also misleading. Within the situation of Newtonian astronomy, based on the observable paths of certain planets, it could have been hypothesized that there is some yet to be discovered planet whose existence would account for deviations in their orbits. A later confirmation of this planet's existence would retroactively show that a statement about there being another planet in the solar system was veridical in that situation (BE 402). Badiou alleges that this is an example of forcing because there is a multiple in the future situation – the planet in question – that would demonstrate, or refute, the statement's veracity. Yet it is also not a very good example of forcing (Badiou does refer to it as a "caricature") because nothing about the method of verification itself is called into question here. What we have is just an untested hypothesis. The situation and its encyclopedia know how to handle such a thing: the planet will be discovered, or not. A radically new future situation – which is usually what is involved in forcing, on Badiou's own account – is not required for an empirical confirmation like this, and within the Newtonian universe a statement such as "there is a yet to be discovered planet" could hardly be said to be introducing a split in the situation.

In another text called "Truth: Forcing and the Unnameable," written a few years after *Being and Event*, Badiou defined forcing as "the point at which a truth, although incomplete, authorizes anticipations of knowledge concerning not what is but *what will have been if truth attains completion*" (TW 127). According to this, there is something undecidable about a truth procedure's knowledge-claims because the very *possibility* of verifying these claims is not there yet . . . and this is because the multiples it is about are not able to be discerned, are just not presented in, the situation in which the truth procedure is occurring. Another example from the history of science, referred to earlier (Galileo's development of "rational physics"), offers a better illustration of the idea. For Galileo's theses were about things that will exist – or better, will have been determined to exist – once the situation comes about in which Galileo's science becomes its own situation and its own encyclopedia.

Consider how this works in a different type of situation, such as art. Take impressionist painting. When it was first being produced, a variety of claims were made about its artistic status, both pro and con. It makes sense to say there was an undecidability to such claims because the works themselves were in an important sense not yet discernible: they were not able to be "seen" by the inhabitants of the art situation in the nineteenth century. Not because of the lack of exhibition space, but for other reasons – because of their newness, let's say. Statements like "these works are of great artistic value" or "this is mere scribbling" could have been made by anyone and everyone at the time. But they can only be considered verifiable (they can only really be decided on) in a situation in which impressionism has a role to play in the discerning of artistic multiples themselves – in a supplemented artistic situation, that is, and not in the art situation from which impressionism emerged.

The next chapter will explore further how and why Badiou links intervention to subjectivation, which is about how interventions affect human beings. This is the topic I opened up at the end of the last chapter and the beginning of this one by arguing that the point in *Logics of Worlds* is that events are measured by their consequences for a world, which depend on what is being done with events by a world's inhabitants. An intervention may sound something like an instant of conversion, or like some kind of revelation: Badiou will speak of it in terms of being seized by an event. But such instantaneous conversions are not enough to bring about a change in a situation. What is required after an intervention is the development of a procedure. Such a procedure goes nowhere, and does not even get started, without an intervention that names the event: yet it is what happens after the intervention that is even more consequential, and this is why a theory of the subject is required in Badiou's philosophy.

In my introduction, I argued that Badiou's main philosophical concern is to provide a defense of the notion of a faithful subject, and equally against the temptations to avoid the disruptions in a human life that a truth entails. His theoretical framework is supposed to provide the basis on which a faithful subject can be considered something other than a maligned *fanatic* subject. Fidelity is not surprisingly then described in *Being and Event* as a careful, meticulous procedure, not as a dogma or a state of mind or even a property of a thinking subject at all (BE 233). We shall see why in the next chapter.

This chapter has dealt with some of the thorniest issues in the systematic part of Badiou's philosophy. That the ontological matters in *Being and Event* lead directly into a discussion of languages and naming is surprising and potentially confusing. And, in what is a recurring problem for Badiou's philosophy, using a notion like decision in a discussion of intervention and fidelity raises the specter of the kind of subjectivism he wishes to avoid: speaking of choosing whether certain elements belong to a truth procedure or not, finding names for multiple, and so on, seems to undercut his theoretical anti-humanism. This is related to the problem I have already alluded to about Badiou's use of a term such as *operation* in his ontology, in which the ghost of the classical philosophical subject seems to be present. I will address this issue in the conclusion to the next chapter, which is devoted to Badiou's theory of the subject.

6
Badiou's Theories of the Subject

Previous chapters have focused on Badiou's laws of being. Badiou calls forcing, with which we closed the last chapter, a "law of the subject" (BE 401). Forcing authorizes and legitimates claims about indiscernible multiples – not proving or verifying them, but giving them a status that is better described as suspended rather than undecidable. Since the subject in Badiou's philosophy is not a conscious thing that *acts* so much as it rather *is* (although we will see this is not quite right) and does not *do*, how is forcing as a law of the subject supposed to be understood? Badiou writes that "a subject measures the *newness* of the situation to-come" (BE 406). The subject, defined by Badiou as a finite part of a truth procedure, is supposed to be a series that stands as evidence of the presence of something new in a situation, something not registered by a situation, yet on the way to creating the conditions for its own situation.

I have made several references already to the presence of a philosophical and theoretical anti-humanism in Badiou's work. This is fairly obvious in his notions of situations and worlds. But it is also present in his theories of truth and fidelity, as well as forcing and the subject. For example, a truth on Badiou's account is an infinite multiple and is therefore more like a being than a property of statements. The term truth describes something that is concrete, and does not serve as an adjective that describes the status of what individuals in a situation might know. For example, a truth in love "is unknown for those who love each other: all they do is produce it" (BE 340). Thus, a truth functions and brings about effects in a world even when individuals wrapped up in such a truth have no idea what it is, and cannot articulate it as such.

Given the contrast between truth and knowledge in Badiou's work, discussed in chapter 5, it should be no surprise that he claims that his notion of the subject does not describe a human person who knows the truth (BE 396). Political militants, for example, do not *know* the truth of their political situation, and may not even have any special insight into it. It is, rather, some aspect of what they are *doing* that produces a series of multiples Badiou calls a truth, because of how this series reveals within the situation its own void.

So, if Badiou is after a philosophy that contests the classical humanist subject's privilege, and if it is the case that the subject for him is not something or someone who knows the truth, or perhaps anything in particular, then why is one of Badiou's primary objectives nevertheless the development of a theory of the subject? Why not drop the topic altogether, and write instead only about situations, events, and truths? If the subject is not a knower, if it is not the one who articulates a truth, why does Badiou persist in using the term subject and in giving the thing a role in his philosophy at all?

Certainly, there needs to be a place for individual human beings and what they do in Badiou's philosophy: the entire apparatus of events and truths in fact requires the existence of historical situations, not natural ones, and historical situations are inhabited by us. Furthermore, the whole theory of naming and of interventions seems to require some account of what human beings are doing with the effects of events on their situations. But what role does the subject play in Badiou's philosophy? If it is the case that the subject is not active in any strong sense, is the subject entirely passive? Is it a mere by-product of a procedure? If Badiou did not have a theory of the subject, would his philosophy really be missing anything? Could it not do with a vague theory of inhabitants of situations, and focus instead on truths and events?

Despite the seemingly trivial, dispensable status that the subject could have in his work, a theory of the subject has been an important part of Badiou's philosophy throughout his career because it is the theory of the subject that allows his theoretical anti-humanism to lead to, and to support, what is in effect his practical humanism. In other words, the notion of the subject serves as the bridge between the systematic part of Badiou's work and the ethical part. Paradoxically, it turns out to be the case that the further one goes down the *humanist* road in theory, Badiou thinks, the more humanity is reduced to the status of a mere living creature, an animal not unlike others, precious and valuable simply for being alive. This has a practical chilling effect: it tends to discourage the kinds of practices that truth procedures are all about. Badiou seems to be arguing that the more humanistic one's theory of human beings is, then, the more one reduces humans to animals who are best off simply pursuing their interests and pleasures, who are best off avoiding anything having to do with truths and fidelity procedures. Therefore, his gambit consists of maintaining that the more *anti-humanistic* a philosophy is, the more it is going to allow human beings to be something other than creatures pursuing their interests, allowing them, say, to risk becoming "immortals": "a truth is that by which 'we' of the human species are engaged in a trans-specific procedure, a procedure that opens us up to the possibility of being immortals, in such a way that a truth is certainly an experience of the inhuman" (LM 80).

In this chapter, my aim is to present Badiou's theory – or rather, theories – of the subject in detail. I have hinted already at my view that the success of Badiou's philosophy depends on how he is able to deliver on what he himself called the "black sheep" of materialism: a theory of the subject that knits together change and structure. And, as I claimed in the introduction, a theory of the subject has always been a guiding concern of Badiou's work. When Badiou wanted to bring the subject into the philosophy of historical materialism, he wanted to do this in order to be able to theorize change adequately. How, and when, does Badiou's theory of the subject manage to do this?

We will see that Badiou has always thought of the subject as a split subject, which was also one of Jacques Lacan's fundamental insights. In *Theory of the Subject*, the subject is portrayed as a double thing, composed of an instant and a process: what Badiou calls a subjectivation and a subject-process. On the basis of these two components, and their relation to the dialectical notions of force and place, he is able to develop his first ethic. In *Being and Event* the notions of subjectivation and the subject-process in *Theory of the Subject* are reconfigured as intervention and fidelity procedure, respectively. Due to its ontological focus, no clear ethic is presented in *Being and Event* and there seems to be only one type of subject possible: a faithful subject. This leads to some problems that become even more manifest in a book that he wrote after the publication of *Being and Event* (entitled, precisely, *Ethics*), which attempted to develop an ethic of truths, an ethic for faithful subjects, using *Being and Event* as a framework. Finally, *Logics of Worlds* presents the subject in a manner basically consistent with *Being and Event*, but this time subjects of different types are envisioned. This is possible because of the different way in which the event is thought in *Logics of Worlds* and because of the development there of a more nuanced, pluralistic theory of change. With this theory, Badiou is able to claim that a truth may induce different types of subjects, corresponding to different modes of living in the wake of an event: there is now an obscure subject and a reactionary subject as well as the faithful subject. So, after *Logics of Worlds*, the faithful subject is no longer the only type of subject going.

The legacy of the philosophical subject

To get a bearing on what Badiou is doing with the subject in his philosophy, it is helpful to consider how the subject in philosophy has, traditionally, always been something of an incarnation problem. The philosophical subject has always been involved in the interaction of two very different orders: thinking and being, or ideality and materiality, or the spiritual or psychological and the physical. Even when the subject is linked to consciousness and constitutional questions with respect to experience, it is still, in its idealist version, about how one order of being – thought, concepts, ideality – goes about interacting with a radically different order of being – matter, objects, the world.

Badiou tries to develop a materialist theory of the subject, but it is still the case that for him the subject is a site where two very different things meet up and interact. Only now the subject is not responsible for the interaction; it is not doing the mixing. It is just the name for the place where a certain kind of mixing occurs. Thus, it will sound like the subject is primarily passive rather than active for Badiou, but we will see that this is not exactly right.

In what Badiou considers to be its idealist version, the subject of philosophy is associated with several properties generally thought to be the privilege of human beings – such as self-consciousness, agency (free action), decision-making, and the use of reason. Descartes wrote that he could be most certain of being a thinking thing. Kant wrote that "the phrase 'I think' must be able to be added to every representation" of the world that I have, suggesting that this "I" is co-present in every human experience, something that is always there, along with every experience and every act of consciousness. Jean-Paul Sartre claimed that every act of consciousness is already an act of self-consciousness, that an awareness of self accompanies every act of consciousness, no matter how dim or vague. Badiou points out that the common feature of these idealist accounts of the subject is transparency: "in the entire great classical idealist tradition, the subject designates this transparent point of being, in the position of immediate givenness to itself, through which passes every access to existence as such" (TS 294). His own elucidation of the subject as materialist and fully post-Cartesian is guided by the idea that "the subject is not given, but must be found" (TS 295). It is neither given to itself, nor given to us by any experience. The reference point, the source of information about the subject, is not going to come from what the French call *le vécu* – lived experience, or conscious experience. Rather, if the subject is something found somewhere in situations, which means that it is something that appears only in certain places, then a theory of the places in which subjects occur is required. The subject is situational for Badiou ("topological" he says sometimes), and if it needs to be found the implication is that it is hiding somewhere, or that it is difficult to discern, and perhaps not always present.

Where it is to be found is in what Badiou describes as a kind of torsion in a structure or situation or world, and this amounts to saying that the subject is the material correlate of change. This will be my basic point, my basic reading, of Badiou's theory of the subject throughout this chapter: the subject, for Badiou, is the real presence of change, of novelty, in a situation. Again, Badiou claims that "a subject measures the *newness* of the situation to-come" (BE 406). This is why it is not entirely correct to say that the subject is simply a passive thing, even though it is not exactly active either. It is, instead, a certain kind of existent linked with novelty. As such, it could well be said to be doing something after all. As Oliver Feltham describes it, it "is not an independent and separate entity that initiates change, like the house-builder, in another being. Rather, [it] consists of the actual material inscription of change" (Feltham 2008: 79).

The subject in *Theory of the Subject*

In *Theory of the Subject* Badiou's philosophical orientation is primarily dialectical, and he reads what in his later philosophy would be called a situation or world in terms of a conflict between forces and positions. There is a conflict between what he calls, in a coinage, the *horlieu* (what is literally "out of place" or "beyond the site") and *esplace* (something like a "space of places"). Much of the book attempts to hammer out the proper relation between the two, which is supposed to be the goal of a materialist dialectics. "Dialectics," Badiou writes, pits "the *horlieu* against *esplace*" (TS 29).

The framework of *Theory of the Subject* is also Maoist, offering a sort of philosophical Maoism, as I have claimed, and it consists of an attempt to describe different possible outcomes of the conflict between the old and the new. The Maoist slogan that "one splits into two" is a recurrent theme of the text (TS 32). The idea is that if you take any system, any situation, any order – a society, say – it is always possible to note how it is fraught with conflict: it consists of rival factions or tendencies jockeying for power and dominance. The conflicts within a system are crystallized in certain elements of the system: the working class, the masses, immigrant labor. A Maoist strategy is, roughly, to find where the social and political fissures are, and to then aggravate them in order to gain clarity on the nature of the struggle.

But this Maoist framework is not the only one Badiou relies on in this text. There is a discussion of Christian theology that is also very helpful for understanding what Badiou is after. Badiou claims that Christianity has taken God himself as one term, correlated to what he calls the *horlieu*, and the finite world as another term, correlated to his notion of *esplace*. The combination of these terms – something like the site of the subject – was posited by Christian theology in Christ, as the infinite God "indexed" and situated (placed, that is) in the finite world (TS 33).

But, of course, the history of Christianity is filled with differing views on how to read the relation between all these terms – Christ, God, and the World. Most noteworthy are what Badiou calls the rightist deviation in early Christianity, according to which Christ was thought to be only a human, emphasizing thereby Christ's finitude and mortality and the complete "transcendence" of the truly divine with respect to him; and another, leftist deviation in early Christianity, according to which Christ's death is only an apparent death, his mortality just an appearance. This is a deviation that emphasizes the purity of God's infinity, and how God, becoming Christ, remained free of any real finite stain, even when he appeared in human form on Earth. (In fact, this Gnostic view held that Christ never really had a body when on Earth, but was more like a ghost.)

At the first Nicene Council, in AD 325, which Badiou describes rather creatively as "the first of the great modern political-ideological congresses," a conclusion was reached that asserted the consubstantiality of the Son with the Father (TS 34). What Badiou admires about this solution is that it posited the relation of the two terms as what he calls a *limit*: it let two strongly opposed terms dwell together in one site. Rather than letting any one of the terms dominate – saying either that Christ is really finite, or that he is really infinite – it asserts both, together, thereby allowing a change to occur to each term. This is why Badiou writes of this position in terms of "limit": the finite puts a limit on the divine, and the divine limits the finite. The infinite God is really placed in the finite world in the man Christ, while the finite Christ is elevated back to the infinite (via Resurrection).

On Badiou's reading, the Nicene Council rejected a circular reading of the relation of the terms, and embraced a periodization that is appropriate for the kind of dialectical spiral movement that Badiou wants to assert is the right way to understand dialectical materialism (TS 38). And it is exactly in these terms that Badiou will configure the relation between *horlieu* and *esplace* in his own philosophy. It is not the case, as in a circular (idealist) version of dialectics, that there is really one fundamental term all along, whose other (the finite, for God) is not really an other at all but just a fallen, inferior version of itself. On the idealist version of dialectics, the fundamental term (God) reunites with itself at a higher, more developed level at the end of a dialectical process: one might say that in this kind of idealist dialectics the true subject all along is the term that is *horlieu*, and that history is about the becoming, the self-development, of this term. Badiou, by contrast, wants to emphasize the persistence of duality in dialectics as well as the strong reality of transformation, such that – to continue using the terms of Christian theology – God and the world are different after they encounter each other, and remain distinct. In this manner, not only does "one split into two," but Badiou can also assert the primacy of "the two" over any "one." God's entry into the world really means that God changes, as does the world after He enters it: yet the world never becomes thoroughly divine.

The adaptation of this dialectical insight from theology into Marxism goes like this: one would have the bourgeois, capitalist state corresponding to the finite world and the proletariat as the infinite force outside of this world. How is the proletariat's place within the bourgeois world to be thought? Just as the dialectic of Christianity was settled by a periodization of the relation between God and Man, each one limiting the other – it was necessary for God to become human, die, and then be elevated back to the Infinite – Marxist theory posits a similar periodization for the proletariat within the bourgeois state. The history of capitalism, then, is the history of the proletariat's attempt to incarnate itself, to become fully present within the bourgeois state – thereby ending the state and class society as such. The proletariat exists because of the bourgeoisie, is shaped by it, and the bourgeoisie will be transformed (destroyed) by the proletariat.

But this periodization also means the real death of the proletariat, as it did for God's becoming-human. Of course, the proletariat is what it is only because of the bourgeois state. Badiou's reading of the role of the party in politics suggests precisely this. What appeared in the failed Paris Commune of 1871 – the proletariat's first incarnation in the bourgeois world, according to Marxist historians – was elevated in the Russian Revolution of 1917 into the political dominance of the working class in the Communist Party (TS 38). Only what failed to happen after that was the death of the party itself, and class: this is why Badiou was intrigued by Mao's Cultural Revolution, which tried to complete this periodization.

In a periodization, then, there is a greater degree of real change for both terms in question (place, force) than there is in the idealist, circular version of dialectics. And Badiou is certainly suggesting that Marxism is not immune to this kind of idealism. The terms do not remain self-identical throughout their development – they become genuinely other. Badiou's is a dialectics that is not guided by some ultimate purpose. It is not the case that a concept is simply unfolding itself through time, becoming what it always already really was: as if the oak tree is already somehow contained in the acorn, as Hegel might put it. The various incarnations that occur change both of the primary terms in a dialectic: the finite and the infinite, place and force, influence each other interminably, in a spiral development, one that Badiou likens to the shape of a snail shell (TS 324). That the development is spiral in shape allows for there to be real setbacks, real regressions, and not constant progress, which is something an idealist, Hegelian dialectic does not admit. For Hegel, there is never failure and never regression. Every move in history is a move toward the ultimate goal (for Hegel, freedom). An illustration of this is found in an earlier text, where Badiou wrote that:

> materialist dialectics will, on the contrary, present deviation as ineluctable, and the existence of the false and the former at every stage of the process as a necessary law. There is not a succession of the new and the old, but a continual battle of the two. Deviations are necessary, and the battle against deviations is a motor force of the development of the whole. (NR 75)

This idea that "deviations are necessary" will receive more attention in my discussion of Badiou's ethics in chapter 7.

Remember that the goal of *Theory of the Subject* is to give us a guide to locating the subject in structures. Where does the subject fit into this discussion of dialectics? Badiou claims that "the subject is neither a cause nor a foundation" of anything (TS 296). The subject is not supposed to be the same as that which causes changes in structures, and it is also not the foundation of structures. This means that the subject is, strictly speaking, neither force nor place, neither God nor the world, neither the bourgeoisie nor the proletariat.

Consider the moment of an insurrection, and the subsequent installation of a new regime. Say that the immediate cause of a new regime is a mass movement, an appearance of the brute force of the masses – such as the storming of the Bastille. By the time a new regime is established, its founding event has faded into the past, and mass enthusiasm typically wanes. Mass movements, then, are vanishing terms in a Marxist theory of history, and Badiou claims that their essence is to disappear, even though when they do exist they exist most intensely (TS 82). Thus, the force that brings the new order about is always a vanished force, and although it is "placed nowhere, vanished force supports the consistency of places" (TS 81). In this respect, what Badiou calls the *horlieu* is "strongly causal" – it is an anchoring and organizing of the system of places; although, as a cause, it is also an absent cause.

What he is calling *subject* is not identical to this vanished force. And, obviously, it is not going to be identical to the structure or system that is transformed by the masses. Ultimately, the "where is the subject?" game is won by finding the subject at a site at which the (absent) cause of structures is linked to the consistency of a structure (TS 301). The subject can then be something like a knot or a crossroads in which these two very different things come together, in what Badiou describes as a torsion. I would point out, again, that this amounts to thinking of the subject in terms of incarnation: the subject is a point, a place, where two very different things come together.

It would have been obvious to identify the subject with what is called in *Theory of the Subject* force or the *horlieu*, but Badiou resists doing this: some type of vitalism might go in this direction, as well as the leftist deviation he wishes to avoid, and Badiou is critical of Deleuze's philosophy for adopting such a position on desire.

Subjectivation and subject-process in *Theory of the Subject*

If the subject were the same thing as force, this would amount to saying that the subject is the same as the cause of change, the cause of a new order, and so on, and this would not be sufficiently post-Cartesian and anti-Idealist. Instead, with his view of the subject as a knot or crossroads, Badiou is able to say that his theory of the subject is rigorously materialist. How is a claim like this – "every subject is at the crossroads of a lack-of-being and a destruction, of a repetition and an interruption, of a placement and an excess" – a materialist theory of the subject (TS 157)? For one thing, the subject names a "network of concepts" and is not reducible to any one of the key concepts Badiou associates it with in this text (TS 301). This seems to make up part of Badiou's materialist point: the subject is a mixed thing. The subject itself is split, and composed.

Badiou uses two terms for the different aspects of this split: subjectivation and subject-process. Subjectivation marks the moment of the subject's emergence, while the subject-process describes the subject's being or persistence, and refers to the process of the creation of some new kind of order, some system of places or placement. "The theory of the subject dictates that the subject is divided into a part that repeats itself and insists in being and a part that interrupts (a non-repeatable moment)" (TS 160). Where subjectivation is a name for something like the subject's sudden appearance in structure, the subject-process is a more drawn-out thing, which entails a recomposition of structure: "subjectivation designates the subject in the principle dimension of interruption, the subject-process in the dimension of recomposition" (TS 276).

So an instant of insurrection does not make a subject. The subject is located not just where there is an interruption in a structure but also where there is a repetition or a recomposition of structure. Again, the theme of *Theory of the Subject* can be adequately expressed by Mao's famous idea that "one splits into two." What the text does is start with a split covered by any dialectical theory worth its salt – a split between the dominant and the subordinate, between the inside and outside, between structure and force – and it splits that split in the following manner: structure is split by force in what Badiou calls a subjectivation, an interruption, and that force itself is in turn split by structuring, or being placed, by being made into a process or re-composition. And these two new terms – subjectivation and subject-process – together form the torsion that is the subject itself.

The final view of *Theory of the Subject* is that the subject "is only the divisible unity of subjectivation and the subject-process. Each of these moments is abstract. It is only acceptable to speak of subject as a process of destruction-recomposition, itself submitted in a second articulation to the dialectic of lack and excess" (TS 293). As the equal presence of two very different things, the subject can also be described as something like the appearance of lack: "*it makes lack be*" (TS 159). Although there are some things that change about Badiou's theory of the subject later in *Being and Event*, this expresses quite well the basic idea of his theory of the subject throughout his work: the subject is something like the real presence of change in a situation.

Subject in *Being and Event*

A subject is defined in *Being and Event* as a finite part of a truth procedure, and this is how Badiou consistently defines the subject thereafter (BE 522). Does this mean that the subject is simply a by-product of a truth procedure? Even though the subject is not a cause of anything in particular (it does not cause a truth, it does not cause an event, it does not cause a fidelity), but is primarily an effect, it is still not just an effect dangling out there in a situation with no efficacy, doing nothing. While the subject is in a sense drained of agency, the subject is still identified with the presence of change and novelty: "a subject is not a result – any more than it is an origin. It is the *local* status of a procedure, a configuration in excess of the situation" (BE 392). And this presence that is an excess is a way of describing the presence of the genuinely new in a situation.

Consider Badiou's claim that in an artistic truth procedure, the series of works produced by it ought to be considered the subject of the procedure (E 44). How can this be? If a series of works are the subject, they are then a finite part of a truth procedure; this much is not difficult to follow. There are infinitely many possible effects of the truth being brought to bear on the art world by a new procedure: any series of works that belongs to this is just a finite part of that. Moreover, a series of works certainly does not represent some idea (it does not "have" ideas: a series consists just of works), or some promise for the new; it does not merely contain some potential for reconfiguring the art world. Rather, it makes sense to say that the works themselves are already this change in their world; they are already a reconfiguration of their art world. Understanding the subject as the real presence of change in a situation means making the subject into something distinct from the truth with which it is associated. A truth is immeasurably more, greater, than the subject because the subject is only ever a fragment of a truth: a particular series of works, for example, or a finite set of behaviors and emotions and beliefs shared among two individuals in love. Badiou, recall, associates truth with an infinite set: a subject is not an infinite set. And, again, this means that the subject does not "know" the truth: "every truth is transcendent to the subject, precisely because the latter's entire being resides in supporting the realization of truth. The subject is neither consciousness nor unconsciousness of the true" (BE 397).

Thus far it may not sound as if there are any significant differences between the theory of the subject proposed in *Being and Event* and Badiou's prior works. The project in *Being and Event* is, like that of *Theory of the Subject*, trying to preserve yet rework the notion of the subject, outside of a Cartesian and phenomenological (idealist) framework. To see the changes from *Theory of the Subject* to *Being and Event*, we need to look at the composition of the subject, and perhaps not its overall situation.

The subject in *Theory of the Subject* was made up of two parts, we saw: a subjectivation and a process. A subject was a knotting together of these two parts, making it a destruction and a recomposition at the same time. In *Being and Event*, the whole idea of a process is taken over by something entirely different, and is decoupled from the subject as such. The process is somehow independent of the subject. And, as we have seen, procedure or process in *Being and Event* is described in different ways, with different adjectives. There are fidelity procedures, generic procedures, truth procedures ... but Badiou does not write there of a subject procedure or process at all.

Can one have procedures like this without a subject? On my reading, if the answer were yes – if there could be, say, a fidelity procedure without a subject – this would mean that the procedure in question is not actually bringing about anything in its situation, because the subject is Badiou's name for the real presence of change. There could be an evental site that is inactive for a situation. What one could not have is a *procedure* that is carrying out the effects of the event on the situation without that procedure necessarily creating a series of multiples that would be called a subject – some works (in art), a being-in-common (in love), a cluster of insights or theses (in science), some slogans or tenets (in politics). So, even though there is no discussion of a subject procedure or process as there was in *Theory of the Subject*, the subject in *Being and Event* is still a component of processes.

What Badiou does in *Being and Event* is link the subject more closely to subjectivation, which is now alleged to be primarily what there is of a subject. Yet subjectivation is not exactly what it was in *Theory of the Subject* either. Subjectivation is now itself split, with part of it turned toward the event (thus making the subjectivation something that does not fit comfortably in a situation) and part of it also having a presence in the situation.

With his theory of subjectivation in *Being and Event*, Badiou is trying to say that something of the subject is present but somehow still not accounted for in a situation. This is because a subjectivation is now something that follows from what Badiou called earlier in *Being and Event* an intervention (BE 393). What effect does this have? Why is it important for Badiou to link subjectivation to intervention? In *Theory of the Subject* things were clearly different. A subjectivation came about from nowhere as far as the situation was concerned, although this nowhere was linked to the concept of force (the *horlieu*, the out-of-site). As he wrote there, "the 'no!' of the revolt is not implicated by local conditions. It is forced by the inexistence of an absolute constraint that would force the submission, in a fashion transcendent to the immediate conditions" (TS 289). Although it is a bit obscure, I think what Badiou is saying here is that the moment of subjectivation – when a revolt begins, say, and when the masses are in motion – is not something that can be deduced or derived from what is happening in the situation. Its source is entirely elsewhere: a subjectivation is not able to be deduced, for example, from a crisis, or from anything else. Even if wages are decreasing, for example, or repression is increasing, a political revolt still may not happen. So, in *Theory of the Subject*, the occurrence of a subjectivation is spontaneous, and this is partly because of its connection to force, the *horlieu*.

Being and Event does not claim that the moment of subjectivation can be calculated from the degree of crisis and conflict in a situation either. But where subjectivation sounds like a pure moment in *Theory of the Subject*, in *Being and Event* it is less pure, and – connected with this, somehow – less affiliated with an absolute destruction of the situation. By making subjectivation a kind of follower to ("consecutive to," Badiou wrote) an intervention, *Being and Event* is able to make the subject itself more bound to the situation, more a part of it, than it is in *Theory of the Subject* (but still not to the extent that it will be in *Logics of Worlds*). This is also because of what a subjectivation leads to: forcing, which, as we saw in the previous chapter, is when an alternative to the situation is constructed within the situation itself, and does not simply come from outside it.

Recall that an intervention is an act that names an event. Since the event "is not," for it to begin to have concrete effects there must be, at a minimum, a name that works as a stand-in for it in the situation. The intervention is, however, still part of the multiple that is the evental site, and is still not a proper part of the situation that contains that site. Thus, as we have seen, the name for the event, while it plays a role in the situation, has a strange status within it. It is an empty signifier for the inhabitants of the situation; it has no referent as far as the situation is concerned. A subjectivation occurs when an inhabitant of a situation starts to bring this name into relation to other multiples in the situation, forcing its presence in the situation.

By contrast to an intervention proper, then, subjectivation, in *Being and Event*, is described as "interventional nomination *from the standpoint of the situation*" (BE 393). What this means is that a subjectivation, unlike the intervention, brings the effects of the event to bear in a situation; it repeats the intervention by directly bringing in to the situation the name for the event decided on by the intervention. This is why Badiou called forcing a *law of the subject*. Only a subjectivation allows a process, rooted in the evental site, to begin; only a subjectivation allows an intervention to become a truth procedure affecting the situation itself. No subjectivation, no truth; only a group of indiscernible multiples.

A subjectivation provides something like a form for the subject, then, and this moment resembles a kind of voluntarist or libertarian moment of freedom. Formally, therefore, the subject in Badiou's philosophy does resemble a classical subject. But it is in his account of the subject's stuff that his philosophy of the subject is clearly at variance with classical theories of subjectivity. The subject's stuff consists of all the particular multiples that have been subjected to an enquiry (BE 394). Thus, the very stuff of the subject is the set of multiples in a situation determined to have been affected by the event – or a finite part of the truth itself, which is precisely his definition of the subject. So, while an event is the ultimate cause of a subject, the multiples that belong to a truth procedure are its very stuff (BE 433). For this reason, the subject is the bringing together of the vanished event-cause and its positive remnants in a situation. Hence my claim that Badiou's subject is a term for the real presence of change in a situation, or the actual existence of the new.

A truth splits but no longer destroys a situation

One thing to add about the theory of the subject in *Being and Event* concerns its relation to destruction. I claimed that the subject in philosophy is usually thought of as some kind of intersection point, some kind of knotting together of different things. As Badiou puts it, in Lacanian terms, "a subject is at the intersection, via its language, of knowledge and truth" (BE 406). Truth, we know from the previous chapter, is strictly opposed to knowledge. Because it involves the creation of something like a new language, the correctness of a truth procedure simply cannot be decided on. One might well ask, then, why the subject is said to be at the intersection of knowledge and truth, and is not put simply on the side of truth. If the subject is a finite part of the generic procedure that is creating an infinite multiple called a truth, what does it have to do with knowledge at all? How does a subject intersect truth and knowledge? (And this is also a tricky question since subjects are said not to "know" anything . . . a subject is not supposed to be a thing with consciousness in Badiou's philosophy.)

Badiou situates the subject at the intersection of knowledge and truth because there is, after all, the assertion of something like knowledge in a truth procedure, as the discussion of forcing in the previous chapter showed. A truth procedure is articulating a series of terms that will take on the status of knowledge if and when a new situation is created. A truth procedure becomes its own encyclopedia if successful. Therefore, the truth in a truth procedure is destined to become something other than truth (knowledge, precisely) as the price of its success. This is the risk undergone by any truth procedure, by virtue of the mere fact that it uses language and thus names multiples in such a way that cannot help but use some of the terms being used by the encyclopedia of the situation. The leftist deviation Badiou writes about tries to keep such a transformation from happening. And the rightist deviation tries to minimize the novelty altogether, making it fit within the already familiar.

One of the more important consequences of the view of the subject as an intersection of knowledge and truth is the effect it has on the link between truth and destruction. According to *Being and Event*, in fact, a truth procedure is no longer primarily a destroyer. It adds. It supplements. Where Mao said "no creation without destruction," and Badiou largely agreed up to and including the publication of *Theory of the Subject*, now Badiou thinks creation is decidedly less destructive: and, in *Logics of Worlds*, Badiou claims that there is no destruction without creation – the emphasis, again, being on creation.

The theory of the subject in *Being and Event* portrays a subject better adjusted to a situation, to the scene of placement, than the subject is in *Theory of the Subject*. This is because Badiou affirms that all multiples in any given situation are also presented in the new situation created after a truth procedure, the one Badiou calls the situation-to-come (BE 408). Impressionism does not destroy realism in painting: but realism does not look the same afterwards. The kinds of beings described by Aristotelian physics are not destroyed by Galileo: they are, however, subject to a different interpretation. Previously, Badiou would have attributed destruction to a truth procedure: and does it not make sense to say that a truth destroys knowledge, that it tears down an old order? Consider what he claimed in *Theory of Contradiction*, a book that preceded *Theory of the Subject*. Truth there is called "the destruction of nonsense" and is said to be "essentially destruction" (TC 16–17). We will see, in chapter 8, where I discuss Badiou's political thought, how death itself played an important role in Badiou's dialectics in the 1970s. He now claims, though, that destruction comes from the other side, so to speak: destruction is a way in which the inhabitants of a situation may react to a truth (BE 408). Destruction, then, is accidental and not essential to what a truth procedure does. It is one of the effects of the new on the old; and what a truth procedure does is now more accurately described as a supplementation of a situation by the step-by-step, multiple-by-multiple creation of a situation-to-come, precisely.

Theory of the subject in *Ethics*

In *Being and Event* the discussion of the subject is actually quite brief. This makes sense, given the goal of the book. After the publication of *Being and Event*, there are scattered discussions of the subject in Badiou's oeuvre until the publication of *Logics of Worlds*. Between these two books, the topic of the subject receives most attention in the short book entitled *Ethics*.

What Badiou wants to achieve with his theory of the subject should be clear by now. Whether he manages to pull off the trick might not be. What is clear so far is that the subject is not supposed to be the same as a free, conscious agent. It is a result of an action and a process of creation that is greater than the subject itself. The subject is not a thinking thing, it is not identical to consciousness – it is not even identical to an individual or a group of individuals. Yet it does depend on the existence of human individuals in an important fashion, and it is this point that will be considered from here on out.

Badiou's exploration of ethics addresses the link between the inhabitants of a situation and subjects. While it is true that the subject in Badiou's philosophy is not the same as consciousness, it would also be wrong to say it has nothing to do with consciousness. It clearly does. It is better to say that the subject is removed from interiority and reflection; it is strictly outside all that in large part because it is trans-individual in every case. The subject has something to do with thought, with conscious activity, and even language, because it is in large part a product of such things. It is not a natural object, but a human, historical object.

Being and Event referred to the inhabitants of situations, those who would receive a truth procedure a certain way, finding it to be nonsensical, undecidable, or promising. *Ethics* addresses the same idea in a different way, referring to the inhabitant of a situation as a "some-one" who is possibly split in two, so to speak, by an event. This splitting is the consequence of being affected by an event; as such, it presupposes a subjectivation.

> "Some-one" can thus be *this* spectator whose thinking has been set in motion, who has been seized and bewildered by a burst of theatri-

cal fire, and who thus enters into the complex configuration of a moment of art. Or this assiduous student of a mathematical problem, after the thankless and exhausting confusion of working in the dark, at the precise moment enlightened by its solution. Or that lover whose vision of reality is befuddled and displaced since, supported by the other, he remembers the instant of the declaration of their love. Or this militant who manages, at the end of a complicated meeting, to find simple words to express the hitherto elusive statement which, everyone agrees, declares what must be pursued in the situation.

The "some-one" thus caught up in what attests that he belongs to the truth-process as one of its foundation-points is simultaneously *himself*, nothing other than himself, a multiple singularity recognizable among all others, and *in excess of himself*, because the uncertain course of fidelity *passes through him*, transfixes his singular body and inscribes him, from within time, in an instant of eternity. (E 45)

The difference between the subject and a some-one who inhabits a situation is this: the subject would be the multiple in excess of the some-one affected by an event, in excess of the some-one who has been subjectivated by an event. That there is something of this some-one left behind, or left out of, subjectivation is where ethics has a job to do, because this difference opens up the space in which it is possible to consider what an individual is going to make of the excess that is occurring through him or her. How do the subjectivated inhabitants of a situation live with an event whose effects are insisting in and disrupting their lives? This is what ethical reflection will be about.

Ethics will turn out to address the challenge of being faithful to fidelity, of a "fidelity to fidelity." The doubling of the term fidelity here is not an oversight: a fidelity procedure itself is already larger than any some-one and is even something distinct from a couple or group. Such a procedure happens, and is not a matter of decision. The same point can be made about subjectivation, of course: a subjectivation is not chosen, it is not willed. For individuals, where choice and decision do enter into play is when they ask themselves whether they are going to let the fidelity continue, or pursue the consequences of a subjectivation. In other words, they face the question: do they remain faithful to the fidelity procedure already going on?

One could argue that it was just such an account of what happens to individuals in situations, how fidelity procedures create trouble for them, how events and truth procedures are occurring, that was missing from *Being and Event*. *Ethics* then is a much needed coda to that book, for without the reference to the effect that events and truths have on individuals, many things about truth procedures in *Being and Event* remain rather obscure, strangely disembodied, and even mechanical, even though they use a very subject-inflected language (with terms like naming, decision, choice, forcing, fidelity, and so on). I will continue discussing aspects of Badiou's ethics in the next chapter.

Subject in *Logics of Worlds*

Before moving to a discussion of ethics, passions, affects, virtues, and vices, it is necessary to address one last treatment of the subject from a formal perspective, as it is presented in *Logics of Worlds*. *Logics of Worlds* gives us the most fleshed-out, substantial theory of the subject yet, because Badiou considers there not how the subject is situated at a junction of an evental site and a situation, or a truth procedure and a knowledge (which is an ontological take on the subject), but rather at how a subject is situated at a junction of an inhabitant of a world and that world itself (which is a logical or objective-phenomenological take on it). This is why the account in *Logics* is also able to include a discussion of affects and a catalog of the different types of responses to events and truths that individuals may adopt. The book closes with a discussion of what it means "to live," and every indication is that this is going to be the direction his further reflections on ethics take him: into discussions of immortality, life, death, and finitude, all put in their proper place.

Up to the publication of *Logics of Worlds* there was basically just one type of subject in Badiou's philosophy, and so it has been possible to make general claims about it – such as my claim that it is the real presence of change. In *Logics of Worlds* there are different forms for the subject. It is still true that the subject as such is the real presence of change; but just as was the case for the event itself, since *Logics of Worlds* is able to offer a more nuanced discussion of change it is also able to offer a more nuanced theory of how this change is present in situations – remember that a study of appearance is what *Logics* is all about. That is, the subject can appear in a variety of forms, but it always remains some kind of evidence of the new. Reactive and obscure subjects, which are now alternative versions for the subject, for example, are what they are because of the production of novelty by a faithful subject: reaction and obscurantism are distinct ways of presenting this novelty, whereas the faithful subject is the only one that presents novelty while also proceeding with it.

Logics of Worlds opens with a distinction between democratic materialism and the materialist dialectics that Badiou wishes to defend. The subject is directly at stake in this difference, so it is a good place to start the analysis of the subject in that work. As I mentioned in chapter 5, democratic materialism is Badiou's phrase for the dominant ideology of the contemporary world, and he finds its essential claim to be that "there are only bodies and languages." His theory of the subject plays an important role in articulating the difference between democratic materialism and dialectical materialism because the former equates individuals with bodies and the use of languages only, which rules out the possibility of access to something other than being – events and truths, the very things to which, for Badiou, a subject is linked. Badiou writes that the exception in his alternative to democratic materialism – which he writes as "there are only bodies and languages, except there are truths too" – "*exists* as subject" (LM 53). To say that the exception ruled out by democratic materialism – the very existence of truths – exists *as* subject is, I think, to say that the subject is still to be equated with the real presence of change: the subject is the presence of an exception to the reign of opinion, and to the exclusive existence of speaking bodies.

Logics of Worlds' specific contribution to Badiou's theory of the subject is found in its account of a "formalism" of the subject. And yet the subject is still linked to a particular type of body, and I want to address that first. A body in this context is of course not always a human, individual body. A body need not be the same as the inhabitant of a world or situation. It is not the "some-one" discussed in *Ethics* either, and Badiou claims that it is "only exceptionally related to the form of an animal body" – meaning ours (LM 76). So, in a discussion of the music world of the early twentieth century, the body in Schoenberg's twelve-tone revolution is described as the musical works composed and performed (LM 90). One of my illustrations of Badiou's theory of the subject earlier used his claim that a series of works would be the subject in an artistic truth procedure. Is he claiming something different here? It sounds as if the works produced by Schoenberg and others would be bodies rather than subjects. What is the difference? Why is the subject still not the same as a body, and vice versa?

A body is defined as a subject's material support in a world (LM 475). In *Being and Event* it was a finite part of a truth procedure that played this role: a subject's body would have been the multiples that incarnate an intersection of truth and knowledge, for example. Since *Logics of Worlds* is about appearance, not ontology, a different account is required. So, in the example of new music in the early twentieth century, Badiou writes that the subject is "the becoming of a dodecaphonic or serial music. [...] It is the history of a new form, incorporated in works" (LM 91). The subject is now said to be what, in a body – a work, a movement, etc. – allows us to read that body's effects on its world (LM 54). Thus, the subject is going to be a certain kind of style of novelty, an appearance of the new: and this is what Badiou studies as the subject's formalism.

So now we have a theory in which the matter of the subject consists of bodies, which define the subject as the presence of the new; yet the form of the subject gives both the subject and the existence of the true and the new itself a particular style, of which there are three types – faithful, reactive, obscure. This means that a subject is no longer exclusively in the service of a truth but that it can also be involved in the denial or occultation of a truth (LM 58). It is because these forms are so closely linked to ethical notions in Badiou's work, as well as affects or passions, that I will discuss them in detail in the next chapter on ethics.

Finally, a split that is a recurrent presence in Badiou's theory of the subject is present again in *Logics*: this time between a body and what he calls a trace. Body names the worldly dimension of the subject, its involvement in the creation of a new present, and trace names what on the basis of the event determines the active orientation of the body. *Trace* in this text seems to be like the name of an event: "a trace is always, in mundane appearance, an existence of maximal intensity" (WL 51–2). The subject has one foot in the world and one foot out of it, akin to the way in which subjectivation was said to be partly of an evental site, and partly of a situation, in *Being and Event*. Now, however, the subject is described as "an indirect and creative relation between an event and a world" (LM 84). Later, Badiou writes that a subject is "a sequence that consists of continuities *and* discontinuities, openings and points" (LM 93). This is reminiscent of the position in *Theory of the Subject*, according to which the subject was a knot and a torsion: as a knot, it was the coming together of "continuity and discontinuity." In *Logics of Worlds*, then, it appears that Badiou is returning to some aspects of the dialectical notion of the subject that he promoted in *Theory of the Subject*.

Conclusion

My guiding thesis in this book has been that Badiou's work can be read as an attempt to develop a philosophical anti-humanism in order to provide a framework for a type of reinvigorated practical humanism. The centerpiece of this theory is an account of what he describes as a constituted, and not a constituting subject: a subject "constituted by a truth" (LM 186). The promotion of a theory of a constituted subject within a philosophy that is all about change and the emergence of the new makes for a dramatic tension in Badiou's work, and one may wonder whether the two parts can really go together.

A strong statement of his orientation occurs in *Logics of Worlds*, when he writes about where his theoretical anti-humanism is taking him. Because he avoids a dependence on references to "human lived experience" Badiou can claim, in a passage already cited, that "in fact, a truth is that by which 'we,' of the human species, are engaged in a trans-specific procedure, a procedure that opens us up to the possibility of being Immortals; in such a manner that a truth is certainly an experience of the inhuman" (LM 80). What I want to address in the conclusion to this chapter is how and whether Badiou really succeeds in avoiding a theoretical dependence on human lived experience.

In this philosophy that is supposed to avoid relying on the notion of a constituting subject for the existence of truths, worlds, events, and beings, we have also seen that many of the key concepts of the philosophical tradition on the subject are retained. For example, Badiou writes that the subject is "that which decides an undecidable from the standpoint of an indiscernible" (BE 407). In *Theory of the Subject*, Badiou even claimed that his account of the subject "should clarify a bit the mystery of decision" (TS 191). I have been claiming that the subject is not a thing of consciousness for Badiou. It is more to be identified with the presence of novelty and creation itself, rather than with an agent who does and creates. This means that the subject is more on the side of being than of things like consciousness and knowledge. Yet here we find Badiou using language according to which the subject is, precisely, deciding and forcing.

A similar problem exists for the notion of an intervention, discussed in the last chapter. Intervention is sometimes described as a kind of decision – maybe a judgment – made by one or more inhabitants of a situation about an event, in which a name for an event is chosen. And I might add that another key concept from the philosophical tradition that remains present in Badiou's theory of the subject is belief, not to mention the faith present in fidelity. "The subject believes that there is a truth, and this belief occurs in the form of a knowledge. I term this knowing belief *confidence*" (BE 397).

Is there any way to reconcile Badiou's claims about the subject being objectless, about the non-Cartesian orientation of his theory (is there anything more Cartesian than a subject who believes?) with these links to things like decision and belief? If the subject in an artistic truth procedure is supposed to be a series of artworks, does it make any sense at all to say that these works believe in a truth?

First, maybe this is not a real problem for Badiou's philosophy and is just a matter of careless language. It should be recalled that truth procedures and events happen only in historical situations. Such situations do presume the presence of conscious human beings, and I have explained that while the subject is not identical to consciousness – not even to many consciousnesses – the subject does depend on conscious individuals. There are four situations that would qualify as historical, as far as we know, and they are love, art, politics, and science. Each one of these names a practice that has for a long time been thought to be distinctly human. And so, even if the subject is not going to be the same as an individual conscious human being, or a collection of them, it is still going to have something to do with such creatures because of the limitation Badiou places on the types of situations in which subjects occur.

Certainly, individuals play some important role in the multiples that are subjects; that is, there is going to be some intersection, sometimes, of human beings and works in what Badiou calls a subject. So that is why it is still entirely relevant to talk about things such as belief and confidence, decisions and choices, even if attributing these things to the subject does confuse matters. It would seem that it is strictly speaking more correct to attribute such things to inhabitants, some-ones, or individuals.

This is why the notion of subjectivation is important. Badiou's subject is anti-humanist: materialist, non-conscious, a multiple, and so on. A subjectivation, however, is like the opening of a humanist

Badiou's Theories of the Subject

window on an otherwise inhuman world, for a subjectivation happens always and only to *inhabitants* of historical situations. That's us: and once there is a subjectivation, there can be a truth procedure. The subject, as a finite part of a truth procedure, is not something to which subjectivations happen, then, and it is not what makes choices and decisions about multiples. This is what inhabitants of situations and worlds do.

Yet in *Ethics*, Badiou writes:

> from which "decision", then, stems the process of a truth? From the decision to relate henceforth to the situation *from the perspective of its eventual supplement*. Let us call this a fidelity. To be faithful to an event is to move within the situation that this event has supplemented, by *thinking* (although all thought is a practice, a putting to the test) the situation "according to" the event. And this, of course – since the event was excluded by all the regular laws of the situation – compels the subject to *invent* a new way of being and acting in the situation. (E 42)

What is troubling is that a subject is again said here to be the one who invents and decides. It is not deciding whether an event occurs, but it is deciding to be faithful. Would it not have been more consistent for Badiou to say that an *inhabitant* decides? How can Badiou's subject – for example, as a series of artworks! – decide on anything?

Certainly, the subjectivation of inhabitants is required in order to bring about the presence of real change in a situation (as the subject proper). This allows us to conclude that without subjectivations there would be no truth for a situation: for it is through subjectivation that events have effects on the situation. If there is no subject, there is also no truth: but without a subjectivation there is no subject either. Passivity therefore turns out to be an important trait of Badiou's subject, despite references to interventions and decisions and forcings which are more appropriate for describing the relation between events and the inhabitants of situations. It is the inhabitants of worlds and situations who are active in their situations, carrying out a truth procedure (or not). A subject is part of what they make.

7
Ethics and Affects

In what way does Badiou account for how and whether an inhabitant of a situation is chosen or seized by an event? A question like this is troubling, because if Badiou says this is the case for only a select few, then this might be the grounds for a strange elitism, perhaps even more extreme than Nietzsche's. I will argue here that, with the developments in *Logics of Worlds*, the question "who is chosen by an event?" is not a significant question, since Badiou's position is that everyone is, although they may not be faithful to it.

Say that a situation is affected by an event. As members of a situation, the situation's inhabitants are also affected: all are, insofar as an event is for an entire situation. There is no inhabitant of a situation who is not affected by an event for that situation. Saying no one is immune to an event, that all are chosen by it or affected by it, amounts to a defusing of the concern about selection. Instead, another question is relevant: what do inhabitants do with it? This is what Badiou's ethics considers.

Incidentally, this position is what will allow Badiou to claim that contemporary religious fundamentalism is in fact a *reaction to* the death of God, and even testifies to that death: "what subsists is no longer religion, but its theater. For it is only in drama, as in *Hamlet*, that specters cast a semblance of efficacy. What this ultimately bloody drama represents to us is something we imagine religion could have been, provided the living God – about whom nobody has the faintest idea – were not dead" (B 13). And this view that everyone is affected by an event, in different ways, with different responses, is what allows him to claim in *Logics* too that any reaction presupposes that something revolutionary is going on (LM 71). In the terms of *Logics of Worlds*, reaction is one of the appearances of change, one of the ways in which the new appears; obscurantism is another, and so is fidelity. Thus, there are different ways in which inhabitants of a world are affected by an event, and this removes some of the troubling language of selection or election that Badiou's philosophy of the event sometimes uses.

Badiou develops an ethics that is at the intersection of the inhabitant of a world and an event. No individual chooses to be seized by an event, and no individual decides to begin a truth procedure. But when such things do happen, all sorts of choices and decisions follow, such as decisions to continue, to stop the process, to be actively opposed to it, to let it die off, and so on. These are all matters for ethics to consider.

Badiou also claims that it is through *affects* that a "human animal recognizes that it participates . . . in some subject of truth" (LM 502). This marks an important addition to his philosophy. I will discuss Badiou's theory of affects in detail in this chapter, but to begin illustrating what this theory of affects is about, consider the affect that he links to the truth procedure of love – happiness. Imagine happiness starts to happen in an individual's life. Badiou is claiming that this affect is a signal to the individual that he or she may be involved in some process – in this case, love – that is already occurring. The affect of happiness, in this case, is a signal to the "human animal" in question that he or she is "some subject of truth." I claimed in the conclusion to the last chapter that there is a good deal of passivity to Badiou's theory of the subject, even though the subject is the real presence of change in a situation. His view of affects is about the impact that procedures have on individuals, and they also therefore involve a good degree of passivity. This also indicates that there is much about Badiou's philosophy of events and truths that is not as intellectual or cognitive as it may seem. Again, a truth procedure is not a matter of knowing anything about an event or a situation; an individual may in fact be surprised that he or she is already involved in one, has already become absorbed by it, without seeming to have actively chosen for it.

It is when individuals become aware of what is happening to them, of the truth procedure that absorbs them, that ethical matters can be addressed. These points will also help to show more clearly how it is possible for Badiou's theoretical anti-humanist philosophical system to be linked to a practical humanism.

On affects and ethics in *Theory of the Subject*: anxiety, courage, superego, justice

Badiou argues that the two components of the subject he addresses in *Theory of the Subject* – subjectivation and the subject-process – have a limited number of possible styles, only a few different ways in which they can be. These are named after affects and ethical concepts. To subjectivation belong the possible styles of anxiety and courage, and to the subject-process belong the possibilities of an attachment to a superegoic law and the pursuit of justice.

Badiou claims, of course, that such styles do not refer to subjective experiences but to *processes* whose combination "defines the region of practical materiality called the subject-effect" (TS 171). To say that anxiety, for example, is not a subjective experience is to say that a subject does not pre-exist this kind of anxiety. If a subject is, it may have anxiety as its style. Badiou calls affects, therefore, the "mode of consistency of the subject-effect" (TS 172). Superego, anxiety, justice, and courage are different ways in which the components of a subject (subjectivation and subject-process) exist and are knotted together. He writes that:

> the four concepts . . . are neither virtues nor capacities. Better: they are not experiences. [. . .] Neither anxiety nor the superego, neither courage nor justice, are states of consciousness. They are categories of the subject-effect. What they reveal to us is a specific material region, ruling every destruction of what supports it. (TS 307)

Subjectivation, I argued in the previous chapter, can be thought of in terms of passivity; the subject-process in *Theory of the Subject* (a precursor to the truth procedure of *Being and Event* and *Logics of Worlds*), however, is active. In the former, there is something like a "decision in me" – it is similar to what Badiou later describes as being seized by an event. In a subject-process, however, things such as choice, deliberation, doubt, and fidelity are to be found. All of the affects and virtues (and vices) discussed in *Theory of the Subject*, and later, presuppose being affected by an event; they presuppose being subjectivated, which is itself something not decided upon and not chosen.

If we keep this in mind, we can see why Badiou claims that anxiety and courage are two styles of subjectivation, and not of the subject-process. Subjectivation was Badiou's way of thinking about the immediacy of an insurrection, for example, or the moment at which some kind of change first emerges. In *Theory of the Subject*, the subject is primarily portrayed as political and collective, so these affects – anxiety and courage – are used there to describe the different styles of a movement's beginning or foundation. Anxiety is a way to describe a "form of interruption" of a social order in which "the real *kills* the symbolic, rather than splitting it" (TS 307). Mass riots, for example, present us with an undisciplined explosion of affect whose demands might not be clear, and not even made ... but it is clear that something is happening (TS 299). Anxiety "brings about the destruction of sense as chaos," Badiou writes, but it leaves something of the social order basically intact, such that the social order continues to beckon at a distance, as a promise of salvation (TS 307). Badiou thinks of this kind of anxiety then as destruction; but it is actually a "destruction of destruction" in "mute and suicidal riots" that are destined to have no longevity, and to be simply temporary outbursts (TS 308). It seems as if anxiety, as Badiou describes it, entails the fading away of a possibility for change as soon as it emerges.

The other style in which a subjectivation might emerge is characterized by courage. This is another way of describing a moment at which a kind of excess appears within a stable social order, but in contrast to riots and other moments of social unrest that are fraught with anxiety, an insurrection characterized by courage does succeed in bringing about a "division" or "interruption" of the old social law (TS 310). The problem with a subjectivation tinged with anxiety, obviously, is that it is purely destructive, and so it fades away as soon as it destroys, and for that very reason, does not really destroy its opponent – an old social order. A subjectivation characterized by courage, however, does succeed in "putting law to the test, instead of calling for its restoration" (TS 311). Thus:

> courage is non-submission to the symbolic order, under the dissolving injunction of the real. From the fact that the real is in excess – courage, in this sense, is identical to anxiety – it inverts values, and is the force of rupture in esplace. Courage positively brings about disorder in the symbolic, breakdowns in communication, while anxiety calls for their death. (TS 177)

It is important to dwell on what is almost an aside in this passage: courage and anxiety are "identical" insofar as in each "the real is in excess" over "placing" (*esplace*). This is because both are types of subjectivation. The purely destructive impulse of anxiety, seeking a total destruction of the possibility of communication, and the social order itself, is replaced by a courageous subjectivation with the risk of a breakdown in communication, a risk that it is necessary to take to enable a new order to emerge.

Justice and the superego are the two styles in which a subject-process occurs. The superegoic style is like the structural or symbolic correlate to anxious destruction. That is, if, in a subjectivation, the force of the real is in excess over the symbolic, in the subject-process we have some kind of symbolic repair work going on. Only, in its superegoic style, a subject-process is engaged in a kind of terror in the name of the law: it is as ferocious in the preservation and enforcement of the law as anxiety was in its pure will to destruction. Badiou cites, in this context, Hegel's famous description of the French Terror, in which death is administered mechanically and everyone is suspect.

Justice – the other possible style of a subject-process – "relativizes law, while the superego absolutizes it" (TS 311). Justice corrodes the law, and says "always more of the real, less of the law" (TS 311). Justice looks like a simple contrast to the superego's style, then, but there is another aspect to justice in which the similarity between the two can be found. "Justice," Badiou writes, "names the possibility [...] that what is non-law can have value as law" (TS 176). In this respect, justice is not opposed to law *tout court*: it brings about a different law. Recall that it is, like the superegoic style, a way in which a subject-process occurs, and that it must therefore involve the reconstruction of a social order. "The superego is the restorative face of recomposition (which does not mean repetitive. Stalin is not the Tsar, Robespierre is not Louis XI). Justice is the face of its establishment. But every instauration restores" (TS 312).

Perhaps it is already clear that there is a natural coupling to these affects. Badiou holds that every subject as such is a knotting together of a subjectivation (which will take shape either in terms of anxiety or courage) and a subject-process (as superego or justice). There are two predominant ways in which a subject can take place in terms of these affects. One is in a binding together of anxiety and the superego (Badiou designates this style with the Greek letter ψ) and one that links courage and justice (designated by the Greek letter α). Other possibilities would be linking anxiety to justice and courage to the superego. Badiou allows for them both, calling the former skepticism and the latter dogmatism (TS 319).

Ethics and Affects 133

The ethic he wishes to promote in *Theory of the Subject* involves encouraging the subject's α-series as much as possible, finding ways to promote a subjectivation styled by courage and a subject-process styled by justice. To flesh this out, he argues that we should be Aeschylean, not Sophoclean (TS 178). Aeschylus and Sophocles, both ancient Greek tragedians, present two very different subjective orientations. The "tragic Sophoclean subject" is presented to us in a play such as *Antigone*, in which the contrast between Antigone and Creon actually forms a couple, each one calling for the other despite their antagonism (TS 179). Badiou uses this play to illustrate the subject's ψ-series, which couples anxiety with the superego. The figure of anxiety in subjectivation is Antigone herself. Seen as an ethical heroine by some – arguably by Lacan in his seventh seminar – Badiou sees Antigone instead as a negative model precisely because her apparently strong resistance to Creon's ban on the burial of her brother is, on Badiou's reading, simply a destruction that secretly yearns for the restoration of what it destroys. We have on the one hand, in Antigone, the "principle of the infinity of the real, unable to be placed in the regulated finitude of the site," while Creon, on the other hand, is a figure for the superegoic law, as a representative of the "deregulated – destroyed – law, by its own native essence come back in excess over the places that it prescribes" (TS 179). In Hölderlin's reading of the play, to which Badiou acknowledges his debt, the German poet claimed that the only possible outcome of such a contradiction is death: no new law or new order can emerge under the conditions of such a strong contradiction (TS 180).

In Aeschylus, by contrast, Badiou sees instead an embrace of the new, and a version of the α-series subject he wishes to encourage. Badiou discusses *The Eumenides*, and how that play contains a lesson about "the recomposition of a different order" (TS 183). In that play, the kind of impasse found portrayed in Sophocles' work (even though Aeschylus preceded Sophocles) is cut through: the play shows how "against the limitlessness of the old rule, it is a matter of engendering the new, and of deciding the conflict" (TS 182). At the end of the play, the goddess Athena descends from the sky and imposes a new order of law on the Athenians: "the new wins out over the old" (TS 181).

On the basis of his reading of Aeschylus – as brief as it is – Badiou starts to work on two different notions of a "reversal" or "turn around" (*retournement*). Against the idea of a "natal reversal, which emerges from anxiety and pretends to cure with a restorative terror" – very much what is found in his notion of a ψ subject-effect, and figured in the play *Antigone* – there is also a sense of reversal found in the notion of exile, where "it is from the denial-by-splitting of the former law that a clarification proceeds, in the guise of the new, of the torsion inflicted on the real. The return of exile revokes the original as barely-real, and restores the real in justice. In this way, it is a total return: let's make a blank slate of the past" (TS 184).

But how exactly is such an ethic supposed to work? Badiou's preference for the α style over the ψ style is clear. But what techniques can be used to promote one inflection of the subject over another?

As a matter of fact, Badiou claims that every subject includes both α and ψ tendencies. Anxiety and courage, for example, are on a continuum: both are styles that a subjectivation can take on, and we should think of a subjectivation as something that is more or less anxious, more or less courageous. The same goes for the subject-process side of the subject: justice and the superego are two styles this can take on. So one is not dealing with two entirely pure things when considering the ψ- and α- series. Any subject can veer off in the direction of one or the other.

What makes a subject become more or less one way or the other is some kind of use of language, and to each pole Badiou assigns a particular type of discourse that promotes that particular pole. He claims, for example, that there is a discourse of elegy that enforces the justice-pole of a subject-process, which claims that what is not placed in a world does nevertheless have a place that can be evaluated: a kind of utopian promise. There is also a discourse of resignation, linked to the superego, which claims that one must do all one can to hold on to the place one has, in a world that is sharply devalued, but preserved as the only thing there is. There is a discourse of discordance, linked to anxiety, that "upholds the *horlieu* of an intrinsically devalued site [*lieu*]" (think of Antigone's insistence on her family bond, on her duty to violate the law and give her brother a proper burial), and finally a Promethean one positing that a "place is to come in a world able to be re-evaluated": this is tied to courage (TS 336). I want to focus for a moment on what Badiou has to say about the Promethean and elegiac discourses, because those are most important to him. And, of course, *Prometheus Unbound* was written by Aeschylus, whom Badiou, we have seen, wishes to champion over Sophocles.

Confidence versus belief

Badiou wishes to skew the subject in the direction of its α-series as much as possible, which would mean cultivating the subject in such a manner that its subjectivation is characterized by courage, and its subject-process by justice. What can be done to ensure that a subject tends toward these, rather than toward anxiety and the superego? A discussion of the differences, ethically, between confidence and belief tries to explain this, via a reading of the political and intellectual situation in France after May 1968. Badiou claims that "the fundamental concept of a Marxist ethic is confidence," and his discussion of the aftermath of May tries to show how many Marxist movements died off largely because there was too much belief, and not enough confidence (TS 327). This endorsement of confidence will be tied to the kind of Promethean ethic he wishes to develop.

There are scattered discussions of the *nouveaux philosophes* in the closing chapters of *Theory of the Subject*, and Badiou's reading of them and their notorious reaction against their former militancy suggests that, according to him, while these figures believed in the movements associated with May, they never had confidence in them, and this was their fatal flaw – his point being that belief is ultimately too shaky a foundation for a subject (TS 341–2). Far better is confidence: "I have confidence in the people and in the working class to the extent that I do not believe in them. Insofar as I believe in them, which always induces the *expectation* of a popular movement, my confidence vacillates" (TS 338). Elegy, as an ethic, aims to support belief, while a Promethean ethic aims to inspire confidence.

To illustrate the difference between these two ethics Badiou considers a famous passage from Marx: "it is not the consciousness of men that determines their being; it is, inversely, their social being that determines their consciousness" (TS 339). According to Badiou, this slogan is elegiac, and is trying to encourage belief. Adopting this point of view, one could rest assured that "communist consciousness will necessarily emerge" when the contradictions in capitalism are aggravated (TS 339). As the "social being" of individuals develops, they will naturally, the slogan encourages us to believe, acquire a consciousness that rejects bourgeois ideology. Marxism, in this manner, *believes* in the inevitability of its success.

To illustrate his Promethean ethic, which is supposed to encourage confidence rather than belief, Badiou presents a famous quote from Mao Tse-tung, who wrote that "Marxism contained many principles, but they can all be boiled down in the final analysis to one phrase: it is right to revolt against the reactionaries" (TS 339). Such a slogan does not require one to believe in the inevitability of a movement's success, Badiou claims. It instead allows one to be confident in the rightness of one's action without being able to claim, or needing to claim, any certainty about what one is doing.

In defense of an ethic of confidence – a Promethean ethic – Badiou proposes another memorable slogan, although he does not explain its sense fully. The slogan is "love what you will never believe twice" (TS 346). I gave a preliminary reading of this slogan in the introduction to this book. Given the context within which it appears, the slogan must have something to do with bolstering the virtue of confidence. Perhaps this is not so hard to see: what it is saying is that where one cannot really believe that one believes, where one cannot fully justify oneself, one must still have confidence on that point. Where one cannot really bring oneself to fully believe (in a mass movement's success, for example), one simply has to be confident. If we keep in mind Badiou's claim that as a compound structure no subject is free from anxiety and superegoic tendencies, belief is also always present in a subject. But it is not belief that is most important, and it should not be primary to a subject's style: as Badiou's discussion of the aftermath of May 1968 shows, making belief central invites reactions against what one formerly believed. The point seems to be that mere belief cannot survive disappointment very well: confidence, perhaps, can, and is inherently more flexible than belief, which cedes too easily to what Badiou describes as dogmatism or nihilism at the first signs of trouble or defeat.

Ethics on the basis of *Being and Event*

What the discussion of ethics in *Theory of the Subject* has already shown is a trait that will remain a constant part of Badiou's philosophy: ethics does not consist of making subjects, or of making events happen (impossible, anyway, as well as unnecessary), but is concerned, rather, with continuing with their disruptive effects, sticking with a subjectivation that has already taken place or persisting in a subject-process that seems to be going nowhere.

Both anxiety and courage, because they are styles of subjectivation, are situated at the point where force is in excess of place (in the terminology of *Theory of the Subject*), and it is easy to see how this idea could be rephrased in the terms of Badiou's later philosophy. Anxiety and courage, justice and the superego, would not describe ways that an event itself is experienced, but ways that an event's effects on its situation are experienced. But the reference to experience here is superfluous. As Badiou would have it, where there is anxiety in a situation is where an event is having a particular type of influence on the situation. The same goes for courage and the rest. These particular effects may or may not exist, depending on how individuals are inhabiting those effects: just as a subject may not come to be at all, if there is no intervention on behalf of the event.

A discussion of ethical matters is not central to *Being and Event*, which is perhaps a weakness of the text but a structural necessity of it as well, given its limitation to a study of the ontological conditions of situations, and the status of truths and procedures. Confidence and faith are discussed there, but the status of an inhabitant of a historical situation is not covered in much detail; the discussion of inhabitants of situations is primarily ontological, not ethical. Since *Logics of Worlds* is concerned with the appearances of multiples, and not just their ontological structure, inhabitants receive more attention there too, and for that reason more is said about the different forms a subject can take on in that volume.

Between the two texts Badiou did take up the idea of an ethics, most notably in *Ethics: An Essay on the Understanding of Evil* (1993) but also in *Saint Paul: The Foundation of the Universal* (1997). The ethic Badiou develops in these years encourages persistence in the pursuit of a fidelity procedure. Badiou calls his ethic an ethic of truths now (it is no longer called a Marxist ethic, as it was in *Theory of the Subject*) and writes that its maxim is "keep going" (E 52). The point is that any inhabitant of a situation seized by an event is going to be tempted to give up and pursue more pleasurable and safer activities, ones whose place in a situation is well established, socially recognized, and so on. An ethic of truths, by contrast, would encourage us to "continue to be this 'some-one', a human animal among others, which nevertheless finds itself *seized* and *displaced* by the evental process of a truth" (E 91). This means that ethics needs to make us comfortable with the fact that we may not be pursuing our best interests sometimes, and that the nature of our activities may be divisive. Badiou writes of a disinterested-interest as a basic feature of life with a truth procedure: this does not necessarily entail a renunciation of our everyday interests, however (E 55).

Ethical ideology – the polar opposite of the ethic of truths Badiou is pursuing – is based on the avoidance of events and truths, and its maxim would be "love only that which you have always believed" (E 52). This is roughly the inverse of the slogan we came across in *Theory of the Subject*, and Badiou alludes to that fact here. That ethic allowed for the sense of astonishment and surprise that an individual will experience at the truth that is occurring. To "love what you will never believe twice," as Badiou put it in *Theory of the Subject*, suggests that one should embrace something one did not experience choosing or deciding on. Retooling Lacan's idea that one should not give up on one's desire, Badiou writes "'do not give up on that part of yourself that you do not know'" (E 47). For:

> the temptation to give up, to withdraw from the subjective composition, to break a loving relationship because of the pull of an obscene desire, to betray a political sequence because of the repose promised by the "service of goods", to replace determined scientific investigation with the pursuit of recognition and awards, or to regress back to academicism under cover of a propaganda that denounces the avant garde as *passé* . . . all of this is exactly what individuals will be constantly pulled to do given the strength of ethical ideology, which tells them to stick with what they know and have always believed. (E 55–6)

The new is always suspect, risky, and perhaps worse than the familiar. But if a life with truth is a distinctly human possibility, it stands to reason that an ethic that is against truth – such is the current and dominant ethical ideology, according to Badiou – is actually dehumanizing. This is an odd claim to make about ethical ideology, especially since that ideology can be portrayed as one that gives every human life a nearly sacred status. Yet Badiou claims that:

> ethics [he means ethical ideology here] is nihilist because its underlying conviction is that the only thing that can really happen to someone is death. And it is certainly true *that in so far* as we deny truths, we thereby challenge the immortal disjunction that they effect in any given situation. Between Man as the possible basis for the uncertainty of truths, or Man as being-for-death (or being-for-happiness, it is the same thing), you have to choose. It is the same

choice that divides philosophy from "ethics", or the courage of truths from nihilism. (E 35)

Ethical ideology is described in a variety of ways in the book – as an ethic of the "service of goods," of communication, of difference, of "the Other," of human rights – but its basic feature is always an insistence on human beings as fragile, mortal creatures whose good consists in the avoidance of pain and death. Ethical ideology "thus defines man *as a victim*," whereas an ethic of truths defines humanity as:

> an animal whose resistance, unlike that of a horse, lies not in his fragile body but in his stubborn determination to remain what he is – that is to say, precisely something other than a victim, other than a being-for-death, and thus: *something other than a mortal being.*
>
> An immortal: this is what the worst situations that can be inflicted upon Man show him to be. (E 10–12)

This reference to being immortal will be explored more in the conclusion to this book – suffice it for now to say that this does not mean Badiou has found religion. The use of the term immortal here is due to what Badiou claims is a truth's eternal status.

On evil: Badiou's practical humanism against ethics

What is evil, according to ethical ideology, is a violation of the right to life, and such violations are usually performed in the name of the very things that allow us to become "immortals" – truths. In a passage I already cited in my introduction, Badiou wrote that efforts to do things in the name of some idea of the Good have been demonized and stigmatized as the stuff of totalitarian nightmares and terrors (E 13). But behind calls to respect others, respect life, and respect difference, Badiou finds a basically de-humanizing tendency. Although such respect sounds noble and uplifting – surely our fundamental right is to pursue happiness and develop our individuality in the manner we see fit – Badiou finds that "every definition of Man based on happiness is nihilist" (E 36). Significant here is Badiou's claim that this seemingly very humanistic ethics is actually a *practical anti-humanism*. Badiou is making the case in *Ethics* that his own theoretical anti-humanism can ensure, on the contrary, a practical humanism, where that humanism might just mean something minimal: permitting humans to live the kinds of lives that make them human, rather than the lives of mere living creatures (animals). Animals we remain, of course: but we also can live as immortals insofar as we are involved in truths.

Ethics begins as a sharp polemic against ethical ideology and its understanding of evil; but it ends rather surprisingly with a redefinition of both ethics and evil, where it had seemed that Badiou wanted to abandon those terms altogether. He concludes that ethics can be retained, as can a reference to evil in philosophy, but each will have to be understood differently. Evil, Badiou argues, is not some kind of radical other to the good, or its polar opposite. Instead, it derives from the very possibility of a good itself, and so also from the fact that "there are truths" (E 61; E 91). An ethic of truths would point this out. Just as the subject consisted of different strands and styles in *Theory of the Subject*, and ethics in that text consisted of somehow encouraging the subject to lean in the right direction, here Badiou is saying yet again that certain tendencies are intrinsic possibilities of a truth procedure. Not bastardizations of one, not things entirely distinct from one, but rather ways in which truth procedures will be constitutively inclined to veer off.

Badiou's ethic of truths can be framed in terms of maintaining certain relationships to key terms from *Being and Event*; what he calls evil is an inverse of each of the preferred relations. There are three of them. One concerns fidelity itself which, in the ethic of truths, is not a fidelity to the event proper but fidelity to having been seized by an event, to the fact that it has done something to you and your situation. It is, thus, something like a fidelity to fidelity. The inverse of this is betrayal. A betrayal is a rupture with the break that the truth procedure itself creates in the situation, leading an individual back to reaffirm the situation as it is (E 80). Such a break may occur because "opinion tells me (and therefore I tell myself, for I am never outside opinions) that my fidelity may well be terror exerted against myself" (E 79). Put this way, the urge to betray is well-grounded, since an individual will always be nagged by doubts about the legitimacy of a truth procedure. Badiou's call for confidence in *Theory of the Subject* was coming from the same concern about reaction, a concern that I have been arguing is a hallmark of Badiou's work.

Another aspect of the ethics of truths involves the status of the event itself: the event's relation to the situation needs to be treated correctly. Mistreatment of this is called by Badiou a simulacrum of an event, and also a terror. Some commentators have taken this to mean that there are possible false events, or that we may be mistaken in thinking something is an event. This is not how Badiou's position should be understood. The point, rather, is to consider how an event's effects on a situation are handled – since that is all we ever have to deal with anyway. Misreading Badiou on this point could support an interpretation of him as a messianic thinker, which he is not. Events are not things *to come*; and they are not themselves true or false, correct or incorrect. There are neither true nor false events, and there is no question of judging whether something is an event or not: judging, truth, and falsehood will occur at the level of the naming of an event, and what makes for a simulacrum is always a certain type of name for an event.

A simulacrum names an event in such a manner that the name evokes the fullness of a situation (E 73). On the basis of such a name, it is "not the void of the earlier situation" that is brought into being in this case but its fullness, by the work of a particular community or group (E 73). So it is not that Nazism (the example Badiou considers in this context) constitutes, or is based somehow on, a false event. Again, there are no true or false events: there are events, and different ways of naming them, of bringing them to bear on their situations. Nazism is based on a particular way of naming what was an event for the political situation at the time, just as Marxism was. Nazism, Badiou argues, is a movement based on a reactive name for the same event as Marxism, and as such it is a phenomenon that arose because of the genuine political events in modern European history – the French Revolution, and the Bolshevik Revolution, from both of which it borrowed the terms "socialist" and "revolution" – but to which it added, fatefully, "national," which negated the otherwise generic and universal character of the egalitarian political procedures (E 72). In this last name – national – its intent and scope were made clear: whatever political event there was at work in the European political situation at the time was corralled into a *simulacrum of truth* attempting to bring a particular collection of multiples in the political situation – the German people – to dominance. A simulacrum of truth – call it a pseudo-truth procedure – will take on the character of a terror because the void of the situation, evoked by the event it wishes to name otherwise, keeps returning. For Nazism, of course, the name "Jew" designated this void, the multiple that needed to be eliminated for the fullness of the national and political situation to be established. (In his discussion, Badiou does describe Nazism in terms of fidelity, even if it is a fidelity to a simulacrum, a pseudo-truth procedure. It is worth noting here that in *Logics of Worlds* this type of reaction will no longer be described as a type of fidelity, but will be assigned its own subject-form, distinct from the form that characterizes the subject of fidelity.)

The third component of an ethic of truths involves the relation of the truth procedure to the situation as a whole, and, again, this actually is more about names for events than it is about events proper (for example, whether there is an event or not). Badiou argues that there are limits to how much of an effect the procedure has on the whole, and transgressing these limits leads to what he calls disaster. A simulacrum is an ethical lapse that emerges from a misunderstanding of the relation of the event to the situation too. It takes the event to be filling in the situation, to be the promise of a restoration of its plenitude. A betrayal is something that happens to fidelity itself, as a break from the break that the event is for the situation. There is one more thing to consider, and that is the relation of the truth procedure to the situation itself, which may be twisted into an evil if what Badiou calls the unnamable of a situation is not respected (E 80). This occurs when a truth procedure takes itself to be able to reorder every multiple in a situation, and to completely redo every opinion in a situation: as if the universality intrinsic to a truth procedure starts to run wild and misapply itself. There is what Badiou calls a "subject-language" used by a truth procedure, and we have seen in chapter 5 how this differs from the language of the situation (the encyclopedia). A truth procedure does manage to change "the established codes of communication" in a situation (E 83). But in the type of evil being considered here, the subject-language takes itself to have "the ability to name and evaluate all the elements of the objective situation from the perspective of the truth-process. Rigid and dogmatic (or 'blinded'), the subject-language would claim the power, based on its own axioms, to name the whole of the real, and thus to change the world" (E 83). Badiou calls this not terror, as he well could have, but disaster.

Faithful, reactive, and obscure subjects in *Logics of Worlds*

Consistent with *Theory of the Subject*, there is one subject in *Being and Event*, and also for *Ethics*: that is, there is one definition of a subject, as a finite part of a generic procedure, situated between the truth that is coming into being and a knowledge that will be. In *Theory of the Subject* the subject was, however, compound, and was described as a knot consisting of different possible styles, a knot that could be made in different ways. Yet, as a subject, all of these ways or styles contained certain definitive features that were the same regardless of the way the knot appeared. In *Logics of Worlds*, the most significant shift is that the basic theory of the subject is not as unified as it is in the earlier texts.

I discussed the structure of the subject in *Logics of Worlds* in chapter 6, but did not explore there the different forms that Badiou posits for the subject. Not only is the subject in *Logics of Worlds* said to have three forms – faithful, reactive, and obscure. On top of that, the subject has what he calls four possible destinations. By this, Badiou refers to the acts engaged in by a subject-form (LM 58). Despite the increased variety of forms for the subject posited by Badiou, it is still the case that one of them seems to be somehow basic, and that is the faithful subject. His procedure for discussing the other forms consists of taking the traits of a faithful subject, with its development of a new present for a world, and looking at possible modifications to that structure. But this does mean that there is no longer only one form for the subject: there are a variety of forms now where there had been only one, even if one of the forms still remains fundamental – that of the faithful subject.

In the introduction, I used Badiou's reference to the Spartacan slave revolt to give an initial portrait of the faithful subject. The key feature of such a subject, as I presented it there, was its production of a new present. But there are other factors as well that play a role in the structure of the different forms of the subject in this text. The trace of an event is another key element of any subject's form. Of course, it is not the case that an event itself is going to make up a part of the subject. It is always, rather, the trace of an event that makes up a part of the subject's form (LM 57). This is because Badiou allows, now, for a gradation in the changes a world undergoes. An event may have no real consequences on a world, as we saw in chapter 4; its effects may be weak, for example. Another component of the subject's form is the notion of a body. I introduced this idea in chapter 6: a body is the bearer of a subject-form (LM 606). I likened this to his idea of a series of works being the subject in an artistic truth procedure: the subject is presented in and through these bodies.

What defines a subject's form is the way in which these three components – a present, the trace of an event, and a body – are related. The present is always going to be treated here as a product: but a present of different types is constructed by different subject-forms. For example, the faithful subject produces what might be called an expansive, supplementary, and new present – what Badiou calls an "evental present" (LM 60). In the case of the Spartacan slave revolts, "the slaves *'en corps'* (as an army) move about in a new present. Because they are no longer slaves. And thus, they show (to other slaves) that it is possible, for a slave, to no longer be one, and to no longer be one *in the present*" (LM 59). A reactive subject, by contrast, produces an extinguished present, or a confused present; yet this is still a novelty, albeit of a reactionary sort (LM 62). That this is still a novelty is an important point: as is the case for the faithful subject, the present produced by this subject is an amended, changed present, different from the pre-evental present and the emergence of the faithful subject-form. In the world being changed by Spartacus, reactionary slaves emerged who benefited from their masters for their inaction, and they could legitimately see the improvements in their situation as the dawn of a new era (LM 64).

Finally, an obscure subject-form creates an occulted present, which is not so much the production of a present as it is the repression of one, the sweeping of a present under the rug. There is something of a return to a past here, but, again, there is novelty in such a return too. Considering Islamic fundamentalism from this perspective, Badiou claims that "it must be seen as an 'absolutely contemporary' phenomenon engaged in occulting the emancipatory gains of the 'post-socialist present' with its calls for a return to a 'full Tradition'" (LM 67–8).

The present involved in the faithful and reactive subject-forms is actually a new present, treated in different ways. The obscure subject-form, however, does not seem to produce a new present at all: its main work is the repression of a new present. It is worth reiterating that this obscure form of the subject does, however, presuppose the existence of a new present, and would not be what it is without it.

So much for the status of the present in each of the subject-forms. What role do bodies and traces of the event play in them? In a faithful subject, the body that bears the subject is described as barred. Bodies have, intrinsically, a split status in this theory because they are partly of the world before the event, and partly of the new world being created – much like the evental site was in *Being and Event*. Thus, "a body is never entirely in the present (*au*

Ethics and Affects

present)" (LM 61). This is because what makes a body a body is the fact that it is an element of a world infected by a trace of the event. Thus, Badiou considers a body in this sense to be subordinated to the trace of the event, which is the cause of the body's split or barred nature. Badiou refers to the non-unified nature of Spartacus's army of slaves to illustrate this (LM 61). As a formula, the faithful subject therefore looks like this:

$$\frac{\varepsilon}{\not{c}} \Rightarrow \pi$$

In this case, ε stands for the trace of the event, the c for the split body, and π for the new present. It is worth remembering that the subject is not any particular element in this formula, but is the entirety of the group. The whole formula is supposed to express the subject. Thus, this theory of the subject is consistent with what Badiou has said elsewhere. For example, it would be inaccurate to say that a subject forms a present. The subject is not on the left-hand side of the formula producing the right-hand side. The subject is the whole thing: trace of the event, split body, and the new present produced by the activity of both.

Similar formulas are given in *Logics of Worlds* for the other forms of the subject, but they are somewhat more complex. This is because each of them is expressed as a modification of the faithful subject-form, and as such each assumes something about that form. The reactive subject even contains the form of the faithful subject in full within it, only in a subordinated manner.

The reactive subject's primary aspect is dominated by something like a negation of the evental trace. Badiou does not wish to say that such a subject involves the negation of a new present, since this form also does create its own new present – albeit a bit of a pseudo-novelty, as mentioned above. (This is reminiscent of some of his points about Nazism in *Ethics* as a pseudo-truth procedure.) His familiar nemeses, the *nouveaux philosophes*, of course enter into his thinking about this form of the subject too (LM 63). The subjective form that brings about what Badiou describes as a cancelled out new present entails, as its chief constituting activity, a negation of the traces of an event. This would make sense: just imagine what your average Roman slaveholder would have thought about Spartacus. Or what a skeptical family might say about a love that unsettles one of its member's lives: "It's nothing. Get over it." In addition to this negation of the event's traces in the world, the reactive subject-form includes within it a repression of the faithful subject-form in its entirety. Thus, Badiou writes the subject-form this way:

$$\frac{\neg \varepsilon}{\frac{\varepsilon}{\not{x}} \Rightarrow \pi} \Rightarrow \bar{\pi}$$

Noteworthy here is the status of the split or barred body of the faithful subject structure. It is under the bar twice, which is Badiou's way of figuring the manner in which a reaction tries to keep its hands clean of the novelty being generated in the world, by holding the split body of the truth procedure at bay. Plus, by writing the faithful subject-form under a bar this way, Badiou wants to say that the faithful subject acts as something like the reactive subject's unconscious (LM 65).

In fact, the appearance of these formulae owes quite a bit to the way that Jacques Lacan wrote out the structure of four different discourses, involving things such as knowledge, truth, the subject, signifiers, and libidinal objects. To put something under the bar in Lacan's formulas was to give it the status of a kind of unconscious motor-force for the discourse. In Badiou's theory, the faithful subject structure had the split body as its unconscious, as its guiding force. The reactive subject takes on its shape through a constant reaction against the faithful subject-form itself. Thus, on Badiou's reading, a reactionary in a sense knows the faithful subject, or perhaps was once involved in a faithful subject structure, but turned against it: like the "new philosophers" of the 1970s.

Finally, the obscure subject also involves a relation to evental traces and bodies in the mode of negation. Yet, as I have already mentioned, the obscure subject does not produce a new present, unlike the faithful and reactive subjects; rather, it involves something neither of those two contain, which is called a full body (represented by a capital C in the formula below). This seems to be a feature unique to the obscure subject. It involves "the invocation of a transcendent Body, full and pure, an ahistorical body, or anti-evental body (City, God, Race . . .)" (LM 68). A full body is called for, or hoped for, by an obscure subject in order to negate the traces of an event in the world, and thereby the negation of the split body that the faithful subject process presents. And all of this occurs to bring about a strict repression of the new present that is now in process. Thus, the obscure subject is written this way:

$$\frac{C \Rightarrow (\neg \varepsilon \Rightarrow \neg \not{c})}{\pi}$$

Rather than producing a new present (π), this formula shows that the obscure subject has the new present itself as its active unconscious – what is truly motivating its machinations.

Subjective destinations

To sum up, the subject in *Logics of Worlds* either produces, denies, or occults a (new) present (LM 71). As we have seen, each is a way of describing the different forms of the subject. Yet subjects are not only forms: they will have some matter too, and Badiou studies this in a section devoted to what he calls the four subjective destinations (LM 70). These will provide the basis for an even more concrete analysis of subjects, for a consideration of how they take place in particular worlds and in their particular involvements with different types of truth procedures. Thus, if we go back to the four truth procedures – art, science, love, and politics – we can see how the different subject-forms are manifested in each.

Any truth procedure consists of a variety of different parts: an ontological foundation, an eventual trace, a body, a "local" present, an affect, and a "global" present. I have covered most of these already, and want to focus on the references to affects and the different presents here. What is the difference between a local and global present? In his explanation of the political truth procedure in this context, Badiou writes that a political truth procedure will always articulate a new egalitarian maxim, one that addresses its particular historical and social context; but, at the same time, this new maxim forms part of a larger, longer series. Egalitarian movements in the twentieth century, for example, can be linked back to the ancient Spartacan revolts and find inspiration in them. They could even see themselves as the continuation of what failed there. In this manner, the truth procedure that began with Marx in the nineteenth century revives the egalitarianism of the Spartacan revolt, but under a new slogan or maxim – "Workers of the World Unite!" (LM 79). A move like this in a truth procedure is called by Badiou a resurrection: the new present being built by Spartacus and his slave army was successfully denied and occulted at the time; but the creation of that present was resumed in the nineteenth century, and presumably at numerous other times. In this manner, what a truth procedure is doing is eternal; it provides a kind of stuff that can always be made relevant again to future situations and worlds.

Every type of truth procedure will have a similar possible resurrection associated with it. So, in this respect, every truth procedure involves a specific, local present, as well as what Badiou calls a larger, global present, having to do with eternals about love, politics, art, and science. In politics, Badiou calls this global series a sequence, but in art, love, and science it is called a configuration, an enchantment, and a theory, respectively (LM 86). And locally, for each particular world in which they appear, these truth procedures will bring about a "new egalitarian maxim" (politics), a "new perceptive intensity" (arts), a "new existential intensity" (love), and "new insights" (science) (LM 86). So we see how novelty has two sides for Badiou, both historical (focused on the "local" concerns of its world) and ahistorical (linking up to previous and other novelties).

Below, I will briefly address the different procedures, leaving out politics, to which the next chapter is devoted.

Art

An event in an art world is a break in the order that regulates what Badiou describes as something like a natural tension between sensation itself and "the calm of form" (LM 81–2). Every art world can be said to impose a preferred form for how what is available to the senses is to be represented. Badiou seems to have in mind here the conventions that dictate what is acceptable practice in any artistic world. By upsetting this organization, an event's traces are where one will find an unformed multiple being presented, being rendered into a (new) form. The cubist innovations in 1912–13 are given by Badiou as a local example of such a process, specific to the art world of the time; yet it fits in with a larger, global process in art that traces back to the Baroque (LM 82).

With this as the basis for a faithful subject in an artistic procedure, Badiou can explain how the obscure and reactionary forms of an art subject also would appear. A reaction would be found in academicism – a defense of the old and familiar against the new. An obscure subject, by contrast, would be iconoclastic – that is, it would seek the destruction of works. As examples, Badiou cites early Christianity's destruction of pagan statues and the more recent destruction of Buddhas by the Taliban (LM 82). By contrast, a resurrection of a faithful artistic subject can be found in what Badiou calls neoclassicism, which consists of attempts to return to a new present that was being constructed previously (LM 82).

Love

An amorous subject contains the following structure. First of all, Badiou describes the world in which a love occurs as a world of an "absolute Two, a fundamental incompatibility" between masculine and feminine orientations (LM 212). Badiou leans heavily on Lacan in his discussions of love. Lacan argued that masculine and feminine are subject structures that are not identical to biological sexuality. He also claimed that "there is no such thing as a sexual relationship," and that this incompatibility is a fundamental truth we try to overwrite in our romantic lives: in other words, we try to find some way to forge a relationship between the two sexes, despite the strict impossibility of a relation.

Assuming this as his background, Badiou writes that an event in such a world would be an amorous encounter between two individuals, structured as masculine and feminine. (Whether this encounter is between two men, two women, one man and one woman matters not to the theory – Badiou claims that every love can be described in terms of such an encounter. In an earlier text, Badiou wrote that "as a truth, as a creation, love operates from the interior of sexual difference, even when this love is homosexual" (P 213).) The event is that despite the incompatibility, a scene for the coexistence of the two emerges, in which it can be said that something common to the two species exists, which he calls a "universal object" that each individual participates in (LM 82). Neither member of the couple can say for sure what this object is, but their love affirms its existence. A faithful subject in love (an amorous procedure) produces "an *enchanted existence* in which is accomplished in an asocial fashion the truth of the Two" (LM 83). This term, enchantment, is also used by Badiou to describe the global referent of an amorous procedure: locally, it creates happiness for two individuals, but globally it can find links to previous loves, taking previous couples (in history, in literature) as models, for example.

The reactionary deviation on this procedure involves trying to find some kind of guarantee for the universal object that unifies the couple: precisely, in the legalistic form of the family (LM 83). The obscure subject of love, by contrast, tries to unify the couple in a transcendent body, in the form of a fusion for which the story by Aristophanes in Plato's *Symposium* provides an adequate model. Badiou refers to Tristan and Isolde in this context too. In obscure love, we have two trying to overcome their duality by becoming one.

Science

Finally, the key feature for a science seems to be an ability to symbolize the real in some manner. Science, according to Badiou, mathematizes appearance, and as such is "entirely indifferent to the naturalness, as to the multiplicity, of languages" (LM 83). That is, scientific knowledge is acquired through a special type of mathematized language, and the knowledge it arrives at cannot really be expressed in natural, normal human languages. An event in a scientific world will therefore involve something that had resisted being written finally submitting to being written or symbolized (LM 86). The body constituted by a scientific truth procedure then consists of the results ("principles, laws, theorems") subsequent to the new way of formalizing appearance (LM 84). The local result, already mentioned, would be the creation of new insights, while the global present that a scientific truth procedure links up to would be the world of theory itself – a new scientific theory that puts itself in a relation to previous theories.

A reactionary deviation on this would involve some kind of insistence that new insights be made consistent with "the epistemological grills" of the "pre-eventual period" (LM 84). Badiou calls this pedagogism. An obscure deviation, however, is concerned with the morality and human meaning of scientific endeavors. Badiou calls this obscurantism (LM 85). Such a movement curtails a scientific truth procedure.

Conclusion: affects and ethics in *Logics of Worlds*

In *Logics of Worlds*, as we see, Badiou presents a fairly detailed account of the different forms a subject can take on. He allows for multiple types of subjects to exist now, and I think that is the major point. In *Theory of the Subject*, the subject was basically of one type or style; it had one nature, but it could be pulled in a variety of directions. In *Being and Event*, the subject is also essentially of one type. There are deviations possible, as the discussion in *Ethics* made clear, but these actually turn out to be false subjects, just as the procedures at their heart are pseudo-truths. It is still the case in *Logics of Worlds* that there is a primary type of subject, and that is the faithful subject. The other types – reactionary and obscure – do presuppose this subject structure. But Badiou does give these two other types of subject more actuality than they had before – a reactionary subject is even said to be creating a new present, after all. The prefix "pseudo-", which stuck to the deviations outlined in *Ethics*, no longer seems appropriate for describing what reactionary and obscure subjects do.

How does an ethic emerge from this discussion of different subject-forms and their contexts? Does the presentation of different types of subjects require Badiou to change anything about the ethics of truths he proposed earlier? *Theory of the Subject* pursued ethics by means of a theory of affects, among which were justice, courage, the superego, and anxiety. *Logics of Worlds* presents a theory of affects too, and these are central to Badiou's ethical developments in that text. First of all, affects are presented as things that are attached to the appearance of a faithful truth procedure. Badiou writes that an affect is one of the "local signs" that a new present is being created, it is "the immediate and immanent experience of the fact that one participates . . . in the becoming of a truth, a creative body-subject" (LM 85). For example, a new egalitarian maxim in politics creates *enthusiasm* among its adherents, art brings about a *pleasure* in the "new perceptive intensity" pursued by the movement, love brings about a *happiness* due to a "new existential intensity" in each individual in a couple, and science a *joy* in the new insights being acquired by the new theory (LM 85). There are, then, four affects associated with the truth procedures: enthusiasm, pleasure, happiness, and joy.

But four very different affects – basically identical to those discussed in *Theory of the Subject* – are introduced when Badiou considers the link between a subject and an individual, and not primarily the link between a truth procedure and its world: they are terror, anxiety, courage, and justice. (Note that what was called *superego* in *Theory of the Subject* is now called *terror* (LM 96).) Once again, Badiou affirms that all four are present in any subject; they are, in fact, necessary components of any subject (LM 98). That means that there is a terror proper to love, an anxiety proper to love, and so on, and equally so for art, science, and politics. Defining them very quickly, Badiou writes that terror entails pushing the "decisive discontinuity" between the truth procedure and its world, such that the subject in question is fully "achieved" and the truth procedure brought to completion quickly (LM 96). Anxiety signals a "desire for continuity" and a loathing for the discontinuous (LM 96). In other words, anxiety is an anxiety about the divisiveness and riskiness of the truth procedure itself. Courage, in contrast to anxiety, "accepts" that "discontinuities are simultaneously imperious and multiform," and is able to put up with the difficulties they entail for life and a given world (LM 96). Finally, justice will be called the "affirmation of the equivalence" of "what is continuous and negotiated, and of what is discontinuous and violent" (LM 96–7).

When Badiou claims that no hierarchy exists for these affects – they cannot be ranked in any manner, and none of them is more fundamental than any other – his point is that a theory of the subject simply needs to see how these all hang together. These affects are necessary aspects of any subject-process, and so it is in a sense out of place to lament the possibility or presence of terror in, say, politics, or anxiety in love, and so on. In fact, Badiou argues that this tendency to lament such things plays a role in the stemming of truth procedures. For example, he holds that it is a fact – one we should not be happy about at all, Badiou writes – that "no political subject has ever achieved the eternity of the truth that it unfolds without moments of terror" (LM 98). This does not mean that terror is ever justified. Badiou's point is rather that a terroristic component is an intrinsic part of any truth procedure. This may just amount to an acknowledgment that any significant social movement is going to have its hard edge. And the reference to terror here need not even mean an interest in real violence: as he defined it earlier, and as he does elsewhere, terror may just entail an insistence on some kind of division, or split, within a world. Surprisingly, he refers to the composer Pierre Boulez to illustrate how someone may promote a kind of "terror of the new" in music, imposing the new music of Schoenberg and others from the early twentieth century on a French audience (LM 97). Such is also terror: not necessarily a will-to-death, but a will to force a discontinuity in a world. From this same perspective, it would be easy to see how love could well exert its own terror on an individual's (former) life.

What an ethics of the subject can do (Badiou states that this phrase is just another name for what he had previously called the ethic of truths) is "find an order of affects that authorizes the *continuation* of the process" (LM 99). And it is ultimately questionable whether terror, with its strict and exclusive promotion of discontinuity, can play a role in encouraging continuation, even if it is an inevitable component of a truth procedure. It may at times be necessary or desirable to highlight a division in a world, given certain circumstances. But it is just as likely that terror would have to be subordinated to justice, or courage. And from what we know of Badiou's position in *Theory of the Subject*, given the resemblance of these affects to the ones there, the combination of justice and courage is probably more favorable to encouraging a continuation of a truth procedure than a combination of anxiety and terror.

What I have tried to establish in this chapter is that Badiou's interest in formal studies of situations and worlds, and the events that have strong effects within them, leads him into ethical considerations that are directly about what the inhabitants of those worlds are doing with the effects that an event has. Badiou insists that any truth procedure, and any subject as its finite part, is a compound structure consisting of competing tendencies, with the possibilities of deviations always in them. This makes sense, given Badiou's constant focus on the multiple: why would a truth or a subject be any different?

8
Politics

Political matters are central to Badiou's philosophy, and, as we saw in chapter 1, equally so in his life history. While politics does not have an officially privileged status – Badiou does not think everything is political, for example, or that a political explanation of matters is always the right one in the final analysis – political examples do seem to be the ones most ready to hand in his work, and there is a deep reason for this. Badiou's reflections on and personal experiences in politics guided the development of his overall philosophical system just as much as anything else – as much as set theory, and as much as his reflections on the history of philosophy.

I will try to explain here how and why Badiou arrived at some of his current political views. It is his long involvement in the history and practice of Marxism that has, ironically, led him to the point where he is now advocating a political activity that has superseded party politics. He even posits the end of the "insurrectionary paradigm" that has guided political thinking and the theory of revolutions at least since the French Revolution. Finally, he even argues for a rupture with the left and the death of the figure or model of the left-wing intellectual. These are the positions I will focus on in this chapter.

On the surface, it may look as if Badiou has effectively joined his enemies, the *nouveaux philosophes*, and turned his back on his Maoist radicalism. While his thoughts on the role of the party in politics and the importance of revolution (at least a certain model of revolution, involving the overthrow of a nation-state) have certainly changed since the time of his Maoism, and while he is certainly no longer endorsing the model of political action he once embraced, this does not amount to a renunciation or a reaction but, predictably, Badiou would argue, manifests a deeper fidelity to it. In a sense, then, this chapter will be discussing, through the example of politics, the structure of fidelity in more detail, and how the right ethic can lead it to embrace something other than dogmatism.

Badiou's views on politics, as abstract and apolitical, uninvolved and quietist as they may end up seeming to many, are consistent with another important aspect of his basic philosophical strategy against the rise of reaction: he wants to show that participation in parliamentary democracy, which seems to be the only way to do politics now, is a kind of intellectual blackmail. It makes political activists expect and hope for a certain kind of change from institutions that by their very nature cannot provide what they seek. Thus, to the extent that the left generally speaking remains wedded to things such as voting, protests, and parties the story of the left, Badiou feels, is going to be one of failure and disappointment. By advocating for something like a psychological detachment from the state, Badiou is hoping to restore an element of surprise to political action. As he put it once, politics is not the "art of the possible" as what he calls "leftist parliamentarians" would have it, but the art of the impossible (TS 333).

Badiou's un-orthodox non-Marxism?

Badiou's political philosophy cannot be considered without a discussion of its relation to the Marxist tradition, in which the nature and role of a revolutionary political party, and that party's relation to the nation-state, is a significant issue. Given where Badiou ends up on this question, it is difficult to say what Badiou's ultimate relation to Marxism is. It is not clear that Badiou can be called any more a simple or straightforward Marxist – whatever that would mean. Yet he remains faithful to Marx, in a paradoxical manner that is never far from amounting to an outright breach with Marxism. The best way to begin to see this is to look at the role Badiou thinks communist invariants play in political history.

Badiou first refers to these invariants in the 1970s, in a book called *On Ideology* written with François Balmès. The two discuss Friedrich Engels's reluctance to admit that peasant revolts in Europe before the Industrial Revolution were articulating communist ideals. Engels, like others, wished to make the full articulation of a communist program specific to the situation of the nineteenth, and then twentieth, centuries, when the historical conditions for bringing such a program into being existed. But Badiou and Balmès find that when mass revolts throughout history are considered, even before the proletariat existed, it is hard to ignore the fact that these revolts articulated the very same ideals also embraced by communism: a radical egalitarianism being chief among them. They write, then, that "communist invariants do not have a defined class character: they synthesize the universal aspiration of the exploited to the overturning of any principle of exploitation and oppression" (I 67).

Some Marxists might want to argue that such ideals had to remain necessarily vague and utopian, and mixed up with a religious terminology even, until a proper theory (or science) emerged to clarify them and explain their proper, economic, conditions of possibility. Badiou and Balmès argue that this is not so, and their claim that there are communist invariants that pop up throughout the history of political movements shows again how a theory of deep structural homologies – a formalism – accompanies Badiou's pursuit of an intelligence of change. And we saw in the previous chapter that Badiou continues to think of this, now in the form of the "global" rather than "local" dimension of a political truth procedure. Structurally speaking, his view is that mass political movements will always refer to communist invariants – equality, freedom from oppression, and so on. But each political situation will require its own *particular* (local) incarnation of these invariants. This point practically requires a break with classical Marxism on Badiou's part, and it is very nearly an ahistorical point, as it amounts to the claim that there is a truth in politics that traverses human history, concerning the assertion of a generic humanity.

His position on the, let's call it trans-historical, function of communist invariants reveals some of the ways in which Badiou is arguably both faithful and unfaithful to Marx: faithful in the sense that communism is a way to think about what Badiou suggests is humanity's fundamental aspiration for equality and a life free from oppression, but unfaithful in the sense that it is not the industrial working class specifically that is the ultimate subject of political history, nor is capitalism the final stage of class conflict. Indeed, on Badiou's understanding, there does not seem to be any place for a final revolutionary agent or an end of history at all, and this is a breach with some traditions in Marxism.

Furthermore, if Marxists would have to be situated on the far left of a political spectrum, by his own account Badiou's political sympathies do not even lie on the left any more, for here is how he defines the left: "let's call 'the Left' the set of parliamentary political personnel that proclaim that they are the only ones equipped to bear the general consequences of a singular political movement. Or, in more contemporary terms, that they are the only ones able to provide 'social movements' with a 'political perspective'" (P 273).

The left is described here as an organ of state politics that finds a place – representation – for mass movements in a nation-state structure. As such, Badiou holds that "'the Left' has been the established order's sole recourse during movements of great magnitude" (P 273). A contemporary political truth procedure would be defined, Badiou writes, as much by its break with the left as by its break from the right (and, needless to say, the center). So, in his most recent work he writes that the political task today is to revamp communist ideals – which may well mean not even using basic Marxist terminology: "Marxism, the workers' movement, mass democracy, Leninism, the Party of the proletariat, the Socialist state; all these remarkable inventions of the twentieth century are no longer really useful to us. In the order of theory, they must certainly be known and meditated on. But in the order of politics, they have become impracticable" (S 150).

Yet some attachment to the communist invariants is to be preserved:

> If it is still true, as Sartre said, that "all anti-communists are dogs," it is because every political sequence that, in its principles or in its absence of principle, appears formally contradictory to the communist hypothesis in its generic sense, must be judged to be opposed to the emancipation of humanity as such, and thus to the properly human destiny of humanity. Whoever does not illuminate humanity's becoming by the communist hypothesis (whatever the words used might be, because the words do not really matter) reduces humanity, as far as its collective becoming goes, to animality. (S 132–3)

Communism, then, is still the name for the basic, ideal form in which humanity can fully be human. And it may remain just that – an ideal form. As such, different vocabularies can be used to incarnate it: the Marxist vocabulary may therefore no longer be of use to a political truth procedure.

Politics as a truth procedure

So, if communist invariants are still supposed to play a role in a political movement, but the Marxist vocabulary for them is no longer operative, what form does Badiou think these invariants should take on now? A contemporary political truth procedure will not participate in party politics; it will not participate in parliamentary structures, elections, and perhaps not even in democracy. A political truth procedure must currently take place, he holds, in a space outside the structure of the nation-state; that is, outside of parliaments, parties, and lobbies altogether. Thus, an entire model of political activity needs to be circumvented – what he calls the insurrectionary paradigm and its presupposition of a representational model for politics.

As a truth procedure, what are the features of a political movement? Consistent with what Badiou holds about any truth procedure, it will have the characteristics of being apparently illegitimate and almost nonsensical for the situation it occurs in; it will be presenting something that has no place in a current political situation; it will be universal, generic; and the political subject would consist not only of a group of militants, but of slogans, happenings, practices, and so on. A political truth procedure, like any other, would involve the patient construction of a new present, outside of the purview of the nation-state.

One way to gloss this further is to say that for Badiou a political truth procedure occurs on the ground, at the grassroots, in a social space outside of state mechanisms. And it continues and builds on a day-to-day practice of innovation and experimentation in living together:

> Politics puts the State at a distance. [. . .] This is the sense in which politics is "freedom". The State is in fact the measureless enslavement of the parts of the situation, an enslavement whose secret is precisely the errancy of superpower, its absence of measure. Freedom here consists in putting the state at a distance through the collective establishment of a measure for its excess. And if the excess is measured, it is because the collective can measure up to it. (Meta 145)

But if a political truth procedure is outside of the state, does this not lead to one of the problems with the insurrectionary paradigm in politics that Badiou argues against: namely, that it conceives of a mass movement coming from the outside and shocking the state?

Badiou's vision of a political truth procedure is able to break with the insurrectionary paradigm when it is described not in terms of a destruction of the state, but in terms of a subtraction or separation from the state. In what follows, I will trace the development of Badiou's thought from destruction to subtraction.

Division as a political strategy

The Maoist tenor of Badiou's early works led him to link political movements with destruction and division. Badiou was not alone among the French in being drawn to Maoism, and he was drawn to it because of the very thing that makes it distasteful to most today: the launching of the Cultural Revolution. As Badiou and other French Maoists saw it, Mao was trying to jump-start a revolution that had become frozen: China was on the verge of becoming another Soviet Union. Mao wrote, famously "where is the bourgeoisie in China? It is in the Communist Party!" So, the Cultural Revolution was seen by Badiou and others as a moment of admirable reflexivity on the part of the communist movement: the Chinese Communist Party was criticizing itself, launching a mass movement to correct itself and purify itself of Stalinist, bureaucratic, and capitalist tendencies. Of course, it is precisely this urge to purify that ended up becoming a problem; it was the terror intrinsic to such a movement. As we have seen, and will see again in the conclusion, addressing and correcting this urge is an important goal of Badiou's philosophy.

However, Maoism, at least as Badiou articulates it, should also have had the tools to avoid this urge toward purification. *Theory of the Subject*, as a text that tries to develop a philosophical Maoism, an introduction of Maoism to the dialectical tradition in Western philosophy, argued that there were two key deviations for any subject-process, described as rightist and leftist. I have already touched on these in chapter 6. The rightist deviation overemphasizes the persistence and continuity of structure and identity (saying something like "there is nothing new under the sun"), while the leftist deviation emphasizes a radical and pure outside (saying something like "there is no place for us in your system"). The proper dialectical position, according to Badiou at this time, consisted of splitting each, and bringing them together in a torsion that he called the subject: knotting together a moment of the destruction of one order and the process of recomposition of another. (I refer readers interested in these matters to Bruno Bosteel's study of Badiou's Maoism in "Post-Maoism: Badiou and Politics.")

Nevertheless, destruction and purification remained crucial aspects of a political movement for Badiou at this time. In an earlier text, citing the well-known Maoist slogan, Badiou wrote:

> one divides into two is not a principle of the engendering of "two" from "one." One divides into two signifies: there is no identity that is not split. Not only is reality a process, but the process is division. The real is not what gathers together, but what separates. What comes to be is what is disjoined. (TC 61–2)

This is why Badiou could argue that the frustrating self-destructive tendency of radical movements to fragment into multiple parties, far from being a sign of weakness, is actually a sign of a movement's strength and vitality:

> Today in France the confrontational diversity of groups translates the *real* state of the movement, and far from being a discouraging artifice, the violence of their ideological conflicts is the very site at which the future is announced. Soaking oneself in these conflicts and taking a clear position on them: the rest is only fallacious unanimity, an ineffective populism or revisionist slumber. One divides into two. (TC 63)

What I wish to say here is that Badiou's philosophical Maoism appreciated the significance of division in theory and in practice. Division, difference, and conflict are simply "what there is" for this view and are not things a movement needs to fear and avoid. This view leads Badiou to endorse a political strategy in which division is seen to have a destructive and purifying role: division strips a political force down to its essence, and the sooner this is achieved, the better. The idea is that the few who remain in a certain group will have an ardor, a strength, and a theoretical clarity that will enable the group to carry the movement forward more effectively than the fragile muddle that is created by coalitions, compromises, and the false appearance of unity. On this basis, Badiou is even able to make a case for "the superiority of the forces of the weakest" (TC 100). A party may be small in number, but quantity is not as important as quality – what the group is, what it stands for, and not how many are in it, is the important thing.

Incidentally, this is a view Badiou consistently holds. In 1985 he wrote that "politics will only be thinkable when delivered from the tyranny of number; number of voters as well as number of protesters or strikers" (PP 68). And, more recently, he has argued for a distinction between "active number" and "passive number":

> why would number have any political virtue? Why would the majority, modifiable at will thanks to the ruse of infinite modes of balloting, be endowed with the attributes of a norm? Such approximations are simply not tolerated in other domains where human thought is at stake. Great scientific creators and innovative artists have been right, contrary to dominant opinion. Even violent amorous passions affirm themselves against mediocre social judgments. Is politics, and it alone, to be condemned to the conservatism of numerical means? (P 93)

What Badiou calls active number is "a number pertaining to demonstrations, mass strikes and, indeed, insurrections" (P 93). Passive number refers to electoral numbers, ballot box results. One of Badiou's complaints about contemporary protests and demonstrations is that they subordinate themselves to "passive number" by trying to influence politicians and electoral politics, attempting to sway public opinion in a certain direction. In the demonstrations in France against Le Pen's appearance on the final ballot for president in 2002, for example, Badiou writes that protestors "'took to the streets.' But their power was laughable, for by love of voting, they proclaimed the active number's servitude to the passive number," whereas Badiou holds that "the active number must be untied from all correlation to the passive number. A meeting, a demonstration, an insurrection: all of them proclaim their right to existence outside any consideration that is not immanent to that existence" (P 94). Thus, Badiou claims that it is somehow counterproductive for a political movement to insist on influencing elections, and to make demands on parties, politicians, and political institutions. I will return to this point when I discuss some other aspects of Badiou's views on the status of a political truth procedure.

Death and destruction

Badiou's philosophical Maoism led him to endorse destruction in politics, claiming that "every truth is affirmed in the destruction of nonsense. Every truth is thus essentially destruction. Whatever does nothing but conserve is also nothing but false" (TC 26). In the same text, he wrote: "the advent of a new process (a new unity of contraries) is made by the disappearance of the terms of the preceding contradiction, that is, at the issue (result) of the destruction of one of the terms by the other, which necessarily leads to the division of the victorious term" (TC 65). For example, "the bourgeoisie destroys the feudal order, but the capitalist order it directs is split right away according to the contradiction bourgeois state/proletarian revolution" (TC 65). The final section of Badiou's *Theory of Contradiction* is entitled "Force and Place," and it opens with a rather troubling discussion of the nature of death in dialectical theory. The idea is that any time a social contradiction – such as class conflict – is "resolved," one needs to consider "who or what dies off" (TC 85). Death is brought up here not just because of the frequent occurrence of real death in revolutions, but also because of Hegel's famous claim that the Absolute endures through the death of its parts and moments. In Hegel's Idealist dialectic, death is real, but also not what it appears to be: what appears to be the dying off of a particular thing – a way of life, the force of an idea – is the sublation of that thing into a higher form, part of the unfolding of its essence within the Absolute, and the Absolute's unfolding of itself. Badiou has a number of things to say about this. Materialist dialectics, as he understands it, is not something in which death is merely "gone through" in this Hegelian fashion: it recognizes instead that there are, and must be, indeed, deaths that leave no trace, deaths in which nothing of the thing that dies off survives in what wins out (TC 87). In a point against what he calls a revisionism, Badiou borrows from the Cultural Revolution again and claims that "the essence of revisionism is the fear of death. [...] The revisionist cannot bear the death of the bourgeoisie," and Badiou claims that it is humanist morality that prevents revisionists from continuing with a political movement, compromising their ability to be successful (TC 87).

It looks as if Badiou is ready to accept the worst. But Badiou does describe different ways in which such a genuine death and disappearance of one pole in a social and political contradiction can occur. A true "resolution of a contradiction," Badiou holds does indeed include "the part of death"; for example, in a communist revolution the bourgeoisie would really die off and disappear as a class, and, along with it, oppression as such.

We have claimed: a qualitative mutation requires an answer to the question "who or what dies off?" Where is the fallen off part of the real? The quantitative thought of force cannot deliver an answer. It tells us apparently what changes (places) in indifference to who dies, and thus to what is born. The revisionist electoral promise follows this path: "power" is going to be replaced by the Union of the Left, the common program will straighten out the situation. But who or what must die off? Listening to them, nothing. And nothing will be born either that is not already there: the party, the union, the government. This history without loss [. . .] awakens our dialectical suspicion. We are being lied to, either because one does not want to change anything, or because one has a horror of any historical birth; or because one is dissimulating the cost, the loss, the death. These are being dissimulated, in fact; because the loss is for the masses, who are submitted, in the practical truth of the promise, to an intolerable revisionist dictatorship, to a mortifying social-Fascism. (TC 92)

A discussion of death in a context in which allusions to the Cultural Revolution and the Khmer Rouge are made is troubling, to say the least. Passages such as this, no doubt, are why many readers of Badiou accuse him of harboring terrorist sympathies. But Badiou may not mean anything more here than the idea that in history ideas and tendencies do die off, and this may be the cost of a political success; something "dying off" may mean nothing more than the disappearance of one side in the resolution of a contradiction. (How many royalists are there in the US today?) The actual death of individuals is not required for a change like this. Indeed, Badiou argues that it is when nothing essential is changing in a situation that death starts to become real, and that it is actual people who end up dying. Thus, Badiou would be able to argue on this basis that the mass executions performed by the Khmer Rouge were precisely a sign of its failure as a movement against the Cambodian aristocracy, and not required for its success.

What should be taken away from this discussion is a rather simple idea. For this period of Badiou's work genuine change, the emergence of true novelty in politics, did require destruction; at least the real destruction of certain political orientations, theses, and so on, by real deaths or not. In *Theory of Contradiction*, Badiou makes both a theoretical and a moral case for this. He uses this insight not only against his familiar enemies, the reactionaries, but also against those within political movements on the left who would balk at destruction (the revisionists, he calls them). The motivation for this is to try to reach a point at which a cycle of oppression comes to an end, at which a repetition of domination stops, in a genuine and conclusive resolution of a social contradiction.

Away from death and destruction: subtraction and separation in politics

The role of destruction in politics does end up being abandoned in Badiou's later political theory, and he wants to put in its place the notion of subtraction:

> Destruction or subtraction? This is one of the century's central debates. Which is the active figure taken by the negative side of the passion for the real? I'm particularly sensitive to the conflict between these two orientations since it has played a decisive role in my own philosophical trajectory. An important section of my *Theory of the Subject* (1982) bears the title "Lack and Destruction." At that time, an altogether prophetic phrase of Mallarmé served as my banner: "Destruction was my Beatrice." In *Being and Event* (1988), I formulated an explicit self-critique on this point, showing that a subtractive thinking of negativity can overcome the blind imperative of destruction and purification. (C 54–5)

I would argue that this self-criticism has already occurred in *Can Politics Be Thought?*, in 1985, although it is certainly not complete there, as we will see.

What effect does this shift have on his claim about death and destruction in *Theory of Contradiction*? What a political truth procedure can do instead – and part of the conditions for its success – is to simply subtract certain multiples from a political situation, making exceptions of them, while letting much about the situation remain intact. In at least one text, Badiou also calls this a separation rather than a subtraction, but it seems to be the same thing: "political process is not an expression, a singular expression, of the objective reality but it is in some sense separated from this reality. The political process is not a process of expression, but a process of separation" (Po 2). The patient construction of a new present, which is how Badiou would have to describe a political truth procedure in *Logics of Worlds*, can accomplish what it sets out to accomplish – a supplemented situation, an alternative present – without an iota of destruction.

The error committed by Badiou's earlier political theories, high on destruction, then, was precisely that they sought to rival or replace the nation-state; as political movements, they sought revolution and were wedded to an insurrectionary paradigm. This is exactly why they had to embrace destruction; and this is the nature of the error Badiou finds in his earlier views. A political truth procedure is now seen to do something other than what a classic revolutionary party set out to do.

Can Politics Be Thought? as the beginning of a self-critique

Badiou's views on politics change quite a bit in the 1980s, and I will mark 1984–5 as a pivotal period for a couple of reasons. This period saw the dissolution of the UCFML (see chapter 1) and its reconfiguration as the Organization Politique (OP). The effects of this dissolution are present in the writing and publication of *Can Politics Be Thought?*, a text that is also the first to use the framework that will emerge fully and clearly in *Being and Event*.

In *Theory of the Subject*, the subject is thought of as a political party that threads together an insurrectionary movement and a social reorganization. In that text, Badiou wrote that "the party is the body in politics, strictly speaking" (TS 306). Badiou's notion of the role of the party changed, fairly rapidly, after *Theory of the Subject*. The book *Can Politics Be Thought?* is a text written in full crisis mode, and he writes there of a retreat of the kind of politics he had been engaged in for a decade. He claims that "the event we are contemporary with is the crisis of Marxism" (PP 21). It had become impossible to support the Soviet Union and the Eastern bloc; vibrant workers' movements (Badiou thinks of the Solidarity movement in Poland here, but also of migrant workers in France) no longer were using a Marxist vocabulary to articulate their demands; third-world Marxism tended to result only in the creation of disastrous "expansionist military states," such as Vietnam (PP 44). So, Badiou writes, "today neither the socialist States nor the battles of national liberation nor the workers movement constitute historical referents capable of guaranteeing the concrete universality of Marxism" (PP 48). Badiou concludes then that "Marxism is not today dead. It is historically destroyed" (PP 52).

The book proposes a new model for politics, and this will be the same model that appears in the general philosophical system

Badiou develops later in *Being and Event*. (This is why I claimed earlier that the source and motive for Badiou's mature philosophical system came from his thinking about and experiences with the political crises and impasses of his day.) Badiou discusses a strike at a Talbot automobile plant in 1984 that, he thinks, crystallized the political dynamic in France at the time. He finds this strike significant because it revealed three fractures in the French political situation. First of all, it revealed the failure of the reforms promised by the Socialist Party's victory in 1981; second, it showed that left-wing parties no longer had a hold on a large segment of workers; and, third, it showed how the extreme right was successful at getting a number of workers to turn against the immigrants in their midst (PP 70–1).

The strike at the Talbot plant is a textbook case for what Badiou will later call a political truth procedure. The incident involved a group that did not really count as far as the French state was concerned, a group whose presence was not accompanied by full membership in the state, and who could therefore well be described as an indiscernible multiple in French politics: immigrant workers. And when they started to come together and make demands, they necessarily ended up using some of the terms from the French political situation from which they were excluded, leading Badiou to claim that the statements they made were "intrinsically irrepresentable" in the political situation of the time (PP 74). As we have seen, a truth procedure in any situation uses a language that is close to being nonsense. Such is the way in which Badiou describes the demands the workers were making, as far as the state was concerned.

The following serves as a neat summary of Badiou's conclusions based on the strike at the Talbot plant:

> Politics begins when one proposes not to represent victims, a project in which the old Marxist doctrine remained a prisoner of the expressive schema, but being faithful to the events to which the victims give expression. This fidelity is supported by nothing other than a decision. And this decision, which promises nothing to anyone, is only for its part connected by a hypothesis: the hypothesis of a politics of non-domination, of which Marx was the founder, and that today must be re-founded. (PP 75–6)

This hypothesis – easily recognizable as one of Badiou's communist invariants – is supported by a decision that "promises nothing to anyone" – an absence that is significant, for it shows how Badiou is starting to move out of what might be called a politics of demand, a politics in which a variety of groups make appeals to the state for recognition and representation. He argues later that "one of the great weaknesses of the century's thought, or at least one of its zones of uncertainty, is that it entertained a representational concept of legitimacy" (C 108).

The example of the Talbot strike already strongly suggests the ideas of the end of the party and the end of the insurrectionary paradigm, ideas that are more clearly and explicitly expressed in Badiou's recent writings on politics. What starts to be proposed here is the end of an entire model of politics and of the structure within which parties make sense, a structure in which parties represent a segment of the population who then exercises more or less leverage over the mechanisms of the state – Badiou also calls this an expressive politics. The structure here is the Lacanian structure of demand, a representational structure in which some big Other is posited who is able to grant recognition and satisfaction. On this model, a grievance is felt, an oppression is suffered, a demand is made to the state; the people clamor, take to the streets, and the state responds or not.

The problem Badiou finds with this representational and expressive model is its clear dependence on the state for the accomplishment of political goals. This is what his analysis of the strike at Talbot was aiming at, although his reading in *Can Politics Be Thought?* ends in somewhat of an impasse: the workers were still primarily addressing the state with their demands, and were not simply proceeding with the construction of their own alternative present. Ultimately, a drawback the later Badiou would see in the Talbot strike is found in the fact that it was a group making a demand, which necessarily requires the representational structure from which he later thinks a political truth procedure is separated. A comparison of the Talbot strike to the example of Spartacus that Badiou uses in *Logics of Worlds* makes this point clearly. The Spartacan slave revolts were not so much demanding freedom as they were presupposing it, and actively creating a new, free present for themselves. In a similar manner, this is what any political truth procedure would be doing: constructing its present in indifference to the reigning situation.

Badiou did claim in *Peut-on penser la politique?* that "we know today that it is a matter of finishing with the representative vision of politics," although the model for this in the text contains some problems (PP 85). The Talbot strike did lead Badiou to realize, it seems, that a certain kind of political activity can only take place outside of the state and outside of a party structure. What he failed to do there was emphasize the importance of what such a movement constructs: as he would put it later, this is a new present, a new possible. And so, for this reason, the politics of destruction is still operative in *Peut-on penser la politique?* at least insofar as the political procedure he posits is still about acquiring power from the state, even if it is not about gaining recognition. When Badiou moves from the model of destruction in politics to that of subtraction, he is able to emphasize that aspect of a political movement that creates on its own what it is about, that does and performs what it says, without recognition and representation from a nation-state – or even the re-founding of one – being requirements for success.

Against identity and for the universal

Badiou's specific political views have long involved paying attention to anti-colonial struggles and the situation of immigrant workers. These views could have led him in the direction of an identity politics, but there is and always has been a strong rejection of identity politics in Badiou's political works. The basic reason for this rejection is Badiou's conviction that a political truth procedure, with its use of communist invariants, necessarily makes a universal appeal within a situation, and this cuts across the identities and positions that define that situation. According to Badiou, identities are always maintained by the state of a situation, and if a political truth procedure must, by definition, be somehow unrecognizable in a situation, it can never have the assertion and recognition of identity as its basis.

A text that makes this case quite strongly is Badiou's reading of St. Paul, subtitled *The Foundation of Universalism*. There are a few different goals in this text. One thing Badiou pursues is a rehabilitation of Paul as a militant for a truth procedure from whom important strategic lessons can be learned. Paul's truth procedure may no longer have any purchase on us, but it was, Badiou claims, entirely pertinent to the social and political situation of the ancient Roman world (SP 5). Badiou claims to have learned from St. Paul that a truth procedure cannot "take root in the element of identity. For if it is true that every truth erupts as singular, its singularity is immediately universalizable. Universalizable singularity necessarily breaks with identitarian singularity" (SP 11). What Paul did was, on the basis of an event that was named the Resurrection, argue that the key distinctions in the Roman world as far as identities were concerned no longer mattered for the new Christian present being constructed. This is the import of some of the controversies covered in Paul's letters, about the relation in general between Christians and Jews: for example, his famous "neither Greek nor Jew, neither slave nor freeman, male or female; for you are all one in Christ" (Galatians 3: 28).

In line with Badiou's move away from destruction as an aspect of a truth procedure at this stage of his work, and toward notions such as subtraction and separation (and eventually to the view that a truth procedure creates a new present), he holds that the new Christian world in St. Paul's work is indifferent to the identities that are.

> For although it is true, so far as what the event constitutes is concerned, that there is "neither Greek nor Jew," *the fact is* that there are Greeks and Jews. That every truth procedure collapses differences, infinitely deploying a purely generic multiplicity, does not permit us to lose sight of the fact that, in the situation (call it: the world), *there are differences*. One can even maintain that there is nothing else. (SP 98)

By giving differences a mundane ontological quality, Badiou is able to argue that differences and identities do not need to be destroyed by a truth procedure. They can persist in a kind of indifferent, uninteresting manner. At any rate, they are not significant.

These points amount to an argument against identity politics insofar as they link identity politics to the kind of reaction against truth procedures that Badiou thinks is characteristic of the contemporary political situation.

> Deleuze put it perfectly: capitalist deterritorialization requires a constant reterritorialization. Capital demands a permanent creation of subjective and territorial identities in order for its principle of movement to homogenize its space of action; identities, moreover, that never demand anything but the right to be exposed in the same way as others to the uniform prerogatives of the market. The capitalist logic of the general equivalent and the identitarian and cultural logic of communities or minorities form an articulated whole.

This articulation plays a constraining role relative to every truth procedure. It is organically *without truth*. (SP 10–11)

Badiou continues to define political events as collective in nature (M 146). That something is collective does not normally mean it is automatically universal; but Badiou thinks it is universalizing, that it is open to all. As we saw in the discussion of ethics, Badiou argues that a collective that is limited to the unity of a particular group is the stuff of evil. He also claims that "politics is an operator for the consolidation of what there is of the universal in identities" (S 89). With his view in *Saint Paul* and *Ethics* that "difference is what there is" – and he has in mind diverse identities, cultures, backgrounds – differences and identities are not as significant or noteworthy as those moments in which the same emerges in a situation in which identities are clearly discernible: say, when diverse demographic groups start to have converging interests, and start to unify under maxims that express communist invariants, an example of which is found in the slogan of Badiou's own Organization Politique – "anyone who works here is from here." Political truth procedures "take no account of any particular interests. They bring about a representation of the collective capacity on the basis of a rigorous equality between each of their agents" and engage the generic in humanity (Meta 97). Identity exists for the individuals of a political situation; it remains what there is and always will be. What makes politics a type of truth procedure is when there is an indifference to these differences, when a generic humanity is asserted, and when different identities start to group together in unheard of and unpredictable ways. Identity politics, Badiou argues, tends to be a defense of existing identities, which is a disaster. This is his point when he claims that signifiers such as "'immigrant,' 'French,' 'Arab,' and 'Jew' cannot be political words lest there be disastrous consequences" (Meta 94). A generic political truth procedure should shake up individual identities, surprising the situation with its revival of a generic idea of humanity.

Against democracy and voting

Why does Badiou argue against a certain use of the term democracy, and also against participation in elections? How are these points linked to his views of a political truth procedure? He writes:

> The definition of democracy poses a problem. As much as one will be persuaded, as the Thermidorians and their liberal descendants, that it [democracy] resides in the free play of group interests, or determined individuals, one will see it ruin itself, slowly or quickly depending on the times, into a corruption without hope. True democracy (if it is necessary to conserve this concept, as I believe it is) is something completely different. It is equality before the Idea, before the political Idea. For example, for a long time, the revolutionary or communist Idea. It is the ruin of this Idea that identifies "democracy" with generalized corruption. (S 122-3)

So there is a contemporary use of the term democracy that Badiou qualifies as fetishistic: it is found in the current interest in promoting democratic governments worldwide, which means not much more than the occurrence of free and fair elections. Thus, this understanding of democracy sees it primarily as a form that states may or may not take on. When democracy is thought of as something other than a form of the state, however, Badiou claims that it is what *"presents equality"* (Meta 93). And for such a presentation – the creation of a truth procedure – elections and parliamentary representation may not be at all important. In fact, Badiou holds that they necessarily cannot be:

> a politics encompassing real decisions, I mean emancipatory decisions, is entirely foreign to the vote, because by deciding for something liberatory you are designated as being hostile to established interests; interests that, despite being in the minority, will make enough of a hullabaloo, and will have sufficient control over the instruments of propaganda, to ensure that you'll be replaced at the next election. And this will be all the more readily done, as people vote to persevere and not to become. (P 91)

This is another way of illustrating the relation of a truth procedure in politics to the state form. It does not present a reigning political situation with a contradiction that could be resolved by having a different group occupy the seat of power. It seems, again, that Badiou is saying it is somehow simply indifferent to the state.

Badiou is not only arguing that participation in elections is anathema to a political truth procedure here; he claims that it debilitates and disorients the militants themselves. "The vote is in essence contradictory to principles, just as it is to every idea of emancipation and protest" (P 91). The slogan "élections, piège à cons" ("elections are for suckers"), used during May 1968, is still obviously dear to Badiou (S 44). He even claims that he is not absolutely in favor of universal suffrage, for "Hitler himself came to power through elections, and it was a regular assembly that elected Petain" (P 94). In *Sarkozy*, he puts his point this way: "I do not absolutely respect universal suffrage in itself; it depends on what it does. Is universal suffrage the only thing one must respect independently of what it produces? And why, then" (S 42)? Elections also produce a sort of illusion:

> The vote is thus productive of a singular illusion. [. . .] "The French have decided that . . ." says the good press. They did not decide anything at all, and, moreover, this collective "the French" has no existence. Why the devil would 51 percent of the French be "the" French? (S 21)

So, with all this, Badiou can actually come up with a formula that equates voting with the abdication of a political truth procedure: "As the libertarians of the nineteenth century said: 'to vote is to abdicate.' More exactly, today one should say: 'To want to abdicate is to vote'" (P 92).

Such arguments can be linked to Badiou's concern about the challenge of a kind of intellectual blackmail engaged in by reaction, even outside of politics. He seems to be aware of the difficulty people would have in following his point. Many would feel tremendously guilty for not voting. But the more people vote, Badiou argues, the more they legitimate the reigning political situation, a situation that is not transformed – fundamentally, anyway – through elections. Yet it is not, apparently, to be transformed through insurrections and protests either – that is one of the most significant consequences of Badiou's calls for an end to the insurrectionary paradigm in politics.

Does this amount to a call to drop out of politics? It does amount to dropping out of political participation in the state, and it is dropping out of a model of politics in which state power is the brass ring. But this does not at all automatically mean dropping out of politics per se, since the site of political action is supposed to be elsewhere to begin with. But, again, there are some problems here. Badiou is concerned that the more people pay attention to election results, and the approval ratings of certain parties and proposals, the more they lose sight of where significant political activity is actually happening. Yet where is it happening, for him? Imperceptibly, on the margins, at the grassroots, in everyday practice and everyday community? On this point, Badiou seems not to have lost his Maoist confidence in the masses.

Conclusion

The abstractness of some of Badiou's political points, and their lack of detail, may be lamentable, yet in fairness it should be noted that this is consistent with what Badiou thinks philosophy should do. He has long maintained that blueprints and programs are politically undesirable: at any rate, philosophers do not have any insight into where a movement is going to lead, what it is going to encounter, what it is going to need, and so on. Moving out of the insurrectionary paradigm also means not developing a theory that is about giving history a push or about speeding along an event. And at any rate, as I have argued, events cannot be pushed. Badiou's position on politics amounts to a focus instead on something like an ethic of movements, which consist of a type of activity that is not about producing events, but an activity that is itself pushed by events, as it were. Thus, it is a theory that is about appreciating the status of a certain type of practice, one that may enhance or enable that type of practice already going on to continue. Badiou describes this as a politics that would be an end in itself, no longer having the takeover of the state as its goal:

> politics would no longer be governed by the question of how to bring about the good State, but would instead be an end in itself. Contrary to what was previously maintained, politics conceived in this way would, in a certain manner, be the movement of thought and action that frees itself from dominant statist subjectivity and that proposes, summons and organizes projects that cannot be reflected or represented by those norms under which the State operates. One could also say that, in this case, politics is presented as a singular collective practice operating at a distance from the State. Or again, that, in essence, politics is not the bearer of a State programme or a statist norm, but is rather the development of a possible affirmation as a dimension of collective freedom which subtracts itself from the normative consensus that surrounds the State. (Meta 84–5)

I think this passage makes it quite plain that Badiou is not a conventional Marxist, and not even a conventional Maoist any more. As Bruno Bosteels puts it, "Badiou was and still is a Maoist, even though he no longer is the same Maoist that he once was" (Bosteels

576). Where he is no longer the same is on the question of the relation of politics to the state. Where he is a Maoist still, I suggest, is in his confidence in what the masses are doing.

It is also odd for a philosopher so influenced by the Marxist tradition that economic analyses never seem to factor in to his writings on politics. Peter Hallward has raised this issue directly. In an interview, Badiou claimed that "any viable campaign against capitalism can only be political. There can be no economic battle against the economy" (Hallward 2003: 237). Later, Hallward himself expresses a concern about what this separation of political matters from economic matters means for the effectiveness of Badiou's conception of politics (ibid.: 284). If, as Badiou seems to concede, only a political battle can do anything to capital, while politics is now outside the state and does not have a seizure of the state as one of its goals, what can it really expect to do against capitalism? Certainly, Badiou is not advocating dropping out and joining a commune. Making a similar point, Barker writes, "Badiou's insistence that politics must be absolutely subtracted from capital-parliamentary norms is problematic, since it appears to count for its combative force on a blind voluntarism where resistance, rather than a politics aimed at concrete transformation, is the only viable option" (Barker 2002: 7). Yet Badiou's politics may not even be about resistance if it is about the concrete production of a new present, something that certainly must be some kind of transformation – if not of the state, of something about communal life itself. This could occur in a mere indifference to the state.

Conclusion

Badiou claims that, in its early days, one of historical materialism's priorities was the undoing of the religious overtones of philosophical idealism. The historical materialism Badiou wants to develop, which he calls a "second materialism, after the one of irreligion," no longer has as its primary task the undoing of the concept of God (TS 203). Badiou, maybe overconfidently, seems to think that this project is finished, and it was a success: not only is God dead, but religion is too (B 23). In light of the rise of fundamentalisms, this is an astonishing claim to make (but it may not be if one considers the philosophical status of God and religions). I have already discussed how Badiou reads the contemporary rise of fundamentalism as an obscure mode of subjectivity, which, as such, actually assumes what it tries to ignore. According to Badiou, the existence of an irreligious present is this obscure subject's "active unconscious," driving it to do what it does. He writes that:

> the God of monotheisms has been dead for a long time, no doubt for at least two hundred years, and the man of humanism has not survived the twentieth century. Neither the infinite complications of state politics in the Middle East, nor the spongy mindsets of our own "democrats" have the least chance of resuscitating them. (C 166)

Badiou's materialism assumes that the critique of religion is accomplished, then; so its task is no longer the undoing of God and religion. What I want to address in this conclusion is his claim that the task is now to do something to the concept of the human: not to undo it, but to undo a certain understanding of it and replace it with another, one with some ironic religious overtones.

A group of thinkers who had an enormous influence on Badiou in the mid 1960s – Althusser, Foucault, Lacan – explored anti-humanism (Foucault himself wrote of the "death of Man") insofar as they promoted the idea that we are to a large extent the playthings of social systems and structures such as language, history, and the unconscious. Badiou points out that their anti-humanism at the level of theory did not prevent these thinkers from being, in their practical lives, very much engaged with the improvement of the conditions of life for human beings, in a manner that Badiou thinks rivals that of many self-avowed humanists of our day (E 7). Badiou makes this point partly in order to assuage any concerns that his theoretical anti-humanism automatically implies an indifference to the fate of our fellow humans; his point about these thinkers is certainly supposed to be a point about his own work too. What complicates his relation to these thinkers is that he is not simply continuing with the theme of the "death of Man" as these thinkers understood it. These thinkers still understood human beings in terms of finitude and mortality, Badiou claims, and from his perspective this is still an understanding of humanity that derives from the religious assumptions of philosophical idealism: as if the "death of Man" in theory in the 1960s still shared the interpretation of humanity found in religions. "It is thus imperative," he writes, "so as to be serenely established in the irreversible element of God's death, to finish up with the motif of finitude" (B 29). Doing this would lead to a proper atheism, which, despite the completion of the death of God, he claims, still remains before us "as a task for thought" (B 29).

Badiou's study of the twentieth century in *The Century* – a study that wishes to explain "what the century thought of itself" – provides a good framework for understanding why he develops an atheism that, oddly, on the face of it, embraces religious themes, such as immortality (C 13). The nineteenth century was, according to Badiou, a century of proposals, utopias, and ideals, accompanied by a faith that these would be attained through the inevitable development of material life and social institutions: "The nineteenth century's Hegelian idea was to rely on the movement of history, 'to surrender to the life of the object'" (C 15). But "the twentieth century's idea is to confront History, to master it politically" by forcing the ideal to come into being (C 15). This is why he characterizes the twentieth century as a period infused with a "passion for the real," a passion that is also a "passion for the new" (C 56).

This passion was not just a matter of trying to transform the world; it was also very much an attempt to create a new humanity. Badiou writes of the passion to "remake man," and he mentions a slogan from the Cultural Revolution in China to this effect, which expressed a wish "to change what is deepest in man" (C 9). Such a passion easily becomes violent. Badiou attributes this to the persistence of a "suspicion" in revolutionary movements that the real, being the new present it is producing, is never real enough, never free of what he calls semblance (C 53). Thus, movements undergo a constant urge to purify themselves and their products: "purging is one of the great slogans of the century. Stalin said it loud and clear: 'a party becomes stronger by purging itself'" (C 53). We saw in the previous chapter how Badiou himself gave purification an important role in political theory and practice. The need for purification never ends, and this is the fatal flaw of the passion for the real that suffused the century: the real it produces is never real enough; the new present is always haunted by the semblance of the past (and present) it wishes to destroy.

Badiou proposes that this passion for the real was the twentieth century's defining feature, and he holds that the century, understood this way, actually ended about two-thirds of the way through (S 143). This places the end of the century at around the time of the Cultural Revolution in China (1966) and May 1968. Badiou places the end of the century here because these dates marked the end of a certain conception of humanity, the end of a certain kind of political project, and the end of one way in which faithful subjectivity was pursued (albeit with a terror-prone inflection). In chapter 7 I discussed Badiou's claims that any faithful subject, be it in art, politics, love, or science, is going to contain, necessarily, something like a tendency for exerting a terror on its world. This particular leaning seemed to dominate the faithful subjectivities of the twentieth century, and it is one of the main reasons for the successful rise of reaction and the obscure against fidelity. After a century of "purifying" disasters – wars, genocides, intolerances of many sorts – it is as if at its (conceptual, not chronological) end the century reached a consensus, which Badiou describes thusly: "perhaps it's the case that today every attempt to submit thought to the test of the real – political or otherwise – is regarded as barbarous. The passion for the real, much cooled, cedes its place (provisionally?) to the acceptance – sometimes enjoyable, sometimes grim – of reality" (C 64). In *Logics of Worlds*, Badiou called this current reigning ideology a "democratic materialism," and he believed it is based on a lesson from the twentieth century. Attempts to re-create humanity lead directly to disaster, which is one of the main points of the *nouveaux philosophes* who play such an important role in Badiou's philosophy. This ideology concludes that "the political will to the overhuman (or the new type of man, or of radical emancipation), has engendered nothing but inhumanity" (C 177). At its conceptual end, then, the century gave way to the dominance of obscure and reactive subjects – the current period that Badiou also likens to the period of Restoration in nineteenth-century France.

The counter-strategy he offers in *The Century* (and throughout his work, really) consists of assuming the in-human and affirming something about it. Badiou wishes to:

> *begin* from the inhuman: from these truths in which it can happen that we participate. And from there, only, envisage the superhuman.
> Of these inhuman truths, Foucault was right to say (as Althusser and his "theoretical anti-humanism," or Lacan and his radical dehumanization of the true) that they constrain us to "formalize without anthropologizing."
> Let us speak, then, of the philosophical task, on the shores of a new century, and against the animal humanism that besieges us, as a *formalized in-humanism*. (C 178)

We have seen much of Badiou's interest in formalizing without anthropologizing: his objective phenomenology in *Logics of Worlds* is the most recent manifestation of this interest. Thinking of this formalized in-humanism in terms of the "death of Man" is somewhat misleading then: for, in Badiou's work, it entails only the death of a certain conception of man, and the invention of another. Badiou claims that the death of God should lead to an affirmation of the infinity and immortality of the inhuman in truths. It is not so much the "death of Man" that is pursued in Badiou's philosophy, then; nor is it a resurrection of man along familiar lines, or a deification of the finite creatures we are (something, arguably, that was pursued by thinkers such as Marx and Nietzsche). What Badiou's work pursues is a reconfiguring of an image of the human, ironically using some of the very terms that the religious conception of humanity deemed essential to humanity's relation to the divine: such as faith, truth, eternity, immortality, and infinity.

Certainly, Badiou is not claiming that human beings are immortal: "to be sure, humanity is an animal species. It is mortal and predatory" (E 11). Yet "being only a form, and as a form – in the sense of a Platonic idea – the subject is immortal" (LM 57). The distinction should be clear enough. After all, the subject is not the same as the human being: it is due to the work of conscious human beings, but it is something apart from them. In this respect, subjects can be called immortal, in a way that other things created by human beings cannot be, and in a way that human beings themselves cannot be. To make some sense of this, recall the notion of resurrection he developed in *Logics of Worlds*, according to which it is possible for a truth procedure in a situation to pick up the legacy of an earlier fidelity – to bring back to life the strands of an earlier process, just as some early twentieth-century movements took inspiration from Spartacus, or some musicians might find inspiration in musical innovations of the past. According to Badiou, a subject process present in the ancient world qualifies as immortal if it is able to later be resurrected. Subjects may well be immortal, then, insofar as they are linked to the creation of eternal truths: sadly, we individuals who work on them remain mortal.

A new subjective paradigm: a theory of living

Nietzsche worried that the death of God would have ill consequences for human life; that it would lead to nihilism. This is precisely how Badiou sees the century ending, with the active nihilism that characterized its passion for the real giving way to a passive nihilism that he describes as follows:

> The figure of active nihilism is regarded as completely obsolete. Every reasonable activity is limited and limiting, hemmed in by the burdens of reality. The best one can do is to avoid evil, and to do this the shortest path is to avoid any contact with the real. Eventually, one meets up again with the nothing, the nothing-real, and in this sense one is still within nihilism. But since the element of terrorism, the desire to purify the real, has been suppressed, nihilism is deactivated. It has become passive, or reactive, nihilism – that is, a nihilism hostile to every action as well as every thought. (C 64–5)

In the same vein, he wrote in 2004 that the possibility of faithful subject-processes seems to be nearly wiped out, and now "we hear of nothing save for human rights and the return of the religious"

(C 165). In both cases "the century concludes on the motif of the impossibility of subjective novelty and the comfort of repetition" (C 66). The claim is that there are only two really viable subject-forms now, the reactive (dominated by an affirmation of the rights of man) and obscure (fundamentalisms and the return of religion). What is currently missing, Badiou claims, is what he refers to as a subjective paradigm that would counteract these two forms. Of course, this is just what he has been working on for years, under the heading of a fidelity procedure.

In a lecture entitled "The Subject of Art" Badiou presents the reactive and obscure forms of the subject in a slightly different way, one that is helpful for understanding where he is going with his exploration of immortality for the subject as a form. This provides a good exercise for understanding how Badiou's theoretical anti-humanism is supposed to pay off practically. His highly formal way of thinking about the subject and its forms allows him to isolate its components. Seeing how two current paradigms of the subject work with these components, he can then describe how a faithful subject-form entails a different configuration of them, ultimately allowing for a different way of thinking about living itself.

Using the vocabulary for the subject that he developed in *Logics of Worlds*, he portrays the subject as the union of a trace of an event and a body in a world. The event itself and the world itself are both, of course, beyond the subject. This means that an event never fully comes to be in a world, and a world is never fully presented as a being either. Democratic materialism – the support structure of the reactive subject – posits that only bodies and languages exist. It emphasizes, then, the link between body and world, and neglects the dimension of the subject that contains traces of an event. (As we saw in chapter 7, a reactionary subject structure involves something like a repression of the faithful subject structure.) Obscurantism works differently: it emphasizes the traces of an event in a subject, but neglects the subject's embodiment in a fragmentary world. So, "in the first paradigm [democratic materialism, reaction] the subject is finally the body itself. In the second paradigm [obscurantism], the subject is completely separated from its body" (SA).

Furthermore, he notes that the ethic of democratic materialism is to "enjoy!" It encourages us to keep working, keep shopping, to see how the present is not so bad and that there is far worse possible anyway; and also to avoid harming anyone, not just physically but also psychologically. The obscure subject of fundamentalisms, by contrast, commands us to "sacrifice!" It tells us that we are not what we could be, we are not what we once were, we have another possible life, in another world, open to us on the condition that we denounce this world. So Badiou claims that "the contemporary world is a war between enjoyment and sacrifice" – with advocates for global capitalism and democracy on the one hand (democratic materialism), and the advocates of fundamentalisms and terror on the other hand (the obscure) (SA).

Badiou's formalist account of the subject has allowed him to discern how the reactive subject structure tries to dispense with the event/trace aspect of the subject, while the obscure subject structure eliminates the embodied and worldly aspect of the subject. One of the important insights his philosophy is able to deliver is that these two paradigms actually have a common root: both conceive of the subject in terms of an essential relation to death. He writes, "we can see in the two paradigms we cannot have something like a real process of production without experimentation of the limits, finally, of death in the life of the world" (SA). And it is on the point of death – thought of as something to avoid at all costs, or at least to experience as painlessly as possible by democratic materialism, and by contrast as a point of glorious transition and honor for fundamentalism – that Badiou's philosophical system can intervene and construct a possible third paradigm for the subject, in terms of fidelity. He claims: "we have to propose something as a new subjective paradigm which is outside the power of death – which is neither enjoyment (that is pleasure beyond pleasure and limits of the body) nor satisfaction in the sacrifice (that is enjoyment in another world, of pleasure beyond suffering)" (SA).

Articulating this third paradigm requires the break with the theme of finitude to which I have already alluded. Finitude is assumed by both sides of the "disjunctive synthesis" offered today by Capital and Terror, reaction and obscurantism (P 35). Badiou's proposed new paradigm for the subject "has to understand completely how a new body can be oriented by a subjective process without separation and without identification" – that is, without the kind of separation from the body sought after by the obscure, and without a strict identification of the subject with the body, which is what happens in democratic materialism (SA). "So," he concludes, this new paradigm will "maintain the distance between the trace of an event and the construction of the body," which means, again, somehow steering the subject clear of two deviations (SA). This should sound a lot like what Badiou has said about the structure of a faithful subject throughout his work: the faithful subject is characterized by its possession of a split body, subordinated to the trace of an event, working to produce a new present.

What bearing does this view of the faithful subject have on the question of what it means to live? Democratic materialism itself has a strong thesis on life: its slogan, consistent with its command to enjoy, Badiou writes, would be "live without idea" since it is precisely ideas (of the good, or the true) that give rise to evil, and trouble our everyday satisfactions (LM 533). This ethic of life, which Badiou would prefer to portray as an ethic of finitude and death, also "claims to be humanist (the rights of man, etc.). But it is impossible to have a concept of what is 'human' without arriving at this (eternal, ideal) inhumanity that authorizes man to incorporate itself in the present under the sign of the trace of what changes" (LM 533). Ironically, an ethic that is supposed to promote life and calls itself humanism is really an "animal humanism" since the difference between animals and humans is negated by it: for, certainly, it is also the case that much of animal life consists of bodies and languages. This is why, in *Ethics*, Badiou claimed that it was "thought" that was a distinctive feature of the human, and he continues to claim this in *Logics of Worlds*. He was already looking in *Ethics* for a way to describe the manner in which humans inhabit their worlds differently from animals: and this need not entail any claims about superiority. It could just be a way to think of the specificity of the human, and Badiou's "formalized in-humanism" is supposed to be able to isolate and affirm this trait better than other philosophical humanisms.

On the basis of this trait – let's call it the capacity for truths – a kind of life is possible that, in turn, would also be particular to human beings. This is what Badiou calls "the faithful form of a subject" (LM 530). The reactive form of the subject replaces living in this sense with "conservation" (persist in the life you know) and the obscure form of the subject replaces it with "mortification" (seek another life). Both are consistent with the humanism described above. Badiou writes that "democratic materialism is a formidable enemy and intolerant of all human – that is to say inhuman – life worthy of the name" (LM 534). His own philosophy is able to affirm, by contrast, that "to every human animal is accorded, several times in its life, and for several types of ideas, the possibility of living" (LM 602). Thus "we are open to the infinity of worlds. Living is possible. Consequently, (re)commencing to live is the only important thing" (LM 536). Badiou's philosophy affirms, then, that by living in this manner individuals participate in immortality

Conclusion

(as a form for the subject) and truth (as an eternal, infinite process), even though individuals cannot claim to be immortal, and cannot even claim to know the truth they are wrapped up in. To use some of the terms that date back to *Theory of the Subject*, it is nevertheless the case that as individuals we can be *confident* that we have a place in them (insofar as we are active in procedures), and we can also perhaps develop the *courage* to continue with their construction.

Louis Althusser wrote once that in his youth, in post-war France, there was no shortage of opportunities to engage in practice as a young Marxist. Strikes were frequent, powerful, and also effective. The French Communist Party was a serious political force. What was missing, Althusser wrote, was a good theory, a good understanding of the situation (Althusser 2005: 21–30). This, Althusser clearly suggests, is partly responsible for the practical failures of twentieth-century Western Marxism.

The contemporary scene might give one the impression that there is now, by contrast, no shortage of theories – and quite good ones. We have access to a multitude of ways of inhabiting and understanding our worlds. It is worth considering, therefore, whether our situation is not somehow the inverse of Althusser's: what is missing is the possibility for a certain type of practice. I take it that Badiou's philosophy is making such a case.

Yet there are also many theories currently that try to influence practice in some way, encouraging people perhaps to live differently or more authentically. I would claim, though, that Alain Badiou offers a fundamentally different orientation on this matter, and a very psychoanalytically informed one. His philosophy in no way offers any instructions about what is to be done. The significant practical point to be taken away from his philosophy is that we need not search around for the right kind of practice: we may already be engaged in a variety of practices whose significance eludes us, much like the meaning of a symptom, or even character or personality itself in Freudian psychoanalysis, eludes us. Badiou's philosophy suggests that we individuals may already be engaged in certain kinds of practices without really knowing it.

That is why his philosophy focuses not on what to do, but on how to continue with practices that we may not be sure we want to continue, especially once we become aware of their existence and what they are doing (and not doing). Thus, rather than offering a typically revolutionary (and always a bit evangelical) theory, which would be all about inspiring people to give history a push (as Lenin put it), or to live authentically (as Heidegger and Sartre might put it), Badiou's philosophy is an important move beyond what could well be called the insurrectionary paradigm not only in politics but in theory and philosophy as well. Badiou's goal is not to trigger events, and it is not about trying to convince anyone to join in any particular movement. Badiou's formalized in-humanism is supposed to show us instead how the new happens, how it emerges; not at all without human practice, but not with the full knowledge and choice and freedom of any of its participants either. And as a practical humanism, his system is supposed to give individuals the wherewithal to continue with these procedures that seize them.

The emergence of the new is not willed or decided on by anyone. So Badiou is doing the work he is doing in order to preserve not the *emergence* of the new (an emergence which takes care of itself, according to Badiou's formalized in-humanism), but to encourage the *durability* of the new, along with the possibility of the kind of life this brings with it – one which may not at all be good for anyone, and may have nothing to do with happiness either. Recall that for Badiou "every definition of man based on happiness is nihilist" (E 37). The contemporary rise of reaction and fundamentalism – each a type of nihilism, for him – is associated with the following problem for the faithful subjects of truth procedures: anyone involved in truth procedures lacks an adequate conceptual apparatus for the support of his or her activity, and is therefore living and working in a time in which the deck is stacked against him or her.

Nietzsche wanted to develop a philosophy that would allow us to affirm the kinds of lives humans actually do lead and are already familiar with: finding joy in becoming, desire, finitude, uncertainty, and so on. This was the point of his re-evaluation of all values, his attempt to write a new table of values. Badiou is also developing a philosophy that he has even described as an affirmationism, but it is built on a very different basis, as I have been arguing. The gamble of Badiou's philosophy is that it is on the ground of the inhuman, on the basis of a theoretical anti-humanism, that it is possible to live and affirm a human life.

Philosophy will never be in a position to tell anyone involved in a truth procedure what he or she should do, and it cannot do anything to assist with the development of the content of any particular truth that is being worked on. Philosophy does not "do" science, art, love, or politics. Philosophy does have some things to say about the form of truth, though – truth is universal, infinite, generic, and eternal as well. It has something to say about the forms and structures of subjectivity. It can study the general conditions of truth procedures, events, and situations. And finally, based on all this, philosophy is able to offer an ethics. In this sense, Badiou thinks the resources of philosophy are required in the service of a struggle against such things as reaction and obscurantism. And, thus, he hopes his philosophy can be of service in the attempt to avoid these two tendencies, as well as the helpless situation of that poor gentleman from the Paris Commune, who lacked not only a theory for understanding his situation, but an ethic that would have enabled him to continue the fragile procedure that was going on there.

Select Bibliography

By Alain Badiou in English

"The Adventure of French Philosophy." *New Left Review* 35 (Sept–Oct 2005): 67–77.

Being and Event. Transl. Oliver Feltham. London: Continuum, 2005.

Briefings on Existence: A Short Treatise on Transitory Ontology. Transl. Norman Madarasz. Albany, NY: SUNY Press, 2006.

The Century. Transl. Alberto Toscano. Cambridge: Polity, 2007.

Conditions. Transl. Steve Corcoran. London: Continuum, 2009.

Ethics: An Essay on the Understanding of Evil. Transl. Peter Hallward. London: Verso, 2002.

Infinite Thought: Truth and the Return to Philosophy. Transl. Oliver Feltham and Justin Clemens. London: Continuum, 2005.

Manifesto for Philosophy. Transl. Norman Madarasz. Albany, NY: SUNY Press, 1999.

Metapolitics. Transl. Jason Barker. London: Verso, 2006.

Number and Numbers. Transl. Robin MacKay. Cambridge: Polity, 2008.

"Philosophy as Biography." *The Symptom* 9. No date. Available at: <http://www.lacan.com/symptom9_articles/badiou19.html>.

Polemics. Transl. Steve Corcoran. London: Verso, 2006.

"Politics: A Non-Expressive Dialectics." Transcribed Robin MacKay. November 2005. Available at: <http://blog.urbanomic.com/sphaleotas/archives/badiou-politics.pdf>.

Saint Paul: The Foundation of Universalism. Transl. Ray Brassiser. Stanford, CA: Stanford University Press, 2003.

"The Subject of Art." Transcript by Lydia Kerr. *The Symptom* 6. No date. Available at: <http://www.lacan.com/symptom6_articles/badiou.html>.
Theoretical Writings. Ed. and transl. Ray Brassier and Alberto Toscano. London: Continuum, 2004.
"What is to Live?" Transl. Jake Bellone. *lacanian ink* 31 (spring 2008): 51–61.

By Alain Badiou in French

De l'idéologie. Paris: Maspéro, 1976.
Logiques des mondes. L'être et l'événement, 2. Paris: Éditions du Seuil, 2006.
Le Noyau rationnel de la dialectique hégélienne. With L. Mossot and J. Bellassen. Paris: Maspéro, 1978.
Peut-on penser la politique? Paris: Éditions du Seuil, 1985.
De quoi Sarkozy est-il le nom? Paris: Nouvelles éditions Lignes, 2008.
Théorie de la contradiction. Paris: Maspéro, 1975.
Théorie du sujet. Paris: Éditions du Seuil, 1982.

Other Works Cited

Althusser, Louis. *For Marx*. Transl. Ben Brewster. London: Verso, 2005.
Anonymous. "10 ans de maoïsme." *Le marxiste-léniniste* 50–1 (spring 1981): no page.
Barker, Jason. *Alain Badiou: A Critical Introduction*. London: Pluto Press, 2002.
Bosteels, Bruno. "On the Subject of the Dialectic." In Peter Hallward, *Think Again: Alain Badiou and the Future of Philosophy*. London: Continuum, 2004, pp. 150–64.
———. "Post-Maoism: Badiou and Politics." *Positions* 13/3 (winter 2005): Paul Patton. New York: Columbia University Press, 1994.
Feltham, Oliver. *Alain Badiou: Live Theory*. London: Continuum, 2008.
Fields, A. Belden. *Trotskyism and Maoism: Theory and Practice in France and the United States*. Brooklyn, NY: Autonomedia, 1988.
Hallward, Peter. *Badiou: A Subject to Truth*. Forward by Slavoj Žižek. Minneapolis, MN: University of Minnesota, 2003.

Index

affects 15, 122, 124, 128–47
  defined 130, 137, 150–3
Althusser 4, 12, 16, 18–19, 49, 176, 178, 183
anti-humanism (theoretical) 8, 12, 15–16, 21, 49, 75, 79, 85, 103–5, 125, 139, 176, 178, 184
  practical humanism and 180
anxiety 130–7, 151–3
appearance(s) 14–15, 32, 39, 67–76, 79–83, 122, 124, 137, 150
  existence and 77
  structure of 73
atomism 33–4
axiom of foundation 42, 44
axiom of infinity 44, 87
axiom schema of separation 61

being 9, 11, 13–14, 26, 29–77, 79–83, 86–7, 93–6, 104, 107–8, 113, 123, 125, 180
  appearance and 69, 71, 76
  being qua being 9, 26, 31, 33–5, 37, 39–40, 44–5, 48–9, 56, 58, 60–1, 64–5, 67
  empty set and 45
  event and 60–5, 67–8

  existence vs. 77
  infinity and 87
  laws of 26, 30, 37, 42–4, 49, 55, 60, 65, 68–9, 75, 104
  multiple qua multiple as 34, 72
  object and 77, 80
  presentation and 14, 33–5, 37, 45, 50
  proper name of 34, 37–8, 49
  situations and 35–7, 39, 45, 64
  void and 9, 33–4, 37–9, 44–5, 49–50, 56, 58–9, 87
belief 126, 135–6
belonging (set–theory) 14, 38, 41–2, 45, 49–53
betrayal 140, 142
body/bodies 81, 91–2, 123–4, 143–7, 150–1, 180–2

capitalism 23, 25, 111, 135, 156, 174, 181
Cartesian 115, 126
  anti-Cartesian 15
  post-Cartesian 108, 113
changes (in worlds) 14, 68, 80–4, 112, 143
chaos 37, 49–50, 56

Index

Cohen, P. J. 46, 99–100
communist invariants 16, 155–8, 166, 168, 170
confidence 101, 126, 135–7, 140, 173–4, 183
count/counting 35–8, 50–5, 59, 70, 88, 90
   count-as-one/count-for-one 35, 40, 53
courage 12, 130–5, 137, 139, 151–3, 183
Cultural Revolution 2, 11, 20, 111, 159, 162–3, 177

death 59–60, 86, 109, 111, 119, 122, 131–3, 138–9, 181–2
   dialectics and 162–4
Death of God 30, 128, 176, 178–9
Death of Man 16, 176, 178
decision 30, 46, 62, 67, 96, 99, 103, 121–2, 125–7, 166
   intervention and 92, 126
Deleuze 3, 27, 32–3, 45, 113, 169
demand (politics of) 131, 161, 165–7
democracy 155, 157–8, 170–1, 181
destruction 7–10, 16, 24–5, 97, 113, 117, 148, 159–65
   anxiety and 130–3
   subject and 113–15, 117–20
   subtraction vs. 164–5, 168–9
deviations 15, 95–9, 101, 112, 151, 153, 159, 181
dialectics 14, 18, 25, 28, 39–40, 109–14, 119, 159
   idealist 110–11
   materialist 23, 109, 112, 123, 162
   structural 22–3
difference 8, 32–3, 72, 74–8, 86, 92, 139, 160, 169–70
   ontological 34
   sexual 149

elegy (discourse of) 134–5
elements (of set) 40–4, 49–65, 73, 76, 80–2, 97, 103

belonging and 41
evental site and 57–65, 81–2, 93
infinity and 88
empty set 44–5, 48–50, 87–8
encyclopedia (of situation) 91, 93–4, 98–102, 119, 142
enquiry 97, 118
esplace 109–10, 131
   see also place
ethics 8, 79, 91, 180, 182
   forcing and 101
   Marxist 135, 137
   of Badiou's philosophy 6, 12–13, 15, 24, 28, 79, 105–7, 112, 120–2, 124, 128–53, 155, 180–5
   of democratic materialism 180
   of truths 9, 107, 137–40, 142, 153
   Promethean 135–6
   vs. ethical ideology 138–140
event 5, 11, 13–15, 25, 30, 38, 46, 50, 56, 60–5, 67–8, 79–85, 89, 92, 103, 105, 121, 126–9, 136, 138, 143, 148–50, 153, 165–6, 169–70, 173, 180, 184–5
   affects and 137
   as being of non-being 64–5, 68
   as cause of subject 121, 124
   contains itself as member 61, 65, 68, 81, 83
   deviations about 98–9
   doubling of 95–6
   evental sites and 54, 60–5, 81, 83–4, 93
   in *Logics of Worlds* 14, 68, 79–84, 102, 107, 122
   inhabitants and 84, 102, 120–2, 127–9, 137
   interventions and 15, 92–103, 117, 126
   point of excess and 50, 53
   presentation and 60, 62–5, 81, 92–3, 95
pseudoevents 66
simulacrum of 141–2

event (cont.)
  situations and 26, 46, 63–5, 80, 84, 92–9, 127, 142
  strong singularity 83–4
  subject and 114, 116, 118, 123–4, 137, 143; event as cause of subject 118, 121
  subjectivation and 100, 116–17, 121, 127
  trace 124, 143–8, 180–2
  transbeing 65
  truths and 89, 92–103, 140–1
  undecidability of 63–7, 92
evental site 13–14, 54–5, 57–65, 68, 93, 95, 116–17, 144
  definition 57
  revisions of in *Logics* 68, 81–4
  subject and 122, 124
evil 6, 9, 139–42, 170, 179
excrescent (multiple) 14, 53–4, 57, 59
existence (in logic) 9, 39, 69, 72, 76–8, 80–3, 124

fidelity 2–3, 7, 16, 25, 95, 103–4, 114, 121–2, 126–7, 129–30, 140, 142, 155, 166, 177, 179, 181
fidelity procedure 97–9, 103, 106, 116, 121, 137, 180
force (in dialectics) 22–3, 25, 106, 111–14, 116–17, 131–2, 137, 162–3
forcing 15, 67, 99–101, 104, 117, 122, 128
  as law of subject 104, 117–18
formalism 3–4, 18, 21, 28, 79, 156, 181
  of subject 123–4
formalized in-humanism 178, 182, 184
Foucault 4, 6, 18, 176, 178
French Revolution 2–3, 154
  as event 62–4, 97, 141

Galileo 99, 102, 119
generic 13, 90–2, 99–100, 141, 156–8, 169–70

generic procedure 46, 98–9, 115, 118, 143, 170

Hegel 24, 75, 111, 132, 162, 176
Heidegger 27, 31, 34–5, 90, 183
horlieu 109–10, 112–13, 116–17, 134
humanism
  animal 178, 182
  practical 12, 16, 79, 85–6, 105–6, 125, 129, 139–40, 175, 178, 182, 184
Husserl 69–70, 74

idealism (philosophical) 15, 40, 71–2, 74, 85, 111, 175–6
identity 30, 70, 74, 76–8, 159–60, 168, 170
identity politics 27, 168–70
immortal/immortality 9, 16, 106, 122, 125, 138–40, 176, 178–9, 180, 182–3
inclusion (set theory) 14, 41, 50–4
individuals 15, 22–4, 36, 84, 94, 97, 104–5, 120–3, 126, 129, 137–8, 151–2, 170, 179, 182–4
inexistent 79–81, 83
infinite
  multiples 75, 86–7, 104, 118
  sets 44, 52–3, 88, 115
  situations 53, 97
  in theology 109–11
  truth and 183–4
infinity 9, 15–16, 44, 85–8, 178, 182
inhabitants (of situations) 5, 15, 84, 101–2, 105, 117, 119–23, 126–9, 137, 153
inhuman (the) 12, 75, 88, 106, 125, 127, 178, 182, 184
insurrectionary paradigm 16, 154, 158–9, 165, 167, 172–3, 184
intervention 15, 25, 67, 92–8, 100, 102–3, 105–6, 126–7, 137
  subjectivation and 116–17

justice 130, 132–5, 137, 151–3

Kant 69–71, 86–7, 107

Index

knowledge
  scientific 150
  vs. truth 94, 99, 102, 105, 118–19, 122, 124–6, 143, 146

Lacan 4, 16, 18, 94, 106, 118, 133, 138, 146, 149, 167, 176, 178
lack (of being) 113–14
language 90–1, 93, 95, 98–100, 118–19, 142, 166
life (theory of) 13, 16, 103, 122, 138, 180–2, 184
limit (in dialectics) 110
limit ordinal 87–8
logic 9, 67–76, 78–9, 81, 86

Mao 20, 119, 136, 159
Maoism 13, 19–21, 155, 159
  philosophical 22–4, 39, 109, 159–61
Marx 16, 25, 56, 135, 147, 155–6, 166, 178
Marxism 6, 18, 20–2, 24, 110–11, 135–6, 141, 154–7, 165, 183
materialism 13, 23, 32–3, 71–2, 106–9, 112–13, 126
  democratic 91–2, 123, 178, 180–2
  dialectical 14, 22, 110, 123
  historical 22, 106, 175
mathematics 10, 18, 21–2, 28
  ontology as 14, 26, 29–32, 39, 48, 60
May 1968 2, 11, 135–6, 171, 177
  influence on Badiou 18–21
metaphysics 30, 40, 45, 86
metastructure 50–1, 53–4
modification (in *Logics*) 80, 82
multiple-ones 35–7, 39, 48
multiples/multiplicity 9, 13–14, 26–7, 30, 32–50, 53–62, 64–5, 67, 69–73, 76, 80–2, 86–8, 90–3, 95, 97–105, 116–21, 124, 126–7, 137, 141–2, 148, 153, 160, 164, 166
  abnormal 57, 60
  consistent 35–6, 48, 53
  event as 60–7, 82

excrescent 54
generic 99, 169
inconsistent 35–6, 48–50, 61
indiscernible 104, 117, 166
infinite 75, 104, 118
multiple qua multiple 34–5, 72
natural 59–60
normal 54
Platonism of 32–3
pure 34–9, 44, 48, 50, 58, 68, 70, 72, 80, 88, 93, 95
singular 54–8, 65

naming 15, 38, 67, 90, 92–3, 95, 97, 103, 105, 122, 141
Nazism 141–2, 145
Nietzsche 84, 178–9, 184
nihilism 8, 136, 139, 179, 184
nomination 92, 117
nouveaux philosophes 6, 22, 135, 145, 154, 178

objects (theory of) 71–80, 82–3
obscure (subject) 107, 122, 124, 142–4, 146–8, 150–1, 175, 177–8, 180–2
one, the 30, 34, 36, 40, 87–8
  is not 13–14, 33, 36, 45–6, 88
  something of 13–14, 36
  splits/divides in two 109–10, 114, 160
ontology 13–14, 29–40, 42–3, 45, 47–50, 55, 60, 62–4, 67, 69, 71, 73, 79, 86–8, 90, 103, 124
operation 34–5, 38, 61, 70, 97, 103

Paris Commune 11, 79, 83, 111, 185
Parmenides 4, 32–3
periodization (in dialectics) 110–11
phenomenology 15, 26–7, 70, 74, 77–8, 84–5
  objective 15, 74, 76–8, 85, 178
phenomenon (in logic) 76–7
place (in *Theory of the Subject*) 22–3, 106, 109, 111–13, 137, 162

Plato/Platonic 10–11, 30–3, 46, 150, 179
point of excess 50, 52–4
politics 2–3, 9–10, 13, 16, 21, 24–7, 46, 83, 89, 98, 111, 116, 126, 147–8, 151–2, 154–75, 177, 184
power-set (axiom) 52
present (in *Logics*) 5–7, 124, 143–52, 158, 164, 167–9, 174, 177, 182
presentation 14, 33–9, 43–5, 50–1, 53–5, 59, 69–70, 81, 93, 95
Promethean (ethic) 134–6
psychoanalysis 18, 22, 94, 183

reaction/reactionary 3–8, 10, 12, 22, 24, 91, 107, 123, 129, 135–6, 140, 142, 144, 146, 148–51, 155, 163, 169, 172, 177, 180–1, 184–5
representation 51, 53–9, 90
  in politics 157–8, 167–8, 170–1
resignation (discourse of) 134
resurrection 147–9, 179
Robert, Hubert 76–7, 80–1
Russell's paradox 61, 81
Russian Revolution 2, 111

St. Paul 19, 168–9
Sartre 4, 17–18, 68, 78, 108, 157, 183
Schoenberg 64, 123, 152
set 40–5, 49–54, 57, 60–5, 81, 87–8, 98, 118
  abnormal 57, 61–2
  infinite 44, 52–3, 88, 115
  natural 43–60
  nature of
  normal 61
  see also empty set
set theory 14, 25–6, 28, 30, 37, 39–50, 52, 61–2, 64–5, 67, 87–8, 90, 99–100, 154
singular (multiple) 54–8, 65
singularity (in *Logics*) 83

situation 5–6, 11, 13–15, 35–9, 48–51, 53–65, 67–70, 79, 84–6, 88–90, 98–104, 117, 120, 126–7, 137, 141, 148, 153, 185
  affects and 127
  art 3, 64, 102
  definition 36–7, 53
  empty set and 45, 49
  event and 14, 46, 60–5, 67–9, 80–1, 84, 92–3, 95–8, 100, 105, 116–18, 127, 137, 140–2
  evental site and 54, 57–65, 68, 81, 93, 95, 116–17, 122
  fidelity procedure in 97, 99, 121, 140, 179
  historical 15, 26, 59–60, 62–3, 84, 89, 91, 98, 105, 126–7, 137
  infinite 53, 88, 97
  language and 90–3, 100, 119, 142, 166
  natural 26, 38, 59–60, 89, 98, 105
  neutral 60
  ontological 35, 37–8
  operation and 70
  political 5, 24–5, 38, 105, 141, 156, 158, 164, 166–72,
  presentation and 35–7, 54–5, 90
  science 99, 101–2
  subject and 23, 104, 108, 114–22, 127, 129
  subjectivation 100, 116–17, 124, 127
  truth and 5, 9–10, 89, 92, 94–5, 98–100, 105, 118–19, 127, 129, 140–2, 158, 166, 179
  types 10, 35, 49, 54–60, 126
  unnameable of 142
  world(s) and 15, 68–9, 84–6, 88, 99, 108–9, 123, 127
some-one 120–1, 123, 126, 137
Spartacus 5, 143–5, 147, 167, 179
state (of situation) 14, 38, 50–7, 59, 63, 65, 90, 97, 168
  in politics 6, 25, 54–7, 110–11, 154–5, 157–60, 162, 165–8, 171–4

Index

subject 3–4, 9, 13, 15, 21–4, 26–8, 30, 67, 81, 85, 98, 100, 103–10, 112–27, 129–37, 140, 142–53, 180–3
  activity and passivity 15, 105, 107–8, 127
  as knot/torsion 108, 112–15, 124, 132, 143, 159
  α-series 133–5
  as real presence of change 15, 23, 108, 114–16, 118, 122–3, 129
  body and 123–4, 151; trace and 180–1
  constituted, not constituting 125
  faithful/fidelity 4–5, 7, 10, 12–13, 25, 28, 46, 103, 106–7, 116, 123, 142–6, 148–51, 177, 179–82; formula for 145
  immortal 179–80, 182–3
  in art 148–9
  in love 149–50
  individuals or some-one vs. 15, 121, 126–7, 151
  in-humanism/idealism/philosophy 40, 70–1, 74–5, 85, 103, 105, 107–8, 110, 120, 125–7; classical 118
  masculine/feminine 149
  obscure 12, 122, 143–4, 146–51, 180–2; formula for 147
  political 152, 156, 158, 165
  ψ-series 134–5
  reaction/reactive 7, 12, 122, 143–6, 148, 150–1, 180–2; formula for 146
  science 150
  truth procedure and 114–16, 123–4, 127, 153; intersection of with knowledge 118–19, 122
subjectivation 23–4, 100–2, 106, 113–17, 120–1, 124, 126–7, 130–3, 135–7
subject-process/procedure 13, 23–4, 28, 106, 114, 116, 130, 132, 134–6, 152, 159

subsets 41, 43, 51–3, 55, 58–9, 64, 70, 98
subtraction 16, 34, 88, 159, 164, 168–9
superego 130, 132–7, 151

Talbot 166–7
terror 2, 6–9, 20, 98, 132, 134, 140–2, 151–3, 159, 177, 181
theology (dialectics in) 109–10
Thermidor/Thermidorian 2–3, 6, 171
trace 74, 93, 97, 124, 143–8, 180–2
transcendent (orientation in thought) 90–1
transcendental (in *Logics*) 15, 69–73, 75–9, 81–3, 88
truth 2–3, 7–13, 15, 26, 30, 46–7, 85–6, 92, 94, 98, 100, 102–5, 115, 122–3, 129, 137, 141, 153, 178, 182–3
  destruction and 119, 161–2
  eternal 5, 8, 13, 139, 152, 179, 183
  ethic of 9, 107, 137–42, 151, 153
  event and 92, 140–1
  evil and 139–40
  fidelity and 98, 104
  generic 13, 92, 184
  immortality and 9, 106, 125, 140
  infinity and 88, 104, 115, 118, 183–4
  inhuman and 88–9, 106, 125, 178
  knowledge and 94–5, 99, 104–5, 115, 118–19, 126, 183
  love 149
  nature of 88–90
  novelty 99
  philosophy and 10–12, 184
  politics 156
  pseudo 151
  simulacrum of 141
  singular 168
  situations and 89, 91, 94–5, 98–9, 105

truth (cont.)
  subject and 105, 107, 114–15, 118–19, 123–7, 129, 143
  subjectivation and 117, 127
  universal 8, 184
  veracity/veridicality 89–91
truth procedure 5–6, 9, 12, 15–16, 27, 46–7, 67, 89, 92, 95, 103, 106, 115–16, 121, 126, 129–30, 137–8, 140, 147–8, 151, 153, 179, 183–4
  affects and 151
  anxiety and 152
  art 115, 123, 126, 143, 148–9
  betrayal and 140
  body and 146
  destruction and 119, 169
  eternal 148
  forcing and 99–101
  generic 170
  intervention and 117
  knowledge and 118–19, 129
  language and 118, 142, 166
  love 129, 149
  names and 100
  philosophy and 184–5
  political 147, 156–9, 161, 164–72
  pseudo 141–2, 145
  scientific 150
  situation and 142
  subject and 104, 114–15, 118, 122–4, 126–7, 184
  subjectivation and 127
  terror and 152–3
  undecideable 102, 120

UCFML 19–20, 24, 165

veridical 11, 89, 91, 100–1
vitalism 3–4, 8, 113
void 33–4, 37, 39, 44–5, 47, 49–50, 54–9, 64–5, 87, 93, 95, 105, 141

workers 6, 19, 21, 25, 157, 165–8
world(s) 5, 7, 9–10, 12, 14–15, 68–92, 99, 102, 105, 107–12, 115, 122–5, 127, 129, 134, 142–53, 168–9, 177, 179–83